T0295988

PRAISE FOR *DATA-DRIVEN PERSONALIZATION*

Zontee Hou has written the essential guide for marketers who understand that data is the key to winning, and keeping, their competitive advantage.
Adam Bryant, Senior managing director, ExCo Group

If you're reading this right now, you already know that data is critical to crafting a better customer experience. You're challenged by the *how*. That's why you need Zontee's excellent, actionable book.
Ann Handley, WSJ bestselling author and Chief Content Officer, MarketingProfs

Zontee Hou provides a straightforward approach to connecting with customers through digital media. With practical case studies and evidence-based insights, this book is a must-have reference for any serious marketer.
Jesse Scinto, Deputy Program Director and Lecturer, Columbia University

Every customer wants to be treated as an audience of one. This is the quintessential guide for making that a reality. This book is comprehensive, clear, and critical for business leaders who hope to capitalize on skyrocketing customer expectations.
Jay Baer, author of *The Time to Win: How to Exceed Customers' Need for Speed*, *Hug Your Haters*, and *Youtility*

Having witnessed firsthand the profound impact that the collection of data has had on the customer experience, it's heartening to observe how Zontee Hou harmonizes a technical subject with human values like empathy and privacy. In *Data-Driven Personalization* she masterfully harmonizes business goals with human yearnings making for a must-read for anyone interested in striking a balance.
Ana Manrique, Vice President, Design, Data & AI at IBM

Zontee Hou's *Data-Driven Personalization* is nothing short of a revolution in marketing thought leadership. This book is the definitive manual for any marketer looking to make the greatest impact. It masterfully decodes the complexities of data to unveil strategies that will not only captivate consumers but also chart the course for the future of personalized marketing that drives business results.

Attica Jaques, Former Head of Global Brand Marketing, Consumer Apps, Google

Our marketing is nothing without data, and our data is a gift from our customers. Using it to enhance customer experiences while being stewards of this information is more critical now than ever. Zontee gives us a strategic and pragmatic resource that will serve as a North Star for marketers and businesses to lead the right way.

Cathy McPhillips, Chief Growth Officer, Marketing Artificial Intelligence Institute

Zontee Hou has delivered more than a great book. She has delivered wisdom.

Mark Schaefer, author of *Marketing Rebellion, Known,* and *Belonging to the Brand*

The word *data* is as impersonal as it gets. Ironically, it's the best way to humanize your efforts and personalize your marketing—dramatically increasing the chances that your customers will say yes to your brand. Zontee Hou spent decades gathering the proof. In her book she demonstrates the value of data-driven personalization via case study after case study. More importantly, she outlines the frameworks, methods and strategies needed to overcome the challenges your brand faces. Read it to learn how you can make magic by connecting data and insights with the content and context around the customer purchase journey.

Rebecca Rivera, Adjunct Assistant Professor, The City College of New York

Every digital marketer needs this essential guide. Zontee demystifies personalization, grounding it in solid business reasoning while making it wholly accessible and practical for everyday marketers.

Robert Rose, author of *Content Marketing Strategy: Harness the Power of Your Brand's Voice*

Data-Driven Personalization

*How to Use Consumer Insights
to Generate Customer Loyalty*

Zontee Hou

KoganPage

Publisher's note

Every possible effort has been made to ensure that the information contained in this book is accurate at the time of going to press, and the publishers and authors cannot accept responsibility for any errors or omissions, however caused. No responsibility for loss or damage occasioned to any person acting, or refraining from action, as a result of the material in this publication can be accepted by the editor, the publisher or the author.

First published in Great Britain and the United States in 2024 by Kogan Page Limited

Apart from any fair dealing for the purposes of research or private study, or criticism or review, as permitted under the Copyright, Designs and Patents Act 1988, this publication may only be reproduced, stored or transmitted, in any form or by any means, with the prior permission in writing of the publishers, or in the case of reprographic reproduction in accordance with the terms and licences issued by the CLA. Enquiries concerning reproduction outside these terms should be sent to the publishers at the undermentioned addresses:

2nd Floor, 45 Gee Street	8 W 38th Street, Suite 902
London	New York, NY 10018
EC1V 3RS	USA
United Kingdom	
www.koganpage.com	

Kogan Page books are printed on paper from sustainable forests.

© Zontee Hou 2024

The right of Zontee Hou to be identified as the author of this work has been asserted by her in accordance with the Copyright, Designs and Patents Act 1988.

All trademarks, service marks, and company names are the property of their respective owners.

ISBNs

Hardback	978 1 3986 1462 8
Paperback	978 1 3986 1460 4
Ebook	978 1 3986 1461 1

British Library Cataloguing-in-Publication Data

A CIP record for this book is available from the British Library.

Library of Congress Cataloging-in-Publication Data

***

Typeset by Integra Software Services, Pondicherry
Print production managed by Jellyfish
Printed and bound by CPI Group (UK) Ltd, Croydon, CR0 4YY

CONTENTS

PART THREE

Fostering Emotional Resonance

LIST OF FIGURES

ABOUT THE AUTHOR

Zontee Hou is founder and President of Media Volery, a digital marketing agency, and Managing Director of the marketing consultancy Convince & Convert. She has nearly twenty years of experience in the marketing industry, and has advised organizations including the International Monetary Fund, Fidelity Investments, Indiana University, and Bentley Motors. She was one of LinkedIn's 16 Marketers to Follow in 2021, one of PCMA's Best in Class Speakers in 2021 and 2022, and she's consistently named one of TopRank's most influential content marketers and top B2B marketers. Hou has been a lecturer at Columbia University and the City College of New York, and she is a sought-after business speaker. She is based in Brooklyn, New York.

Introduction

In my first marketing role, just after I had finished my undergraduate degree in business, I had the good fortune of getting to sit in a lot of meetings with the executive team. I got to hear how the people who led the company made decisions about promotion, product development, sales, and operations. The company's leaders were part of the family that owned the company and they had spent their whole careers in the arts and crafts business. It was what they knew. In some ways, it gave them a strong understanding of the customers and their gut instincts often served them well. In other ways, being far removed from the real customers made it hard for them to see the changing landscape for what it was: Blogs were just starting to become the go-to sources for information, retail brands were starting to lose their footing, brands were having to rethink how they promoted their products.

Luckily, my boss at the time, Ilana, was determined to introduce a modern, digital-marketing approach to the company: Building a robust email subscriber base of nearly a million people, spearheading an ecommerce business, and giving me free rein over the development of a social media program, podcast, video program, and even influencer program (way back before "influencer" was a term—this was the late aughts and early 2010s) through which we were able to not only hear from customers directly, but get their feedback in real-time. We were able to build an understanding of our customers, who ran the gamut from young indie crafters who described themselves as "makers" to retirees, leaning into beloved handicrafts as a means to connect with others. And we were able to build a thriving brand that defined customers' expectations of the crafts and hobbies space. What I've experienced first-hand is the power of building a digital marketing engine that is powered by a positive feedback loop of testing messages and content, based on the motivations of your customers, getting their feedback, and then refining your marketing approach based on what works and what doesn't work.

In the years since—in my role as an agency owner that works with small and medium businesses across the US, as an advisor to major global brands, as a speaker at industry events around the globe, and in my classrooms at Columbia University and the City College of New York—I've built and presented frameworks that help marketers and business leaders hone their marketing strategies. But at the core I'm a practical marketer who believes in following the evidence. I believe in making recommendations that you and your team can actually put into practice. I believe in not wasting your time or your resources. I believe your customer has the answers to your questions—if only you ask them, listen to what they say, and then deliver on the ask. And you'll see that throughout this book.

Why Should Marketers Have a Seat at the Data Table?

If you're reading this book, you get that marketing can and should be driven by data. You get why marketers need to use customer data to meet the expectations of customers in order to gain a competitive edge. But perhaps you've also noticed that, traditionally, data isn't necessarily "owned" by the marketing team. Perhaps it sits with the sales or operations team. Perhaps it's decentralized with many different teams touching various facets of data. Yet, as we get further into the digital age—with technology like machine learning and artificial intelligence (AI) pushing customer expectations even higher—marketers need to play an active role in the collection of data to do their jobs.

This means that marketers must help shape the strategy around what data is collected, how it's collected, why it's collected, and how it's used to serve the customers. Whether you're a marketer, a marketing communications (marcomm) professional, in a hybrid sales and marketing role, or a business leader with marketing responsibilities, your role is to persuade the customers that your brand and your products are right for them. Knowing why and how they buy in your business category is vital. Speaking to their unique needs will help to break through the competitive noise and achieve business growth. But to do that, you need to root your work in what is true about your customers, not just gut instincts. That requires you to make the case for why you need a seat at the table, when it comes to shaping data practices within your organization.

What to Expect in This Book

The customers are at the heart of data-driven personalization, so throughout the book we'll explore the behavioral economics (how customers make decisions) and behavioral psychology (why customers think what they think) that impact their actions. Understanding how our audiences think is just as important as understanding what marketers do about that thinking. We'll also take a look at case studies from a wide variety of brands and hear from marketing leaders from businesses across organizations, both large and small, so that you can see what these frameworks look like in action. Even if your organization is in an entirely different industry, I encourage you to suspend your skepticism and see if there's something that each example can offer you. I've often given talks at events where someone says that their company is business-to-business (B2B) and so they didn't relate to my business-to-consumer (B2C) examples or vice versa. But even if the examples aren't exactly applicable to your business, hopefully they will help you understand how the work can be done in principle—and I've included examples from B2B, B2C, and institutional organizations, so that marketers of all stripes see themselves represented.

Because my team at Media Volery, a boutique marketing agency I own in New York City, works with small and medium businesses, I'll share examples from some of our current and former clients. I'll also share examples from my team at Convince & Convert, a digital marketing consultancy that works with major brands that I also lead, so you can see how global brands and institutions approach these challenges. I'll reference research conducted by myself and my teams as well as from trusted sources throughout the book—to make sure you not only understand what's true but can also make the case within your own organization.

Resources and action plans

A few weeks into my very first year teaching a course for Masters candidates at the City College of New York, one of my students asked if I could supply suggested resources to help him and other students dive more deeply into each week's topics. It's a suggestion that I've implemented into every course I've taught since, and it's one that's incorporated into this book. Because there are a lot of topics that we could spend an entire book on, at the end of each chapter I've made sure to include recommendations on books and other resources that do just that. I've also incorporated a summary and action items into each chapter, so that you can use the book as a workbook. You'll also find an overall summary, final exercise, and even FAQs in Chapter 24 to help you get the most out of the materials.

Building Your Strategy

So, how do we achieve a data-driven approach to personalization and to marketing? You've heard that famous adage about planting trees: That the best time to plant one was 20 years ago, but the second-best time is today. So it goes with collecting data. In the ideal scenario, your organization has already been collecting a wide variety of data about your customers and bringing them together in such a way that the data can be queried and used. However, if you haven't been collecting much data and/or you know that you have a lot of room for improvement, the time is now.

Ultimately, this book's topic is bigger than data and personalization—it's really about rethinking your marketing strategy, your approach to customer experience, and achieving a true competitive advantage. The goal is to know more about your customers than your competitors do *and* to do something about it. If that approach rings true to you, read on!

01

The Case for Data-Driven Personalization

Picture your inbox in the morning. How quickly do you scan your emails for junk mail, then highlight those messages that fit the bill, and delete them? It's probably a split second. Similarly, how quickly, do you scroll past irrelevant content on social media without a second thought? You probably do that all the time. That's no surprise when there is so much content that you're exposed to every day. On average, in *every minute of the day*, there are 157 million videos watched on TikTok, 5.9 million Google searches, and 2.1 million people active on Facebook (Heitman, 2022). The volume of content that we are all bombarded with is immense. It's no wonder that our customers, like us, are quick to dismiss messages that don't immediately hook them.

In this environment, which brands stand out for becoming the de facto choices for customers? It's the brands that make it easy for customers to say yes, because they anticipate their needs and offer a seamless experience. Think about brands like Netflix, whose streaming platform became dominant because of its content recommendations algorithm. Or think about mega-store Amazon, which aggressively adapts every page of its website and app to the behaviors of customers. The thing is: Most of us don't have Amazon's budgets. But the good news is that you can build a strategy that allows your brand to communicate with your audiences in an intuitive and responsive way at nearly any budget.

Throughout this book, you'll read case studies from organizations large and small and hear from experts who work with clients in just about every industry. Their experiences help illustrate why and how investing in a data-driven approach to personalization is necessary to build a competitive advantage. For instance, you'll hear from folks like Robbie Fitzwater, founder of digital market agency MKTG Rhythm, which works with small/medium ecommerce businesses across the US, who said in our conversation, "I always say: Our goal is not to out-scale Amazon. Our goal is to out-*human* Amazon. For the businesses we work with, we can really work to connect the data and insights we have on their customers with content and context around their purchasing and customer journey. And when we can connect those two, that's where we really can create some magic" (2023).

What Fitzwater is describing is our opportunity. When we know more about our customers than the competition and we use that knowledge to deliver more relevant messages, content, and product recommendations based on their needs or circumstances, they say yes to our brands. But knowing more about our customers takes work. Even as we all have access to more opportunities to measure and track, many businesses still aren't using their data to their fullest potential.

Why Now is the Time to Improve How Your Marketing Team Use Data

Since I started in the marketing industry nearly two decades ago, the number of digital touchpoints has continued to increase. That means that our marketing efforts are more measurable than ever and marketers are expected to be able to connect the dots between marketing campaigns and business results. Furthermore, we're working in an environment in which marketers are expected to do more with our resources. Content Marketing Institute/MarketingProfs' annual report (2021) found that 67 percent of marketers surveyed agreed that, over the last year, their content team had been asked to do more with the same resources. It should be a no-brainer to use data to find efficiencies and eliminate wasted efforts. And yet, when I work with marketers and business leaders across organizations both large and small, I often find that the marketing metrics that are reported out are about reach or general engagement, not about consumer insights or customer lifetime value. What will drive our business forward is our ability to learn about our customers, deliver more relevant messages to them, and improve their relationship with the brand through insights.

How Marketers Are Using Data

If you're feeling discouraged because your organization still faces significant limitations when it comes to how you're using data, don't fret. You're not alone. To help you better understand what other organizations are facing and doing currently when it comes to data-driven personalization, I—along with my team at Convince & Convert and our friends at ICUC, a leading social media and online community agency—surveyed 319 marketers in both B2B and B2C industries in August 2023.

ABOUT THE SURVEY

The 319 marketers represented a fairly equal distribution across industries including agencies (advertising, digital, content marketing, PR), education, financial services/banking/insurance, healthcare/life sciences, manufacturing, professional services, publishing/media, retail/ecommerce, technology, and travel/tourism/hospitality.

About 40 percent of respondents represented companies with 1,000+ employees. About 36 percent represented companies of 100–999 employees. And just under 12 percent represented those with 10–99 and 1–9 employees each.

Three-quarters of those surveyed were located in North America, about 15 percent in Europe, and the rest were located in Asia, Africa, Australia, and South America. This survey was fielded by Convince & Convert and ICUC (2023).

We found that:

- About a quarter of marketers feel that their companies are very mature or somewhat mature when it comes to using data to drive personalization. Another 22.57 percent say they're moderately mature, 18.5 percent say slightly mature, and 9.09 percent say not at all mature.

- Only 25.16 percent of marketers strongly agree with the statement "My company is able to effectively analyze our owned customer data to generate valuable customer insights for marketing." Another 39.31 percent somewhat agree and the rest either disagree or "neither disagree or agree," demonstrating that there are a lot of brands that need to improve to stay competitive (see Figure 1.1).

- More than half of marketers feel that they are not collecting enough data or only a moderate amount of data (see Figure 1.2).

- It's no surprise that the most common types of data collected are customer relationship data (66.88 percent) and demographic data (64.98 percent),

FIGURE 1.1 Only a quarter of marketers confidently agree that their companies are able to effectively analyze their owned customer data to generate valuable insights—that means there are a lot of companies with room for improvement

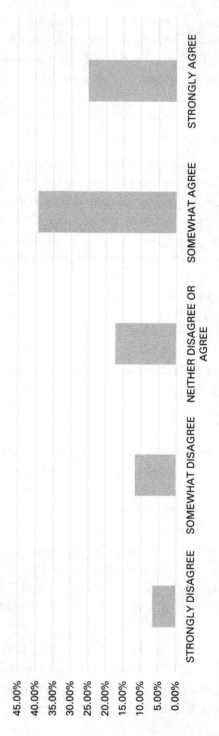

Agree or disagree: My company is able to effectively analyze our owned customer data to generate valuable customer insights for marketing

SOURCE Reproduced with permission of Convince & Convert/ICUC (2023)

FIGURE 1.2 Fewer than half of marketers surveyed said their companies collect "sufficient" or "more than enough" data

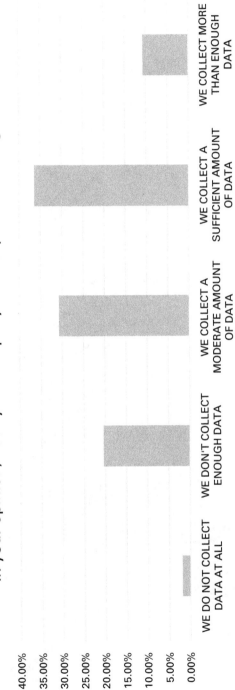

In your opinion, does your company currently collect enough data?

SOURCE Reproduced with permission of Convince & Convert/ICUC (2023)

FIGURE 1.3 Organizations rely heavily on their websites and emails to collect data, but are missing out on the opportunities within many other channels

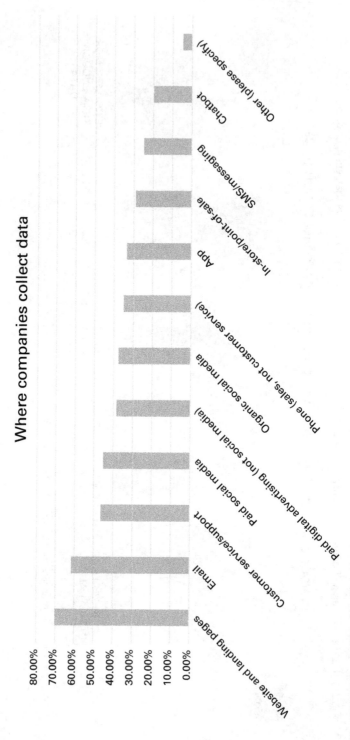

Where companies collect data

SOURCE Reproduced with permission of Convince & Convert/ICUC (2023)

but it *is* surprising that these numbers are so low, considering how basic they are. This discrepancy could come down to marketers' access to how their organizations collect data (see Figure 3.1).

• It's also unsurprising that website and landing pages and email are the most common channels where brands collect data. But fewer than 50 percent of those surveyed said that their companies collect data via customer service support, as well as paid channels. These channels cost money to run and should be integral parts of the data-collection ecosystem, so that companies can collect insights to improve efficiency and customer experience (see Figure 1.3).

The survey showed that while data is part of the way organizations are running their marketing programs, there's a great deal of room to grow. And most marketers feel that they both need more data and have the opportunity to improve how data is used within their organizations. To give you frameworks for making these improvements, throughout this book we'll take a closer look at where and how data should be generated and prioritized.

Why Personalization Matters

Our opportunity is to use data to better understand our customers so that we can make better business decisions and provide more relevance to customers. How we demonstrate that relevance is through content and messages that speak to the specific needs, motivations, and attitudes of our customers. I spoke to Chris Lu, co-founder of Copy.ai—an AI-driven platform for copywriting, designed to help businesses scale their work—about how he sees the usage of data in marketing in the coming years. He told me, "Data is important to help you target and personalize. We believe marketing will become even more relevant and more personalized in the future. Ultimately, a business solves a problem, marketing shares the solution to the world. Marketing will be able to make sure the solution is most relevant to every potential buyer" (2023). The potential is there, and now, with more affordable and accessible technology, more brands than ever before can take advantage of personalization.

Most marketers understand the potential. In fact, my research found that an overwhelming majority—80 percent—of marketers agree that data-driven personalization is very or extremely important for improving customer experiences. Furthermore, nearly 85 percent agree that data-driven personalization would provide a competitive advantage to their companies. Marketers understand that there are many ways in which personalization fulfills the needs of their audiences, while also providing benefits to their brands. In the survey, I asked what are the top three benefits marketers associate with data-driven personalization, and Figure 1.4 shows what they said (Convince & Convert/ICUC, 2023).

The challenge marketers face isn't just about building the strategy to achieve an integrated approach to using data and personalization in their marketing. It's also about getting organizational and executive buy-in, nurturing a culture that cultivates strategic data usage, hiring for people who can execute upon the vision, implementing the approach with the right tools, and having a seat at the table to actively play a role in how data is collected, analyzed, and used. This book will not only help you tackle those challenges, we will also explore and address each of the benefits shown in Figure 1.4:

- *Improved customer experience:* Tailoring your customer touchpoints to the unique needs and specific motivations or attitudes of the customer makes it easier for them to learn/shop/engage with your brand and more relevant to their lives. (See Chapter 9 for more on customer experience.)

- *Deeper customer insights:* Understanding your customers (especially specific segments like best customers or most loyal customers) allows you to uncover the opportunities to get more out of your relationships with them and improve your customer lifetime value (CLV). (See Chapters 11, 12, and 19.)

- *Competitive advantage:* As technology continues to increase the expectations around personalization, knowing more about your customers and delivering better content, messages, and products to them will allow your brand to gain a competitive advantage and become the go-to choice for your customers. (Chapter 5 explores how to set the strategic foundation, but we'll look at this throughout the book.)

- *Improved customer retention:* Customers want to engage with brands that provide them with what they're looking for. The more your brand provides that highly relevant experience, the more they will stay with your brand. (Parts Three, Four, and Five go into this in-depth.)

- *Higher conversion rates:* Offers, messages, and resources that speak to the specific needs of your customers improves conversion rates. (We also touch upon this topic in Parts Three, Four, and Five.)

FIGURE 1.4 Marketers particularly value the improvement in customer experience, but also cite deeper customer insights, competitive advantage, and improved customer retention as top benefits

Top benefits associated with data-driven personalization

SOURCE Reproduced with permission of Convince & Convert/ICUC (2023)

- *Enhanced relevance:* The more you know about your customers, the better your content marketing and merchandising can address the specific needs of your audience. This goes hand-in-hand with improving the customer experience and increasing engagement. (Parts Two and Three lay out the tools to increase relevance.)

- *Cross-selling and upselling opportunities:* Understanding your customers' past behaviors allows you to identify more pointed opportunities to cross-sell or upsell relevant, related products or services. (Chapter 19 discusses this topic.)

- *Improved marketing performance or efficiency:* Focusing on customers that are more likely to convert within each channel, specific to their needs and/or behaviors, allows your marketing teams to publish fewer marketing messages while improving performance. The goal is to do more with the same resources by focusing on the places and the messages that are most likely to resonate. (Parts Five and Six examine these opportunities.)

- *Improved marketing return on investment:* More strategically deployed marketing tactics that result in stronger performance should increase return on investment (ROI). (Parts Five and Six also consider this theme.)

- *Increased customer engagement:* As customers find more of what they're looking for at the right times, customer engagement should improve in your most effective channels, providing your team feedback on the places to focus resources and energy. (We'll touch upon this idea throughout the book, but particularly in Part Two.)

GAINING EFFICIENCY THROUGH BETTER INSIGHTS

Making the most of limited resources isn't just about deploying marketing more wisely, but also about supporting sales teams effectively (particularly in B2B marketing) I spoke to Tessa Barron, Vice President of Marketing at ON24, a webinar and virtual event platform (see Chapter 4 for a case study), about the role that marketing insights can play in sales enablement. "It's about increasing the propensity for sales to make that connection and continue the conversation. That's what marketing's job is now in this world—how we can help our sellers understand the buyer before they meet them, so that they can use their time more effectively. And we can have a higher conversion rate as we scale our reach" (2023).

Customer Expectations Around Personalization

The good news is that the benefits of data-driven personalization align with customers' expectations of brands. These expectations are higher than ever before, and brands—in response—must evolve to stay relevant and to break through. As we've seen, marketers and brands are struggling to collect enough data, glean meaningful insights, and act upon the data that they collect. And yet, customers believe that brands should be offering them meaningfully differentiated and personalized experiences based on what those brands know about them.

What do those expectations look like? In addition to the aforementioned research, I worked with my friends at Researchscape (2023)—a market research consultancy that produces custom and omnibus surveys—to ask a panel of 1,048 US adults about their views and expectations around personalization by brands:

- We found that 88 percent of respondents said it was somewhat to extremely important for a brand to remember past interactions and engage with them based on that shared history.
- We also found that 85 percent said it was somewhat to extremely important for brands to share personalized recommendations with them.
- 80 percent of respondents also said they were somewhat to completely likely to select a brand over its competitors if the first brand offered more personalized messages, offers, and recommendations.
- 58 percent of respondents said that AI technologies have increased their expectations around personalized messaging from brands.
- When asked about how they value privacy and convenience, when it comes to how brands track their behaviors online and offline, we found that respondents skewed towards preferring convenience over privacy (see Figure 1.5).

Our Opportunity and the Impact of Personalization

This book explores our opportunities to meet customer expectations head-on. It draws from my years running digital marketing teams, advising organizations big and small, and building frameworks for folks from graduate students to executive leaders. It showcases examples from leading brands

FIGURE 1.5 44 percent of respondents said they preferred convenience, 25 percent said they preferred a balance of convenience and privacy, and 31 percent said they preferred privacy

When it comes to brands tracking your behaviors online and offline, do you prefer more convenience or more privacy?

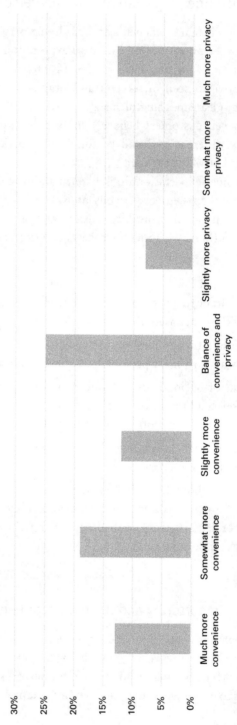

SOURCE Reproduced with permission of Researchscape International (2023)

across industries, as well as interviews with people whose businesses are bringing personalization to life. Throughout the book, we'll look at how we can personalize better—ranging from broader customer segmentations and personas to truly personal one-to-one messages. We'll also look at the impacts on your business, how to build a discipline around data and personalization in your marketing organization, as well as the impacts on the bottom line. This book is divided into six parts, each a necessary building block of a holistic digital-marketing approach that is grounded in your customers' needs and built on the data that allows you to take shrewd action based upon your knowledge and learnings. Let's get started.

RESOURCES RELATED TO THIS CHAPTER

DataDrivenPersonalization.com—Find the research featured in this chapter, videos, and a webinar-version of some of the takeaways from this book, along with a book trailer and other resources on my website.

CHAPTER 1 SUMMARY

Most marketers want to do more with data, but the vast majority aren't getting nearly as much out of their data as they would like. In this chapter, we reviewed the research on how marketers and their organizations are collecting and using data, as well as what customers' expectations around personalization truly are.

Actions

▢ Review your organization's current data collection: Are you collecting enough data? Where do you collect your customers' data? What are your strengths and weaknesses?

▢ Identify the opportunities that you want to explore in terms of using your data: Make a list and use them as a reference as you read this book.

▢ Want to get more out of reading this book? Find a book buddy—reading with a group or an accountability partner will help you stay on track.

PART ONE

Understanding Your Customers

02

Starting With the Right Audiences

As a marketing consultant and speaker, I'm often invited to present at industry events on digital marketing best practices. Many years ago, I was leading a marketing workshop at a conference and trade show for the needle arts industry (that's knitting, crochet, embroidery, cross-stitch, and the like), and when it came to the Q&A part of my workshop, a gentleman stood up to ask a few questions about how to build an audience from scratch when you're a new business. He and his wife were opening a yarn store in Florida, and they weren't sure how to go about building a customer base. To better answer his questions, I asked him to describe the customer base he was going after: "Who are you targeting? What's your ideal customer?" He replied with a shrug, "Anyone who wants to shop at our store."

Perhaps you've had a similar conversation with someone in your life. There are a lot of people who believe that their business has something for everyone. But let's be honest—unless you're a mega-store like Amazon or have many multiple lines of business like Google, it's pretty difficult to provide everything to everyone. In responding to the gentleman, one key piece of advice that I shared was to work on defining his target audiences, whether that meant doing market research or experimentation to learn which audiences are most valuable (that could be most profitable, easiest to acquire, or the best fit) to him and his business.

Most marketers know that understanding your audience gives you the ability to communicate more effectively with them, because you understand what they care about, what's relevant to them, and what drives them. Throughout this book, we'll look at what behavioral psychology tells us about what persuades people and how behavioral economics impacts how they make decisions. But understanding your audience is also strategically important because we as marketers don't have unlimited resources. To effectively deploy our time and energy to persuade audiences to take the actions our organizations want them to take—whether that's buying, subscribing, donating, or changing their minds—we need to understand who are our most valuable audiences and most persuadable audiences. Then we should put our energy and resources into going after these best audiences, rather than going after everyone.

Recognizing the Right Customers

When you hear the word "personalization," it may give you visions of targeting every single customer with value propositions tailored to that individual. In theory, you could then appeal to every individual and serve every customer. But, as I like to say, marketing isn't magic. You may be able to tailor your marketing messages to each individual but, as we discussed, you're unlikely to have a product, service, or expertise that appeals to every person. It doesn't make sense for your organization to expend time and energy on customers that aren't a good fit or aren't in the market for what you offer.

So who is the right customer? Oftentimes, the relationship between the brand and the customers comes from the brand's positioning statement and its core insight into the audience it serves. In other words: *What does your brand offer, to whom, and for what purpose?* As we'll see in later chapters, what your brand offers often goes beyond product features into emotional resonance, beliefs, and even a sense of community.

Identify Your Key Audiences Through Segmentation

To start on the road to personalization, the first step for most brands is weeding out the people for whom the brand *is* versus the people for whom the brand *isn't*. This categorization homes into the attributes that relate to the brand's positioning statement and core audience insight. For example, consider customer/brand fit. Think about lifestyle brands or home furnishing brands which have different aesthetics; if you're not into contemporary aesthetics with a mid-century flavor, then a brand like West Elm is probably not for you. Other examples would be attributes such as: Profitability or price point—think about a luxury accessories brand like Rolex; attitudinal considerations—an example would be beauty brand Lush, which is focused on body products with integrity and ethics; or behavioral considerations—such as vacation rental company Vrbo emphasizing the ability to rent a full property to differentiate themselves from Airbnb and other home-sharing platforms. These attributes might even be around timing—products aimed at people in specific life stages, ages, or at pivotal moments.

As we think about personalization, we also have to think about capturing the attributes that allow us to target customers and prospects that are right for our brand. This means both organizing our data structures to parse these key attributes, as well as making sure that our marketing teams are leveraging these attributes in how they segment, personalize, and tell stories.

EXERCISE
Brainstorm the Attributes That Define Your Customers

Working with your team, list the attributes or considerations that make a customer a good fit for your product or service. Don't get boxed into basics like job title, income, or location—rather, focus on what they need and how that relates to what your brand offers. Are there specific psychographic (attitudinal or personality traits) that make them a good fit? Is there a kind of use case or life stage that makes them right? Do they have needs that your brand can uniquely fulfill?

Once you have these attributes, use them as a basis to audit what data you collect about your customers. We'll explore this further in Chapter 3, but consider what you are currently collecting and what you're missing. Identify what information you need more of in order to better understand your customers based on these attributes.

CASE STUDY
How Mars Petcare Builds Relationships With its Core Audience
and Collects Data That Makes an Impact

With well-known pet nutrition and pet food brands such as Pedigree, Whiskas, and Iams, Mars Petcare has a wide variety of product lines that serve different audiences who have different approaches to pet parenthood or pet ownership. But across all of these different brands, they recognized that a pivotal time to build the relationship with these prospective customers is at the initial adoption of a pet. In an interview with AdAge (2023), Jean-Paul Jansen, VP of Marketing and Chief Marketing Officer for North America of Mars Petcare, shared that they focused on how they could provide value to these new pet parents while also capturing key data that they would be able to use for future marketing. By making recommendations for local veterinarians or nutritionists, in addition to the obvious pet food samples, Mars Petcare offered these new pet parents pertinent resources to get their questions answered at this critical (and confusing) new stage of their lives.

Because these resources were so meaningful to consumers, Mars Petcare saw opt-in rates of 80 percent or higher and they found the quality (in other words, the accuracy and relevance) to be very high. This data—organized based on the needs of pet parents—also then served as a backbone to their data strategy, focused on supporting these new pet parents where they were in their customer journeys (see Chapter 7 for more on customer journeys). Identifying that new pet parents were a core audience to influence because of their thirst for information and their desire for guidance allowed Mars Petcare to focus their resources on tailoring their messaging and content to move the needle.

Challenging Your Assumptions

In my work as a consultant I advise marketing teams of all sizes, and what still surprises me is how little marketers truly know about their customers. I've spoken to many teams at large, multibillion dollar multinational companies who admit that they don't have formal customer research or that the research they have is out of date and not truly leveraged by their teams. The thing is, we as businesspeople often make assumptions about our customers. We think we know when, how, and why they make buying decisions, but we haven't actually done the analysis to find out the truth. We may measure certain aspects of these customers—perhaps a few of the attributes we just talked about—but we don't have a full picture of them. Therefore, we may miss what's truly important to them. Throughout this book, you'll find me balancing what behavioral psychology and behavioral economics tell us about people against the practical research and data collection techniques that allow us to truly understand our unique customers. As my friend Alex, a statistician, likes to remind me: Averages are true only in aggregate; they don't hold true for each individual. In other words, you may know what's generally true for your customers, but it may still not apply to the individual customer.

To obtain a better understanding of our customers than our competition has, we need to do more than the competition to get to know them. That requires us to know our customers on a one-by-one basis. That does *not* mean that we don't consider segments. We still need to create audience segments to build our strategy, create our frameworks, and collect the right data. But once we have those segments, we layer personalization on top, using the data we have that's specific to each individual.

Furthermore, it's not always about going after the biggest audience segment. Nor is it about going after the biggest spenders. Sometimes, it's about going after the customers who are most likely to be loyal, or the customers who are the easiest to acquire. It may be a combination of those attributes and others. In Chapter 19 we'll talk about increasing CLV and the way the three components (average purchase value, average purchase frequency, and average customer lifespan) can be influenced.

Scaling Your Audience Outreach

In a world where data and technology allow us to scale our marketing efforts, we can more effectively go after our key audience segments through messages, content, and resources that speak to each individual's unique preferences, needs, and shared history with our brand. We'll take a look at how AI, lead generation platforms, testing engines, and content serving platforms can help us increase the reach and efficacy of our audience outreach efforts. But don't be intimidated if your organization is small or has a limited budget—these tools are getting more affordable and accessible to organizations of all sizes with every passing month.

Keeping the Right Customers

Although it can feel like marketers are mostly tasked with acquiring new customers, keeping your high-value customers is an extremely important part of the equation. After all, conventional wisdom holds that it's much more cost effective to nurture your existing customers than to acquire new ones, since customer acquisition is commonly the most expensive part of the sales cycle. Data-driven personalization is a powerful tool for keeping your customers because they value brands delivering information to them based on who they are and what they care about. In the research study I conducted with Researchscape (which we explored in the previous chapter), we found that 85 percent of US adults said it was somewhat to extremely important for brands to share personalized recommendations with them. In addition, 88 percent said it was somewhat to extremely important for a brand to remember their past interactions and engage with them based on that shared history (Researchscape, 2023). This should be no surprise to anyone who has engaged with customers; they have high expectations for relevance and personalization. It also means that brands who do a great job of delivering on these expectations should out-compete the competition. In fact, my research found that 80 percent of US adults are somewhat to completely likely to select a brand over its competitors if the first brand offers more personalized messages, offers, and recommendations. That's an advantage worth pursuing.

Going From Segmentation to Personalization

Once we understand what our ideal customers look like and what audience segments are most valuable, we can then start to build a framework for capturing the right data for our organizations. The goal isn't to collect every piece of data under the sun; rather, it's about collecting every piece of data that *matters*. Customers want to receive messages, offers, and recommendations that help them live better lives and achieve their goals. They're not looking for personalization just for the sake of personalization.

Think about it this way: If you see an old friend for lunch, you appreciate them asking about your hobby that you've previously mentioned. You might find it somewhat bizarre and mildly creepy if they ask you about your cat's health if it's a topic you've never discussed together, even if you share photos of your cat on social media. One is a contextual piece of information that helps you and your friend converse about shared interests. The other seems like an invasion of privacy, *despite* being publicly available information that your friend may have noted. Personalization by companies is perceived in a similar fashion: Customers desire relevance and appropriate context. They are put off by overly personal references that don't seem to serve a purpose (more on this in Chapter 10).

Collecting Data to Personalize

To capture the right data, we need more than just the categories of data (which we'll cover in more detail in the next chapter), we also need to understand the ways in which we should collect data:

- *First-party data:* Data owned by your company will be the highest quality and likely most relevant because you can control the inputs, the data fields collected, and the data cleanliness (issues including errors, inconstancies, duplications, etc.). First-party data can be collected through contact forms, lead generation forms (such as forms to download non-public content—also called gated content), purchases, contests, and memberships.

- *Second-party data:* Collaborating with trusted partners with whom your organization has disclosed data-sharing agreements can be another valuable way to collect information from prospects and current clients. This may take the form of video content created with a thought leader or influencer that's gated; for example, in your own life, perhaps you've attended a webinar offered by a brand you engage with. It may look like sponsorships of events; for instance, you may have received an email from a sponsor the last time you attended a conference. Or this may take the form of a contest; when was the last time you entered a sweepstake and received emails or follow-up materials from one of the sponsors?

- *Third-party data:* Third-party data is collected by an entirely separate entity; for organizations, this may look like purchasing lists from a data broker. The challenge of third-party data is that its quality and relevance to your organization's needs and audience parameters will be limited. For instance, I gave a workshop at Content Marketing World in 2023 on this topic, and an audience member asked me how to deal with the fact that the data they purchased from a data broker was often either incomplete or less high-quality than they were originally led to believe. While I believe that, in certain cases, third-party data can be valuable, it should only be used as a starting point to build the relationship with the customer and collect more valuable (read as: accurate and high-quality) data.

Understanding the Shift to a Cookie-Less World

Online, there was a long period when third-party cookies (cookies that tracked customer behavior over third-party websites) were highly valued by marketers because they allowed marketers to understand customers' behaviors and preferences over a wide variety of different properties. But as brands like Apple and Google have made moves to limit their usefulness to marketers and increase privacy for customers, they are becoming obsolete. As we continue to get further and further into a cookie-less world, first-party data and tracking become more important. This means that the brands that build high-value ecosystems that keep customers engaging with their content will have the most insights about their customers.

Think about a brand like Google. If a customer uses Google Maps to find local businesses to visit, uses Google search to do research, and uses Gmail to communicate about their lives, Google has a ton of data that it can leverage to make sure that its offerings are highly relevant and personalized to that customer. In Chapter 9 we'll explore the ways in which brands like Nike and Marriott are creating more touchpoints for collecting customer data to gain this competitive edge. How can your organization compete in this increasingly data-driven world?

Ask yourself: Is your organization thinking about how it can create an ecosystem for collecting valuable data about your customers? In a more competitive environment, we need to know our customers' behaviors, attitudes, and preferences better than our competition does. We need to think about their omnichannel experience with our brand. And we need to be deliberate and strategic in getting our customers to deanonymize their presences (in other words, use logged in accounts to engage with our brands). It puts a great deal of burden on marketers to provide more value to customers than ever before. And that's why data-driven personalization isn't just about data—it's about your entire strategic approach to connecting with your key audience segments.

RESOURCES RELATED TO THIS CHAPTER

Customer Understanding: Three ways to put the "customer" in customer experience (and at the heart of your business) by Annette Franz—An easy-to-follow resource on customer experience, Franz's book focuses on understanding your core customers, researching them, developing personas, and using customer journey maps to document your company's touchpoints with these customers. We'll talk about some of these concepts in this book, but if you're interested in digging more into the customer experience piece of the puzzle, this book is a good option.

CHAPTER 2 SUMMARY

Being deliberate in identifying our most important audiences allows us to be strategic in how we collect data and for what reasons. For some companies, it may be difficult to decide which challenge to tackle first, as you may not yet have enough data to identify your key audiences (a challenge we'll address in Chapter 4). But for most, having a clear understanding of what customers your brand wants to pursue gives clarity in terms of how to identify those customers through data and personalization.

Actions

☐ Using your positioning statement, identify what attributes make for your most important audience segments.

☐ Consider what data you need to collect in order to accurately segment your audiences.

☐ Acknowledge what you *don't* know about these customers that should be captured to add context and depth to your knowledge.

☐ Consider what data your brand could collect to make your marketing more relevant.

03

Researching and Segmenting Your Audiences

Once we have our customer segmentation defined (which we explored in the previous chapter), we need to enrich these segments so that they provide strategic direction from a marketing perspective. To better connect with our customers, we need to have a rich understanding of how they behave and what they value, in the context of our brand and our products/services. And while consumer behavior has long been a part of the marketing curriculum at higher education institutions around the world—I've even taught a course called "Consumer Behavior and Persuasion" at the City College of New York for many years—marketers have used limited tools in understanding their customers. One such tool is the persona. Over the last two decades, we've seen organizations in all industries and of all shapes and sizes embrace personas as a way to bring our customers to life. The common wisdom goes: By creating a profile of a person with the specificities of an individual, we can better imagine the customer we're serving—and, therefore, be more strategic in our approach to communicating with them or marketing to them.

Yet, personas—as they've often been developed—aren't really personal. They're often audience segments masquerading as deep knowledge because they include more "human" details like their supposed habits, names, or family makeups. While lackluster personas can help us plan more broadly, without more detail on each individual consumer's needs within these broad buckets marketers are often left making assumptions about what people will value in the communications they receive from brands.

Furthermore, many organizations see personas as an exercise to be done and ticked off the list. I've seen many organizations over the years which use the same personas for many years without any updates. While there are quite a few industries where the customers' needs may not radically shift over time, the world around our customers is constantly changing (just look at technology in the last three decades); therefore, we cannot rest on our laurels when it comes to understanding our customers.

To truly get specific in our communications with our customers, we need to first do the research to understand our customers in meaningful ways (more on that in Part Two). Second, we need to continuously collect the right data to be able to deliver personalized messages that resonate with them based on our understanding. In other words, we need to treat our understanding of our customers like an ongoing fitness routine: Something we need to do consistently for the health of our brands, to build strength, and to tone our marketing muscles.

Building a Robust Picture of Your Customers

Even in the development of personas, in my work advising marketing teams for major brands, I still encounter many organizations that build their personas on limited data or on the knowledge and assumptions of their employees, rather than on research. Personas or audience segments that are not built on robust research are flawed by the biases that their creators bring to the table, as well as their limited purviews. In other words, their writers include what they know (or think they know) and exclude what they don't know. To create a more rounded picture of our customers, we need a lot of information about how they think, behave, and interact with our brand categories in the world. Building this kind of profile through discovery and investigation is more akin to market research.

Market research is often a discipline held within the product development function within an organization (when it exists), whereas marketing communications teams are often brought in once the product or service is fully developed. Therefore, marketers may not automatically seek out voice-of-customer data, even when it is available within their organizations. For example, as I've been writing this chapter, my team at Convince & Convert has been kicking off work with a new client—a large healthcare organization. And in our discovery session, when I asked what customer data they use to inform their digital marketing efforts, they admitted they don't use any specifically. Yet, when I asked them what kinds of customer data their organization has about sentiment, attitudes, priorities, and behaviors, they noted that their organization collects a great deal of patient feedback including that kind of information. The obvious question was: Why didn't the marketing team think to pull in this information as they were going through their own planning process?

Again, what I see again and again is that marketers often don't use their customer research as a component of their ongoing strategic planning, but by skipping this step we fail to ground our strategy in our knowledge of the customer. In other words, leveraging your customer data allows you to not only get more specific in developing your marketing strategy, but also in developing marketing tactics that help you collect more useful data to create a virtuous cycle of feedback.

Voice-of-Customer Data

Before we get any further, let's understand: What is voice-of-customer (VOC) data? This term refers to sources of information that capture the opinions, feedback, experiences, and priorities of customers. This information, when captured and analyzed, gives brands the ability to not only better understand what matters to current customers but also make improvements to their communications to anticipate the needs of their customers going forward. Some of the common sources of VOC data include:

- *Surveys and feedback forms:* These may include market research surveys, customer satisfaction surveys, net promoter score (NPS) surveys, and other types of feedback forms. Feedback may be collected via email, website pop-up, short message service (SMS), and even direct mail.
- *Customer service interactions:* Tracking, coding, and analyzing the issues that come up in customer support or customer service interactions is one of the front lines of understanding customers in their own words.
- *Customer reviews:* Reviews on owned, partner, and third-party websites can be extremely valuable for understanding strengths and weaknesses of the product/service, as well as friction and pain points in the customer service process. Keep in mind that most reviewers tend to be on the extremes, though: It's the vocal minority of extremely happy or extremely unhappy customers who write the reviews, not the ones who had an acceptable or unmemorable experience. (See the end of this chapter for a further reading suggestion on this topic.)

- *Social listening:* Collection and analysis of both branded and unbranded terms on public social media channels can not only provide a snapshot of perception of your brand and its competitors through sentiment analysis, but it can also allow you to spot trends among your customers, such as new use cases, new users, and new sources of referral (such as when a product starts gaining momentum on a platform like TikTok). In addition to monitoring social media channels, monitoring content on blogs, websites, and forums is part of the social listening arena.

- *Search analysis:* Analyzing search behaviors on search engines and your owned brand websites gives you a great deal of insight into the terminology, topics, and related questions that your customers use in learning about your category, product, or service.

- *Community or forum engagement:* Whether you're monitoring questions on public forums such as Quora and Reddit or actively polling a private, owned community (such as a private Facebook group or a Slack channel), engaging with online communities to better understand the priorities of your customers is a valuable source of insights.

- *Customer interviews:* One-on-one or group interviews can be a powerful way to delve more deeply into the experiences, circumstances, attitudes, and cultural considerations that might impact how your customers engage with your brand. (For more on this topic, I've also included a further reading recommendation at the end of this chapter.)

With VOC data in-hand, brand teams can develop (or flesh out) robust personas that reflect the realities of their customers and identify the key differentiators that set apart these customers. These personas should include key details that make clear what are the defining characteristics that set these customers apart from other personas (in other words, what differentiates them), as well as what behaviors make them worth focusing on for the brand (such as their brand loyalty, their purchase cadence, or their willingness to try new products). When done right, personas serve as a building block for your strategic marketing framework, helping you to deliberately speak to the needs and motivations of your key audience segments (as we'll see in this next example). They should also help to shape your organizations' approach to collecting customer data to segment your audience and provide more relevant interactions with these key customers.

WHEN LESS IS MORE: FOCUSING ON THE ATTRIBUTES
THAT MATTER IN YOUR PERSONAS

While we often hear examples of audience segments based on demographics, spending behaviors, or life cycle stage—think of "young professionals" or "retirees" as possible audience segments for a financial services brand, for example—what may truly differentiate your customers may be their lifestyle, preferences, and attitudes.

For instance, the team at Sam's Club (the chain of members-only warehouse stores owned by Walmart and former client of Convince & Convert) shared that one of the core audience personas they target are what they call "Happy Hosts," in an interview on Convince & Convert's flagship podcast Social Pros. This persona loves to entertain, and they see entertaining as a way to express their affection and showcase their personality. They're focused on creating memorable experiences through food, décor, and fun—and they do so on a regular basis. What the Sam's Club team recognized is that this is a persona that is more about attitudes and shared mentality than about demographics like age cohorts or family makeup (Baer and Brown, 2023).

Because they are focusing on this desire to entertain, they are able to create campaigns that speak to a variety of different ages or even geographic considerations (campaigns for people in cooler or temperate areas may look very different from campaigns aimed at populations in desert locations), but that all share a similar emotional core around the motivations of the happy hosts. (For more on motivations, see Chapter 5.)

Customer Segments That Inform Our Data Collection

While I think that most personas fall short of the ideal state, I still believe in them as a tool. Why? It's because I believe the inherent framing of personas is human-centric—more focused on the motivations and needs of the customer than the generally broader approach of customer segments. Often, customer segments are based on how the company organizes customers for internal purposes (such as the product/service consumed, the life stage, and/ or the frequency of purchase).

But to get the most value out of your personas, they must be used as a *starting point* for planning your marketing strategy and building an approach to collecting more data; remember that it's only a starting point. To shift from personas to personalization, we need to then fill in the gaps about what's uniquely true to each customer and their relationship with the brand. We must collect data that helps to increase the relevance of our messaging, content, and offers to our customers, and we must treat the collection and updating of that data as an ongoing process.

Nine Types of Data to Collect

As you are developing your personas, you'll find that they will include a variety of details that represent the broad categories of data that you have about your customers, from your research. For each brand or organization, the categories that play the most important roles and are most useful within the personas will vary. But it's likely that your brand will both need to have research/underlying data in each of these areas *and* collect data in each of these areas to effectively conduct your marketing personalization. For the purposes of this book, I've categorized the types of data as:

- *Demographic:* Population-based data such as age, race, gender, employment, income, marriage or family status, birthdates, etc.
- *Geographic:* Physical location, but also geographic attributes such as urban versus rural, proximity to major metropolitan centers, and even proximity to physical store/business locations.
- *Customer relationship:* Data relating to the interactions between the brand and the customer, such as marketing, content consumption, lead generation, purchase and sales frequency, as well as customer service.
- *Behavioral:* Data relating to how customers behave in terms of the product/service category, their research process, their purchase process, their usage, as well as their rate of repurchasing.
- *Psychographic:* Attitudes, opinions, and beliefs that impact how the customer views the brand, the category, and related products/services (in Chapter 5 we'll look at more detailed ways to consider parsing this type of data, based on motivations).
- *Channel preference:* Attitudes towards communications channels used in marketing and general communications between the customer and the brand.
- *Technographic:* Referring to the technology stack that the customer has access to/uses, such as iPhone versus Android or specific software

providers (particularly valuable for B2B brands, as well as software/technology brands, video game brands, and smart home brands).

- *Social media:* Usage of social media channels, connected social media accounts, as well as preferences for social media channels.
- *Consent and preference:* Referring to the legal permissions and stated communications preferences that have been implicitly or explicitly agreed to.

Your Opportunity to Build a Competitive Advantage

In my research in conjunction with Convince & Convert and ICUC, we found that while the majority of organizations are collecting the basics of customer relationship data, demographic data, and consent and privacy data, only 44.5 percent are collecting behavioral data and just under 30 percent collect psychographic data (Figure 3.1).

As we'll see throughout this book, the opportunity is to get better than your competitor at providing highly relevant messages, content, and offers to your customers, and there is no better way than understanding these customers' mindsets. In Part Two of the book we'll more deeply explore how brands can create mechanisms to understand the motivations and attitudes of their customers. By doing so, brands can increase the lifetime value of their customers through more purchases, more frequent purchases, and/or more loyalty.

How does this come to life? Let's take another look at Sam's Club. In 2023, the company announced that they were rolling out a new display advertising platform, Sam's Club Member Access Platform, that leverages first-party member data, advertising data, and behavioral insights from Sam's Club. It allows third-party brands to advertise and precisely target Sam's Clubs members with offers that are unique to their mindsets, their purchase histories, and their interests in real-time. With this tool, these advertisers are able to leverage Sam's Club's deep knowledge of its members to build interest in new products, retarget people who have considered a product but haven't yet purchased, or even to remind past purchasers that it's time to buy a product again. Essentially, Sam's Club has taken its deep knowledge of its customers and turned that data itself into a new product offering—one that has the potential to provide its customers with more tailored, relevant offers. This is a competitive advantage that not only gives Sam's Club a new revenue stream, but also improves its customers' experience when shopping in its stores or on its website (Walmart, 2023).

FIGURE 3.1 We surveyed over 300 marketers and asked which of these categories of data they collect

Types of Customer Data Collected by Companies

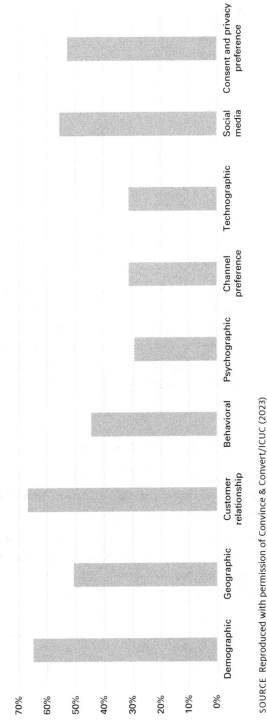

SOURCE Reproduced with permission of Convince & Convert/ICUC (2023)

RESOURCES RELATED TO THIS CHAPTER

Hug Your Haters by Jay Baer—Customer reviews are a powerful form of VOC data and a rich source of learning for every brand. If you're interested in how to learn from your reviews and how to engage with your customers to turn reviews (even the negative ones) into a valuable asset, this book is a must-read.

Interviewing Users: How to uncover compelling insights by Steve Portigal—This essential read is a valuable resource for anyone conducting user and customer interviews. Although it's written with design research or user research in mind, it makes qualitative ethnography accessible.

CHAPTER 3 SUMMARY

To make human-centric customer segments that truly allow us to speak to our customers' unique motivations and attitudes, we need to incorporate research that allows us to dig into what they truly say and think. That's where VOC data comes in. By digging into what customers say and then creating (and iterating upon) personas, marketing teams are then able to better understand what data should be collected on an ongoing basis to inform marketing efforts.

Actions

- Review existing customer segments or develop new customer segments.
- Augment these customer segments with VOC data.
- Shift from a brand-centric framing to a customer-centric framing with personas.
- Describe the data that needs to be collected on an ongoing basis to identify and segment customers going forward, paying particular attention to behavioral and psychographic data.

04

Gaining Insights When Your Resources Are Limited

In an ideal world your organization would make the necessary investments in high-quality customer research without hesitation. But I recognize that in the real world our organizations have limited budgets and time, and it can feel like a step backwards to say that we need to research our audience in order to move our marketing strategy forward. So how can we fly the metaphorical plane while we're building it? Let's take a look at three different approaches that you can use individually or in combination with each other to strengthen your personas and make strategic decisions on the types of data that will be most useful to collect and use in your personalization efforts.

Leveraging Third-Party Research

Although conducting your own first-party research allows you best control of the questions asked of your audiences and the way the research is analyzed, it's also often the biggest investment of time and resources to produce. Therefore, many organizations may elect to use third-party research as a starting point. How do you select research that is aligned with your organizational needs?

In the classes I taught at the City College of New York and Columbia University, my graduate students would take a similar approach in their assignments: Developing personas and customer journey maps (more on those in Chapter 7), without the ability to conduct real-world first-party research. Each semester, I would inevitably have a few students who would start with age cohorts and bring back data about the behaviors, needs, and interests of those age cohorts. For instance, they might find reporting on the technology preferences of Gen Z or the financial considerations of Boomers. While there are, of course high-quality research pieces that delve deeply into the needs of these specific age cohorts, such as the analyses from AARP Research (a client of both Convince & Convert and Media Volery) or reports from Pew Research, this reporting doesn't necessarily align with the best ways to segment your audiences. Unfortunately, this kind of data may be too broad or non-specific to be valuable for shaping your customer segments and personas. As we saw in Chapter 2, your audience segments will often relate to purchase behaviors, changing life stages, and/or attitudes, rather than age or other demographics. So, start with data that's highly pertinent to your audience's needs and use case, rather than making assumptions based on demographics.

To that end, I recommend leveraging industry research: What research has been conducted within the specific industry in which your brand operates? Industry-specific technology brands often publish reports based on their owned data. For instance, if your organization is in real estate, you might leverage the home-buyer reports that Zillow has produced. Trade industries are another good resource for reporting. If you are in the events space, you might leverage the data produced in conjunction with the Professional Convention Management Association (PCMA, a Convince & Convert client).

Many vendors provide reports specific to industries or even geographies. For instance, you may consider reports from IBISWorld, which offers an in-depth overview of a variety of different industries. Or if you have physical locations, you may consider purchasing reports from Esri, which offers detailed demographics and psychographics for populations in specific geographies.

Finally, you should also leverage digital audience insight tools that allow you to understand audience cohorts based on the topics they discuss and even the websites they frequent. For instance, SparkToro and Audiense Insights are two tools that identifies the online and social media behaviors of audiences, based on content they already engage with. I've used tools like these to help clients identify the skills and interests, geographies, content consumption patterns and demographics of their likely audience—based on people who follow certain accounts online, visit competitive websites, and/or discuss certain topics online. (These tools can also be used for social listening purposes, focusing on your brand's own audiences.)

While there are costs associated with sourcing high-quality, highly relevant third-party research to develop out your audience research, segmentation, and personas, it's absolutely worth the time and effort. This research grounds your audience work in the specifics of what your audience values, what channels they frequent, and who they trust. It helps you to be more strategic in what data you collect moving forward and how you analyze the behavioral signals from your customers throughout their relationship with your brand (which we'll explore in Part Two).

Capitalizing on AI and Large Language Models

While research will provide you with a great deal of direction and allow you to add depth and specificity to your personas, you may find that it still leaves questions unanswered. Furthermore, you may prefer to be able to dialogue with your customers to learn more and test hypotheses further. In the next section of this chapter, we'll look at how we can build content that helps to fulfill this roll, but short of that, what else can marketers do to get more in-depth insights into what our key personas think, feel, and do?

With the increased accessibility of AI tools built on large language models (LLMs), we all have the ability to leverage the wisdom of the crowd. Because LLMs are built upon scraping reams and reams of human language and, by their very nature, predict what are the likely words related to each word provided, they are good mimics of people—pulling from the language that people use when describing specific situations. These tools can be good brainstorming partners when you give them relatively detailed prompts or inputs.

My friend Andy Crestodina, founder of Orbit Media and an expert in content marketing and technologies for marketing, walked through the process of using AI to support persona development in a blog post on his company's website, "How to create AI marketing personas with 8 powerful prompts" (2023). In it, he suggests feeding ChatGPT (or a similar chat-based AI tool) the basic parameters of your customer segment (such as job title, business category and mission, company size and geography, and business objectives) and then asking ChatGPT to provide the goals, pain points, and decision criteria of this persona. The benefits of this approach are that, because LLMs have read thousands if not millions of pages of content from people who fit your parameters, it can provide a relatively cogent description of the goals, pain points, and decision criteria that people like this have described online. Crestodina then takes this approach further by using the tool to ask questions about the words that this persona might use to describe their marketing challenges and solutions. He also uses Bing to suggest resources that this persona might use in their research process.

All of these exercises allow you to gather more detail that approximates the types of responses that customers like yours might share based on their unique situation. (While it's not perfect, it can give more depth and specificity to your thinking about your customers' needs and motivations.) Once you have your persona revised, you can even input it into your AI and ask it to answer questions in the guise of this persona. With that capability, you have a feedback partner that can give you insights into how to make your marketing messages and content more relevant to your core personas. Ask your AI persona to rewrite descriptions or headlines to be more appealing to that persona. Ask it to give you feedback on key questions your customers may need answered. But remember: Just as with the third-party research, this is an exercise that gives you a starting point, not the official personas you should use forever and ever. Instead, treat the personas you refine with AI as hypotheses to test with real customer feedback.

Testing With Live Customers

That brings us to our final category of testing: Engaging with customers in the real world and learning on the fly. Because working with live customers is potentially costly in terms of resources and potentially risky in terms of reputation, testing with live customers should only be done once you have a strong starting point. That being said, testing should be an ongoing part of your customer segmentation and persona-building process. As I've said before, organizations must continue to revise these frameworks over time, as circumstances and audiences change.

What does testing with live customers look like? If you've ever stumbled upon a new restaurant in your neighborhood, you may have wandered in to try it out and you may have been told that they're in the "soft opening" phase. This is a period when the restaurant is open, but not yet promoting their opening, so that they can test their menu and their staff and work out the kinks. Similarly, there are many software companies that launch new product offerings in "beta" to gather feedback prior to the official launch.

Beta periods can also be a useful time to gather customer feedback on messaging and offers. Many brands test out various messages, offers, and pricing models using experimentation or multivariate testing tools to measure which versions resonate best with customers.

But beyond just putting messages passively in front of customers and waiting to see which ones resonate, your organization can also take a more proactive approach. Consider paying for survey panels to give feedback on specific offers or messaging. With the accessibility of platforms like SurveyMonkey and Cint, recruiting panels that fit your audience criteria is more affordable than ever. If you want to further engage with customers who are specifically interacting with your brand, you may consider offering discounts or gift cards to prospective customers in exchange for participating in surveys or focus groups. Using exit intent pop-ups (those windows that pop up on a website as your mouse moves out of the window) to showcase single-question surveys can also be a useful way to get feedback on specific questions that may be on the minds of your team. Lastly, ask for feedback after your interactions with customers. While many of us are aware of NPS surveys as a customer experience feedback metric, incorporating open-ended questions that encourage customers to share their feelings can give you more insights that help. (I would recommend only putting one question in front of customers at a time to increase participation and show respect for your customers' time.)

GET MORE OUT OF YOUR CUSTOMER FOLLOW-UP MESSAGES

In your follow-up communications, consider asking your customers:

- What motivated you to choose our product/service today?
- Who would you recommend our product/service to?
- Were there any challenges or issues you encountered in purchasing our product/service today?
- When you were deciding to purchase today, what's the one thing you wanted to solve for?
- How would you describe our product/service to someone considering it?
- How can we make your buying/shopping experience better?
- What can we do to help you get more out of your purchase over the next few weeks?

In addition to testing through surveys or feedback mechanisms, how customers engage with content is also a valuable mechanism for learning. In the last two decades, content marketing (the providing of valuable resources for free to customers to build brand affinity and trust) has become the backbone of many digital marketing programs. With good tracking and measurement, your organization should be able to see what content pulls in traffic to your website, as well as what traffic results in conversions to actual sales.

Creating content—on social media, on your website and landing pages, in emails, and in other channels—based on your assumptions about your core audience's needs and motivations is a useful way to test what truly resonates. Using your personas and an experimentation or multivariate tool, you can test various aspects of your content, analyze what resonates, and refine your assumptions based on what performs best. Things to test include:

- headlines
- sub-headlines
- calls-to-action (CTAs)
- meta descriptions and/or short summary statements
- value propositions or framing
- types of appeals (see Chapter 5 for more)

The goal is to understand what your customers care about and respond to by seeing what they engage with, how they engage with that content and how it impacts their relationship with your brand. For instance, perhaps your brand is a commercial bank looking to understand the priorities of your professional Millennial core customer. You may test content about building a budget to save for a new home, building a budget to save for a dream vacation, and building a budget to make a career change stress-free. By seeing which of these value propositions resonates with your audience most strongly, you may be able to develop additional content for social media, for ad campaigns, and for further nurturing those customers.

WHY MORE MARKETING QUALIFIED LEADS AREN'T ALWAYS BETTER

It's worth noting that, often, the content that drives eyeballs and traffic isn't the same as the traffic that drives sales. That's because most organizations create content broadly to attract the most traffic at the top of their sales funnels and build general awareness. And yet, there are many organizations that still gate this top-of-funnel content. Gating content refers to making customers fill out a form to obtain the content behind the gate (think of it as a paywall, but your customers provide identifying information, rather than money). When you gate top-of-funnel content, you not only decrease the access to the content itself, but you also generate a lot of marketing qualified leads (MQLs) that are not sales qualified; in other words, they may be in your marketing funnel, but they are nowhere near ready to buy or to hear from your sales team.

While our goal throughout this book is to generate more data for our organizations to understand our audiences, recognizing that all leads aren't equal is vital. In fact, we'll see in the case study below the value of scoring our leads based on the specific signals they give, rather than treating all leads as valuable from a marketing or sales point of view.

Content that educates your customers and helps them to prepare for taking action is particularly valuable, because it tends to demonstrate a desire to take that action in fairly short order. For instance, when I was getting ready to purchase my first home, my husband and I attended an event from the real estate listing website StreetEasy (owned by Zillow, Inc.). Brand partners of that event could be assured that attendees were not simply looking at real estate, but rather, making a concerted investment in their own knowledge to make a purchase. This kind of behavior is a strong signal of intent. I believe events (virtual and in-person) are particularly valuable for brands, because they not only signal high intent but they also give brands a medium to interact with customers and ask them questions in real-time. This allows brands to particularly test their assumptions and gain insights that can refine their audience knowledge quickly and efficiently. What are some ways that marketers can leverage this kind of high intent, educational content effectively as part of our audience research process? Let's take a look in this next case study.

CASE STUDY
How ON24 Empowers Brands to Capture Buying Signals at Scale

"Why are you running a webinar? Why are you doing an event? Why are you creating this landing page? What's the reason?" Tessa Barron, Vice President of Marketing at ON24, told me that she always starts her conversations with clients by asking them to dig into the behaviors they're trying to elicit and the insights that they're trying to capture. As a webinar and virtual event platform, ON24 helps its clients to run virtual events smoothly. But beyond that, they focus on making easy to connect those virtual events with the post-event marketing and sales process.

Barron told me, "What we've done is we've been able to allow for our customers to create dedicated calls-to-action within a webinar or event experience, so that that hand raiser activity can be extracted. We then allow for different mechanisms to capture that buying signal." She helps their clients think through on-screen polls or surveys for event attendees that go beyond speaking to a salesperson to signals such as unhappiness with their current vendor or searching for a solution to specific business problems. This data then improves the ongoing marketing and targeting that her clients are able to conduct, because they're more knowledgeable about the needs of the customers, as well as the appropriateness of the prospect to their sales team.

"Because everything is digital, we now have this unprecedented opportunity to learn about buyers before we've ever met them and enable those insights to help [the sales team] continue a conversation versus start cold. And I think that—what's happened in digital marketing overall is—we have suddenly been able, with the push of a button, to drastically reach more people and interact or engage at scale. But different channels have different levels of engagement, and therefore, the data that they're producing is also at different levels. Some channels are going to provide a greater opportunity to learn about a prospect and therefore qualify them and some are not," Barron noted (2023). Utilizing the right channels to learn about your customers as part of your ongoing marketing practice allows you to continue to refine and improve the accuracy of your personalization and the relevance of your marketing.

As we've seen throughout Part One (Chapters 1 through 4), building an understanding of your audiences, identifying your key customer segments, and building mechanisms to learn more about your customers is vital to both your marketing strategy and your overall business strategy. With a deep understanding of your customers, you can begin to build your toolkit for personalization, which we'll explore in Part Two. We'll then explore how to get even more nuanced and resonant with audiences by tapping into their emotions and communities in Parts Three and Four. Finally, in Parts Five and Six, we'll circle back around to how we put this work into practice through our infrastructure and teams. Let's get to it!

RESOURCES RELATED TO THIS CHAPTER

"Generative AI for content marketers: 10 ways to use artificial intelligence for productivity and performance" (orbitmedia.com/events/webinar-ai-for-content-marketers) presented by Andy Crestodina—If you want to learn more about how you can use AI to support your development of your persona, be sure to tune into this webinar from Crestodina. It's a detailed and very actionable walk-through.

"How to create a content marketing strategy in 7 easy steps" (convinceandconvert.com/content-marketing/how-to-create-a-content-marketing-strategy) by Anna Hrach, Jenny Magic, and Jay Baer—This blog post walks through Convince & Convert's approach for building a content marketing strategy, including its framework for mapping your core audiences to their journey steps to their key questions (5x5x5).

CHAPTER 4 SUMMARY

While conducting first-party research is the ideal state, not every brand or marketing team has the time and resources to do so. What should you do when you can't conduct first-party research? Leverage highly relevant third-party research, use AI based on LLMs to add nuance and bring personas to life, and/or test your content with audiences through content marketing and experimentation.

Actions

- ☐ Review your customer segments and personas to identify gaps in your knowledge.
- ☐ Source high-quality third-party research that can provide insights and augment your segmentation and personas.
- ☐ Use AI as a resource to add nuance and turn your personas into a planning and brainstorming tool.
- ☐ Identify ways to incorporate testing of your hypotheses into your content.

PART TWO

Building the Toolkit
for Personalization

5

Preparing for Personalization

The Strategy Behind the Data

Once you have a strong understanding of your audience, you need to build a toolkit that allows your organization to truly personalize your customer's experience across different touchpoints. Data—enough of it, and the right kinds—is the next step. But what data do you need?

Beyond the basics of identifiers like name, email address, address, phone number, etc., you'll need a variety of information to help make your messaging more relevant to customers. Before deciding what types of information you'll need, it's important to take a step back to understand what kinds of personalization will resonate with your audience. What matters depends on the nature of the product/service/transactions they engage in with you and the psychology of that decision-making process. So let's first take a detour into the realms of behavioral psychology and rhetoric.

Working With Limited Cognitive Bandwidth

Have you ever—after a long, busy day at work—gotten home and been asked by your significant other, spouse, roommate, or family member, "What do you want for dinner?" You respond, "I don't know!" And perhaps, if you're like me, you feel a little resentful that they're asking you the question at all, because you feel burnt out from every other decision you've already made during the day.

That mental exhaustion is normal. We all have limited cognitive bandwidth for decision-making, and as the day wears on, it's more and more difficult for us to make decisions. To help extend our mental bandwidth, our brains use heuristics (or mental shortcuts) to help make decisions more quickly where possible. These mental shortcuts are an example of one of the modes of thinking we use to make decisions.

In his influential book *Thinking, Fast and Slow*, psychologist Daniel Kahneman describes two systems of thinking—one that is quick, based on intuition, and emotion-driven, and the other which is more deliberate and logic-oriented—which coexist in our minds. Kahneman calls the instinctive mode "system one," and outlines it as relying on habit, estimation, and the unconscious—whether that's emotion or expertise. He calls the deliberative mode "system two;" this system is effortful, requiring analysis and reflection. Kahneman explains that how we make decisions is an interplay of these two systems, where sometimes one system dominates and in other cases the two systems work together (2011).

Using System One: Forces of Habit

Imagine going to the grocery store or supermarket for your weekly food shopping. Imagine yourself entering the store, walking through the produce aisle, the dairy aisle, etc. You can probably already conjure up exactly what you would pick up in each section. You know the brand of your favorite yogurt and the design of the boxes of snacks that your family always grabs.

Now imagine coming to an exciting endcap or display in the store. It would probably only take you a few seconds to decide whether or not to give this new product a shot, based on the brand, the type of product, the price, and what you know about your family's preferences. Unless you have specific dietary limitations, you might not even look at the ingredients or read the label too carefully. You might go on the box design, the brand, and your general knowledge of the product type. It's a snap judgment, based on your gut. That's a decision that uses system one thinking. Why? Because groceries are relatively low-cost items, you won't waste a lot of energy making your decision. Instead, you'll go with your instincts or habits and move on.

Now let's imagine that you run the marketing team for this grocery store. And you're crafting out a personalized offer from the store as an email or SMS to a regular shopper to get them to add something new to their basket. What kind of language or offer might be compelling to them? It might highlight a product that's from a brand they already trust. Or perhaps it would showcase a product that the store says lots of families like theirs tend to buy but that they haven't yet tried. Or perhaps it describes a product that's complementary to their diet—say guacamole, because they buy a lot of chips and salsa. In other words, the language or offer that would capture their attention would likely tap into their grocery shopping habits, behaviors, and considerations.

On the other hand, you probably wouldn't cite an academic study or create a graph about the relevance of guacamole to their diet. You probably wouldn't send them a three-page essay on the features of the product either. Your message would focus on demonstrating trust in simple ways (e.g., brands they already trust, testimonials from others like them, citations of shoppers like them). And you would make the key benefit of their purchase crystal clear. Basically, you would likely make it easy for them to use system one to make the decision. By aligning the personalized offer to their needs and the ways in which they make decisions about this particular product, this message would make it easy for them to say yes.

System One Throughout the Customer Journey

In the previous example we looked at how an offer might work at the end of the customer journey, when you're about to decide to purchase something. However, you'll also see personalization aimed at system one thinking throughout the customer journey. For instance, if you've ever shopped with Amazon (and in this day and age, who hasn't?), you know that the company showcases related products in a wide variety of ways. From items "inspired by your shopping history" to "related products" to "frequently bought together," each Amazon page highlights a ton of different ways to explore additional items. It's how Amazon keeps you browsing, even if the item on this page isn't the exact one that you're looking for. Amazon recognizes that you might not yet be ready to buy, but they sure as heck want you to buy with them when you find the perfect thing.

This type of cross-merchandising makes it easy for someone to use their fast mode of thinking to explore products as they work through the "consideration" phase of their customer journey. And, in fact, it's become so common that even small businesses on ecommerce platforms like Shopify or WooCommerce can take advantage of these basic types of tools. While Amazon is using complex algorithms to tailor its recommendations to each individual user, even off-the-shelf ecommerce platforms are often showing related products or offers based on simple rules. For instance, if you're looking at sneakers, the platform may show other sneakers as related products. But as AI gets embedded in more and more off-the-shelf ecommerce solutions, we'll also see an increase in the level of specificity of recommendations for stores of all shapes and sizes—suggestions based not only on what you're looking at now, but what you've previously purchased, what colors you like, and the price points that you tend to shop at.

Appealing to System Two: Taking it Step-by-Step

What kinds of decisions trigger you to use your system two thinking? In general, these decisions tend to require more resources and have a larger impact. The purchase might be expensive (say, a car), very important to the customer (such as their child's day-care), or have a lot of stakeholders involved (for instance, hiring a service provider for your business). Because these purchase decisions are higher value, your brain activates this more effortful and deliberate way of thinking. System two requires you to take the time to weigh options, do research, and mull. In fact, the process of research feels necessary to making a good decision. Therefore, to make a decision, you'll tend to seek out enough information to feel comfortable to make a call.

Purchase decisions that require system two thinking can be found among both B2B and B2C businesses. At my agency, Media Volery, all of our clients tend to fall into this category—they're not specifically B2B or B2C, but rather, they're organizations whose customers have lengthier customer journeys. They range from engineering firms and consultancies on the B2B side, to architecture firms and fine jewelry companies in the B2C space, to higher education institutions. For organizations like these, they know that their prospects will engage in a lot of research and deliberation, so it's vital to get the right messages in front of them to help these prospects build the case for saying yes. Furthermore, it's important to have enough information available—these firms can't rely solely on package design or associations. They need to have strong arguments.

THE ESSENTIAL NATURE OF EMOTION IN DECISION-MAKING

While it may seem like the head would overrule the gut, when it comes to system two decisions, science actually shows that emotions are vital to decision-making. In fact, those who have brain damage to the parts of the brain that control emotions have trouble making even basic decisions.

In his noted book, *Descartes' Error: Emotion, reason, and the human brain*, neuroscientist Antonio Damasio shares the story of Elliot, a businessman who—after undergoing surgery to remove a brain tumor pushing on his frontal lobes—found that his life fell apart. Despite having his language and intelligence faculties intact, he could no longer reach decisions effectively, because his emotion centers were damaged and he could no longer feel strong emotions about anything. Instead, he would deliberate and deliberate without being able to come to any resolutions. His lack of emotions limited his abilities to choose based on the information at hand. Neuroscientists have documented other cases with similar results; where the emotion centers are damaged, decision-making is impacted (1994).

The takeaway for us as marketers and communicators is that appealing to emotions is always essential, even in decisions that seem like they should be purely rational.

Having a fundamental understanding of how your audience makes decisions about your product/service/category is extremely valuable to understanding what information they will prioritize receiving. This, in turn, will allow you to be strategic in how you prioritize the data to collect and the personalization you provide.

Crafting Persuasive Messages Like Aristotle

If you've ever taken an intro to philosophy course, you may have encountered the Greek philosopher Aristotle's model of rhetoric. In his influential work *On Rhetoric* he identifies four types of appeals: Ethos, pathos, logos, and kairos.

Ethos is persuasion based on credibility. The audience should believe in the presenter of the information. This type of persuasion can be based on reputation or familiarity, signals of trust and expertise, and third-party validation. For brands or organizations, ethos can come to life through testimonials, press coverage, customer reviews, third-party accreditations or awards, showcasing experts within the organization, or endorsements by other trusted sources.

Pathos is persuasion based on emotional resonance. The audience should feel moved by the presenter. In marketing communications, this comes to life through relevance—does the emotional appeal align to the audience's beliefs, experiences, and/or desires? Brands such as Patagonia, which focuses on a purpose-driven approach to business, consistently leverage pathos in their messaging. For instance, as part of their 50th anniversary campaign, the brand included this statement on their website, "For our 50th year, we're looking forward, not back, to life on Earth. Together, we can prioritize purpose over profit and protect this wondrous planet, our only home" (Patagonia, 2023). This framing helps customers see themselves as part of this mission and part of a community driven by this desire.

Logos is persuasion through logic. The audience should believe that the information, evidence, and use cases presented are right. Brands or organizations will often showcase product features, case studies, and demonstrations to aid in this type of persuasion. However, data and research, particularly around the behaviors and needs of the audience's peers (e.g., people like you save two hours in their workday by using our tool) can also be powerful logos appeals.

The final type of appeal is kairos, or persuasion through timeliness. The audience should feel moved to action because of how the timing is framed. You often see limited time offers and discounts based on holidays. Even B2B businesses might offer sharper pricing at the end of a quarter or focus on their clients' end-of-year goals as a way to message the importance of moving fast or striking while the iron is hot. All of these are examples of appeals based on timing.

These four types of appeals make up the ingredients that convince your audience to act. Picture them as criteria on a spider chart (sometimes called a radar chart)—see Figure 5.1—where the mix might be different for each

FIGURE 5.1 Example spider chart of the appeals that might resonate with two different audiences

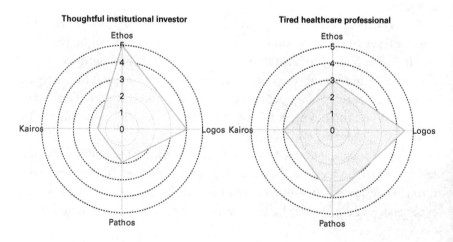

scenario, with arms pulling more towards one or more of the four appeals than the others. For some audience segments, you'll need to be heavy on logos and ethos—for instance, for an institutional investor choosing an asset management firm. For a brand like this, you'd need to demonstrate the benefits, processes, and capabilities of the firm, as well as prove the trustworthiness and stalwart nature of the organization. For others, you may need to focus more on pathos and logos. For instance, for sneakers aimed at healthcare professionals, you might focus on the unique challenges (long days and exhaustion!) of healthcare professionals, as well as the impact of the feet on full-body comfort and health.

Hitting the Sweet Spot With Rhetoric and Personalization

How does this mix of appeals come to life in terms of data-driven personalization? Here's an example from my own life: As the mom of a baby, I've been preparing for my child to start eating solid foods. As I've been browsing content on where to start and what to do, social media platforms like Meta are tracking the content I engage with through their platform to identify my interest in these topics. Advertisers who use Meta, such as Amazon, are then able to target me with items such as baby-friendly bowls, cups, and spoons. I recently purchased a set of silicone cutlery and bowls inspired by some ads on Instagram (owned by Meta). Because of this purchase, Amazon's database was updated with that shopping behavior and interest category as well. So the next time I logged into Amazon, it showed me another featured product based on my recent purchase: A 13-in-1 food processor for baby food with all the accessories you need. How convenient! It even had a red tag that highlighted a limited time deal: 33 percent off this product for the next 24 hours. Plus an orange tag indicated that this item was the #1 bestseller in this category. And of course, like all Amazon products, it included the item's star rating prominently in this featured box. Reader, I bought the food processor.

What Amazon did was successfully leverage the right mix of ethos (high star ratings), pathos (aimed specifically at parents), logos (strong value proposition, clear product features), and kairos (limited time offer, featured prominently just after I had purchased related products) to make me act. Not only did they create an argument that was persuasive based on my experiences and needs, but the timing of the presentation and the limited time nature of the deal made it so that it was top of mind and irresistible for me. Pulling all of these different arguments in a highly personalized way isn't just the territory of large organizations like Amazon, it's also the basis of techniques such as account-based marketing (ABM), which is a methodology in B2B marketing to target highly relevant accounts, one-to-one, with highly compelling content. Whether your brand is large or small, having the data to help you shape this kind of personalized messaging is the key to driving more relevant engagement with customers and more sales.

Aligning Audience Needs With Data Collection

Once you know how your audience thinks—fast or slow—you'll understand what kind of information they'll tend to seek out or respond to and how much information they'll need to make a decision. Understanding rhetorical appeals allows you to shape the right messages to move them to action. These concepts are two sides of the same coin and they help to define the story that your audience needs to hear and the supporting arguments that will make the case. As you consider the data to collect, keep in mind how your audience segments think, as well as what kinds of appeals will matter to them. If you're not sure, go back to Chapter 3 to review the steps for defining and researching your segments as a foundation to determining your data needs.

Of course, your brand will need to collect basic demographics and identification information for your customers, but what else can/should you collect to help you appeal to ethos, logos, pathos, and kairos? Let's consider them one by one.

Ethos

Within this category, demographic, geographic, channel preference, and customer relationship data will be highly valuable. Here are a few examples:

- *Industry:* To demonstrate your relevant experience, to provide case studies and testimonials.
- *Size of organization:* To show that you understand organizations like theirs.
- *New or return customer (relationship to the brand):* To gauge the level of familiarity.
- *How they learned about your brand (referral source):* To tailor communications based on what they might already know or have heard.

Pathos

For appeals of pathos, making sure that you have psychographic data is obvious, as is preference data, but customer relationship and social media data can also be valuable to round out your understanding of customers. In addition, consider the following:

- *Interests:* Whether stated or inferred; in addition to leveraging stated interests on your website, advertising using lookalike audiences and then tracking user behavior on-site (such as in the Amazon baby food processor example) can be a good way to create a feedback loop on interests, when you don't own that data yourself.

- *Priorities:* Whether stated or inferred; while you can ask customers directly what their priorities or challenges are (through on-site quizzes, email welcome series, etc.), you can also infer this based on content they engage with by developing content tagged based on specific priority areas.

- *Goals:* Similar to their priorities, you can use a mix of stated and inferred information to identify their goals; for brands with a hands-on sales/business development process, goals should also be tagged using a standardized schema to help facilitate scaled personalization and make the data more usable.

- *Identity or affiliation:* Depending on your product or service, how they identify (e.g., new mom, healthcare provider, vegan, casual dresser) or their affiliations (alumna/alumnus, organization member) can be another powerful piece of knowledge to show emotional connection and relevance in messaging.

- *Brand affinities:* As with the earlier grocery shopping example, knowing what brands are preferred by your customer can be valuable, whether you carry multiple brands or if you're a family of brands (think of Gap Inc. with Gap, Banana Republic, Old Navy, and Athleta).

Logos

Because of the factual nature of this type of appeal, making sure that you have demographic, customer relationship, channel preference, and technographic data (how they use technology to engage with your brand) helps you to be highly relevant. Specific examples include:

- *Role:* To help you showcase relevant examples, evidence, use cases, and also to help them make the case to other stakeholders.

- *Team/group/family size:* Similar to role, this helps you showcase information that's specific to their needs.

- *Content consumption behaviors:* Tracking how individuals engage with your brand's content on-site and off-site is highly valuable to inferring much of the information above; while it's not always possible to track behaviors off-site, building in calls-to-action that drive them to click on tracked links can help bridge that gap.

- *Sales process engagement behaviors:* This can include points of contact (e.g., chatbot, phone call, live demonstration, customer service outreach), as well as topics discussed; this information allows you to demonstrate to the customer that your brand cares about the interaction history and their purchase journey so far.

- *Purchase behaviors:* When, how, what, how often, and how much they've purchased; for products, this should come from your ecommerce system, but for services, making sure that your customer relationship management (CRM) system is integrated into your marketing tools is vital to using this data for customization.

Kairos

Once again, behavioral data, customer relationship data, and also social media data can be valuable to understanding relevant timing for messaging. Specific ways you can bring that to life include:

- *Account age:* To offer status for loyalty, to identify newer or older accounts for special offers or reactivation.

- *Key dates:* Think of birthday discounts, children's ages, or even key industry dates to determine the right content/products to showcase.

- *Recent behaviors:* Recognizing correlations between the timing of behaviors can often help you better tailor when certain messages will resonate, as with my baby-food processor example.

Thinking about your data based on the appeals may not feel as intuitive as using the traditional categories we cover in Chapter 3, but I hope you see that the value of doing so helps you to clearly unite the data with its marketing purpose and the impact on customers. By turning how we think about data on its head to start with audience needs, we can become more mindful of the opportunities for personalization and persuasion. After all, the value of the data is not in having the information, but rather in informing your marketing to be more effective at converting your customers.

EXERCISE

Audit Your Current Data Streams

These are just a few examples of the categories of data that you may want to collect to take to capitalize on these four types of appeal. Audit the data that you currently collect within your organization. Is there a category that's relevant to your business in which you collect very little data? Identify the gaps, create a list, and prioritize the opportunities to build up your database.

RESOURCES RELATED TO THIS CHAPTER

Thinking, Fast and Slow by Daniel Kahneman—Many of the ideas that Kahneman and his long-time collaborator Amos Tversky developed are now a part of everyday business discussions and behavioral psychology terminology, but the original book is a useful and thoughtful read that's worth revisiting.

Thank You for Arguing: What Aristotle, Lincoln, and Homer Simpson can teach us about the art of persuasion by Jay Heinrichs—In this engaging read, Heinrichs gives useful examples of how rhetorical appeals can be used in everyday conversations.

CHAPTER 5 SUMMARY

Based on your audience research and personas, your team must set the strategy for data-driven personalization by looking at data collection from the point of view of what information is relevant to persuade your audience segments. Understanding the behavioral psychology of your audience segments and starting from their considerations will allow you to not only collect more valuable data, but also to deliver more convincing messages.

Actions

- Align audience needs with data collection through ethos/pathos/logos/ kairos.
- Audit current data streams to identify gaps in information and prioritize additional data to gather.

06

Setting Up Data Systems for Today and Tomorrow

Collect more data. If there's any obvious takeaway from this book, it would be that. But beyond just *more* data, I want you to think about more *useful* data—and preferably data that will continue to be useful to you far into the future. Your data must serve as the backbone of your marketing approach, even as customers' expectations continue to evolve in the coming years. And in case you haven't already noticed, it doesn't matter whether you're a big company or a small business. It doesn't matter if you're B2B or B2C. It doesn't matter if you're selling sandals or offering heart surgery. Customer expectations is a rising tide that all brands must learn to navigate.

For example, over the years, I've worked with many large organizations in regulated industries, from financial services to insurance to healthcare. And the marketers within these organizations often tell me that they know their organization is behind when it comes to digital marketing disciplines, but they also know that their competitors are no better. This may be true, but their customers don't just compare the marketing they receive from these brands to their direct competitors—they compare them to the messages they're getting from their favorite clothing store or the ads they receive on their preferred social media platform. It's not good enough to keep apace of your competitors, because you are competing for your audience's attention and their cognitive bandwidth. And as discussed earlier in the book, cognitive bandwidth is limited—and the amount of content and messaging coming at your audiences shows no signs of slowing down. In fact, digital consumption patterns have grown significantly over the last several years. During the Covid-19 pandemic, digital consumption patterns rose 30 percent and research indicates that these trends had a lasting impact on behaviors (Clapp, 2021).

In addition, in the last several years, we've seen a huge shift in the way brands are able to leverage third-party data as Google and other major platforms have shifted away from cookies. The more difficult it is to use third-party platforms to identify customers by behaviors and interests, the more important it is that your organization consistently identifies and tracks customers and prospects across its own omnichannel ecosystem. This is just one example of the macro trends that have huge impacts on businesses. Without preparing for these inevitable shifts, your organization can easily be left behind as other competitors more rapidly adapt to major changes in the digital landscape.

Furthermore, as the pace of AI tools integrated into analytics platforms, business intelligence tools, and CRM platforms continues to increase, your ability to learn from your data continues to increase. But your ability to extract insights is only as good as the underlying data itself. You may not always know when these tectonic shifts in the digital landscape will happen, but even when you do, you and your organization may not necessarily have established an approach to stay forward-thinking. What must your organization do to better use data today and stay adaptable to new market conditions in the future?

Start With Your Foundation: Unify Your Data

If your organization is like most companies out there, it's likely that you have many different sources of data that you use for marketing and personalization. You may have CRM, an email service provider, an advertising platform, an ecommerce platform, plus social media analytics, website analytics, direct mail reports, etc. Perhaps you have some of this information pulling into a data studio or business intelligence dashboard to view key metrics in one place. But still, this method doesn't necessarily unify the data in a way that allows you to query across sources meaningfully. To make the most of your data and allow for more relevant, accurate, and impactful personalization, it's imperative to bring your data together into one source that allows you to analyze it in multiple ways. Furthermore, it's only with one single view of your customers as a whole that you can deliver experiences that demonstrate that your brand knows them, you know what you've been through together, and you know what they want to see.

While there are different considerations in terms of speed, flexibility, and usability depending on your organization's sophistication and capabilities, the key takeaway is that it's vital to move towards a central data repository as soon as possible. One single source of truth—driven by automated connections rather than spreadsheets that are prone to human error—will allow you and your team to pull more accurate and usable insights out of your data.

DATA LAKES VS. WAREHOUSES VS. MARTS: A PRIMER

You may have heard of data lakes and data warehouses, but what are they and how are they used?

- A data lake is a raw or unstructured repository where data is fed from multiple sources, but the information has not been organized or processed for analysis. This raw form allows for real-time analytics, as well as machine learning use cases.

- A data warehouse similarly contains large amounts of data from a variety of sources, but whereas a data lake is not structured, a data warehouse stores *structured* data, which is highly curated and whose purpose is defined.

- A data mart is a sub-type of data warehouse designed specifically for the needs/questions of a specific business unit (e.g., marketing or operations).

Most organizations will have a mix of data marts and data warehouses or lakes; this allows their teams to share a single source of truth while also accessing faster insights, based on specific teams' needs.

CASE STUDY
How FreshDirect's Unified Data Allows
it to Adapt With its Customers' Needs

Started in 2002, American online grocery company FreshDirect serves the New York metropolitan area, delivering brand name groceries and meals to its customers across New York, New Jersey, and Connecticut. It's so popular in Brooklyn, where I live, that you'll often see its signature reusable shopping bags on the shoulders of locals running errands or at the park.

What sets FreshDirect apart from its competitors is a high level of sophistication when it comes to its omnichannel customer experience. From shopping on its website to its use of SMS, email, and direct mail, FreshDirect is truly an organization that has implemented data-driven personalization in a helpful and engaging way for its customers.

This approach has come from years of investing in technology to help unify its data and deliver personalized experiences to customers (Selligent Marketing Cloud, 2020). In an interview with IBM Cloud Stories (2015), Dave Gerridge, Senior Director of Marketing Operations for FreshDirect at the time, described how their aim was to meaningfully segment their customers and identify customer needs. They wanted to bridge the gap between data across sources such as online purchase history, survey responses, browsing behavior from their mobile apps, and data from third-party providers. By doing so, the organization was able to build highly personal, relevant communications, not only on their website and app, but also in email and SMS.

This clarity in terms of customer behavior has also allowed FreshDirect to identify the best channels for each stage of the customer journey, from direct mail for customer acquisition to email and SMS for retention.

Invest in Data Quality

Once your data is unified, the next thing your organization must invest in is data hygiene. Regularly cleaning (e.g., removing duplicates, removing old records, correcting errors) and updating your records allows you to maintain the validity and usability of your data. Particularly when your data is being pulled together from multiple sources, as we discussed in the previous section, there is often room for error and inaccuracies that create poor customer experiences.

To illustrate: My husband and I have a membership at our local botanic garden, and because it's a five-minute walk from our apartment, we often go visit. Recently, my husband received a direct mail piece from the botanic garden; thinking it might be a message about his status as a frequent visitor, he opened it. But it was, in fact, an appeal to him as a neighbor of the botanic garden to join as a member. He was a little offended that the garden, which he often visits twice a week during the warm months, didn't even know that he was a frequent visitor. There is no reason that their direct mail lists shouldn't have been compared with their existing database to be de-duplicated. Furthermore, the garden had the opportunity to use this additional comparison to identify hyper-local members for communications personalized to their needs.

To ensure that your data stays clean and errors (such as unusable email addresses, incorrectly formatted phone numbers or addresses, etc.) are kept to a minimum, be sure to enforce data entry standards using rules and standardized abbreviations or fields. Case in point: Instead of allowing users on your website to type in their state, province, or country, use a drop-down menu so they can select from standard options. Similarly, be sure to use data validation/verification tools wherever possible; these tools can ensure information is correct, even allowing you to cross-reference your data with third-party datasets (such as email and company records—particularly useful for B2B prospecting) to ensure that your data is high quality.

Finally, your organization must make sure that data audits are a regular part of its processes. This can allow your team to identify errors and correct them before their impact is too widespread, and it ensures that your organization does not allow embarrassing errors that undermine brand trust. As an example: When Twitter transitioned to X Corp, I received an email about the transition addressed to a name that was unfamiliar to me; it made me double-check that the email wasn't a phishing scheme (it wasn't). Two days later I received an email apologizing for the error, but with no personalization within it—perhaps they were afraid of making the same mistake twice. There's absolutely no reason that automated emails, which pull in data, should ever be addressed to the wrong person's name—the most basic information brands should associate with an account. Don't make this simple, but reputationally costly, mistake. Regularly scheduled data audits should review data entry standards and processes, spot-check data quality, and review how data is being used.

How can your organization stay on top of data hygiene? Be sure to establish data governance policies that identify data ownership, data quality standards, and identify use cases. Write them down, distribute them, socialize them with your team through regular trainings, and update them based on new and changing industry considerations. In addition, it's important to make sure that staff are trained on data hygiene and maintenance. So many teams will touch your data and data structures—from sales and marketing to customer service to IT and engineering. Be sure that you have clear lines of sight when it comes to who is responsible for what, and make sure guidelines and policies are accessible and shared.

Leverage AI and Machine Learning

To get the most out of your data, knowing what questions to ask is key. Andrew Pole was a statistician for the big box store Target back in 2002 when he was asked by the marketing department if he could figure out a way to identify pregnant customers based on behavioral data, even if the customer had not identified as such. Capturing customers during their second trimester of pregnancy—when new mothers start to shop for pregnancy and baby-related items—was the goal (Duhigg, 2012). In an article for *The New York Times Magazine*, Charles Duhigg describes how Pole and the team at Target ran test after test to identify the patterns that correlated with pregnancy—including things like purchasing unscented lotion, purchasing particular supplements, and buying some other specific products.

Not every company has a large data analysis team like Target's, which can parse the data in multiple ways and test their hypotheses again and again. Luckily, as AI becomes more accessible and affordable, these technologies make it easier to ingest and interpret data quickly—and with high rates of accuracy. Organizations of all shapes and sizes will be able to spend more time identifying key questions and using natural language interfaces to pull out the answers from their own data sets. Already, tools such as Google Analytics—the free website analytics tool from Google—have introduced insights tools that can respond to natural language queries.

However, machine learning technologies will allow teams to go a step further—enabling machines to learn from data to solve problems, automate tasks, and make decisions. In the healthcare field, doctors are already using machine learning to personalize cancer screenings and improve patient outcomes (Gordon, 2022). Leveraging larger data sets to train on, machine learning might allow your team to identify patterns of behavior that impact buying, returns, cancellation, or loyalty well before they occur, so that your team can take action and communicate in meaningful ways. In the example of pregnant customers, machine learning will make it easier than ever for teams to identify the purchases that past customers made while pregnant and then identify new pregnant customers in the future.

IMPLEMENT ADAPTIVE METHODOLOGY

To paraphrase the Greek philosopher Heraclitus: The only constant in life is change. To make sure that your organization stays ahead of—or at least on top of—the shifts in consumer behavior, technology, and policy that we've discussed throughout this chapter, it's important to research in a way that's adaptive.

In their article on adaptive methodology in the *International Journal of Social Research Methodology* (2021), researchers Kristof van Assche, Raoul Beunen, Martijn Duineveld and Monica Gruezmacher describe the value of adaptive methodology in research, stating that this approach relies on learning that is taking place within the research itself, as well as broader knowledge or learnings from the researcher or team. In other words, you should iterate your research design and continue to change how and what data you seek out, collect, and analyze along the way—rather than taking one static approach over time.

To prepare for future changes, it's imperative that your team take an adaptive approach to researching and understanding your customers, their preferences, and their usage patterns. Research cannot be one and done; it must be a living, ever-changing part of your data collection and improvement process. This approach allows you to adjust based on new learnings and new assumptions, keep questioning the bias in your data, and evolve your analyses to reflect the moment, not history.

Identify and Interface With New Behaviors

Now that we've got the data housekeeping done, let's talk about your customers and potential changes in how they behave. The good news is that, if you're using the frameworks in Chapter 5 to identify types of personalization that will resonate with your audience and collect data to speak to those customer needs, you're already laying a strong foundation for future-proofing your data. That's because you are collecting data that allows you to appeal directly to the ways in which your audience makes decisions.

But, often, how your audience makes decisions may be impacted by changes beyond your control. Outside forces change what your audiences prioritize. As smartphones became more and more prevalent, their presence in the hands of in-store shoppers changed the way people browsed products. Rather than asking a salesperson to help them find products, many people (especially Millennials and Gen Z) adapted to relying on their phones to augment their shopping experience. For example, shoppers at beauty retailer Sephora are often observed looking at their phones when browsing its aisles. Several years ago, its executive team took note, and they conducted research to understand what behaviors they were engaging in. According to a case study from Think with Google (Adams et al., 2015), their team discovered that most of their customers were looking for past-purchase information (i.e., what color or formulation they had previously purchased) or looking up reviews for the products they were considering. Based on these learnings, Sephora developed their mobile app and mobile website functionality to align with their customers' behaviors in these specific instances.

In addition to better serving customers based on those behaviors, the mobile website and app allow Sephora to capture key information, such as brand preferences, colors purchased, frequency of purchase, purchase history, etc. This provides the company with detailed first-party data that is then useful to customize the offers and messaging that can be served to each individual—whether in-app, in-store (at the cash register), or through other channels, such as email or SMS. What Sephora recognized was that there was a shopping behavior within their purchase journeys (checking their phones for information) that customers were engaging in that the company could facilitate or participate in.

Incentivize Your Customers to Engage

For Sephora's customers, the benefit of the app was that it allowed them to keep track of information they would want handy for cosmetic shopping. When it comes to cosmetics, knowing which colors you usually purchase or which formulations agree with your skin is very important—so the brand was able to tap into a pre-existing behavior and capitalize on it as they developed the functionality of their app. The inherent incentive is purchasing the right product that suits the customer's skin. But what if your customers don't have an organic need like this?

How do you incentivize your customers to engage with an app or other digital touchpoint in that case, in order to capture this valuable first-party data? Again, look to how customer behaviors are shifting. According to McKinsey & Company (Gerards et al., 2018), the apparel industry has had to use historic levels of promotion to fight against declines in customer traffic. With this trend in mind, it's no wonder that Japanese casual clothing retailer Uniqlo, which also has an app for its shoppers, is using push notifications to capture in-store shoppers' attention with exclusive offers and timely discounts. This in turn allows them to connect their customers' in-store and online shopping behaviors, allowing them to offer incentives more accurately and drive future shopping behaviors. With speed and convenience paramount post-pandemic, large brands including Sam's Club—the warehouse club chain owned by Walmart—as well as smaller brands like New York City specialty supermarket chain Fairway Market use their apps to help customers speed up their shopping process by offering scan-and-pay within the apps. As with Uniqlo, it allows them to connect in-store shopping with interim behaviors like building a shopping list. Whether you're helping your customers save money or time, the incentives should tap into the motivations of your customers within the category.

This approach to tapping into emerging customer behaviors goes beyond B2C applications. In the late 2010s, global technology company Cisco noted that its reseller partners were investing more into their digital marketing efforts. To that end, it developed its Marketing Velocity program, an online education platform, and worked with our team at Convince & Convert to develop live, cohort-based marketing education for these resellers. This program not only allowed Cisco to better serve its partners, but also to learn from them and identify highly engaged resellers for whom they could offer further resources. By adapting to the shifting practices of their customers, Cisco was able to build reseller loyalty and also support sales.

Recognize Trends and Behavioral Shifts

In the last few decades, we've seen drastic changes in consumer behaviors—from the rise of short-form video (TikTok, Instagram Reels) to shopping behaviors reconfiguring during the Covid-19 pandemic to increased accessibility of AI to all industries. What will be next? Will we see voice-activated technologies finally become a staple of everyday life as AI bolsters its utility? Will we see virtual reality transform how we gather and shop, just as the internet did before it? Unfortunately, I don't have a crystal ball.

As you saw with Sephora and Cisco, there are a lot of micro shifts in behaviors that can create new opportunities to collect data and intervene in your customers' journeys. At the same time, there are macro shifts in your industry, such as with Uniqlo and Sam's Club, that brands must grapple with and adapt to in order to stay competitive. How should you recognize these trends so that you can get ahead of them?

First, question the trends that you're seeing in your quantitative data. It's not enough for your team to notice that certain metrics are trending in a specific direction month-over-month or year-over-year; it's also important to question why they're trending that direction and what it means. For instance, when smartphones became ubiquitous, most websites saw that more and more traffic was starting to come from mobile devices, but organizations that identified what were the most important activities that customers were likely to engage with and why they were using the websites on the go were able to adapt their content to suit the needs of their audiences in a meaningful, high-value way—and to identify the personalization opportunities that would keep customers coming back.

For example, some years ago, we worked with a large regional home builder whose mobile website was simply a responsive version of their desktop website. But because the desktop site was busy and had a lot of extraneous information, our team at Convince & Convert identified the opportunities to streamline the mobile experience to focus only on the key activities that people were likely to engage with on their mobile devices, such as finding open houses in specific communities or browsing home listings for later. But how could they have taken this experience further through personalization? What if—based on the observation that open houses got the most traffic, especially on weekends—the mobile website offered up potential itineraries to view several houses in the chosen neighborhood? What if the home page only showed listings based on customers' saved criteria, each time they returned to the website? Could they have driven more foot traffic into open houses and/or shown more relevant homes to people who were already primed to visit? Those small tweaks would have driven significant business results.

In the previous example, we can infer a great deal from which pages and functionality were being used on the mobile website. However, the most forward-thinking teams are pairing quantitative research with qualitative research—using surveys, focus groups, and even in-field observation to learn what behaviors may be changing in real-time. They understand that existing data isn't going to give you all the answers. In fact, relying on existing data can create blind spots—we don't know what we don't know.

Think Like an Anthropologist

As we saw with the Sephora example, it was employees standing in the stores who flagged the behaviors of customers in the aisles. They identified that this behavior was common enough to warrant discussion. They then, presumably, followed a line of questioning around why customers were stopping and what they were doing when they stopped. Essentially, they were acting as anthropologists do—seeking to observe and study their customers' behaviors and their experiences to identify patterns and develop explanations for their cultural practices. Organizations including those such as Intel employ cultural anthropologists to identify how products are really used by customers in their daily lives and how those products are currently failing to meet their needs (Singer, 2014).

To identify new behaviors that will impact your customers, it's vital that your team is empowered to observe your customers out in the wild and to ask questions about why and how they behave. That might look like shadowing your customer service team, sitting in on sales meetings, or working the floor of their local brick-and-mortar. For marketing teams, building panels of trusted customers—and rewarding them for their time—can be a great way to test hypotheses and get in front of new behaviors. For example, when I worked in the arts and crafts industry, my marketing team built email lists specifically of customers who opted in to take occasional surveys to help us conduct market research, in exchange for rewards. Investing in the mechanisms that allow your team to stay ahead of rapidly shifting consumer behaviors is vital to keeping your data set ready for the future. Ultimately, setting up your data systems for success—both now and for the future—is about building processes and tools, yes, but also about making sure to establish a culture of data integrity—hygiene, quality, and policy— and curiosity about the customer.

RESOURCES RELATED TO THIS CHAPTER

The Power of Habit: Why we do what we do in life and business by Charles Duhigg—Duhigg explores the importance of habit in consumer behavior and shares some fascinating examples of consumer research in a wide variety of industries.

CHAPTER 6 SUMMARY

Most organizations have data coming from multiple sources, but there's no time like the present to improve data quality, build the needed technology systems, and set guardrails. This will require your organization to bring together a cross-functional team to build a plan to lay a strong foundation for success with using data—to personalize, analyze, and inform. While this goes well beyond the purview of your marketing team alone, it's a worthwhile endeavor for organizations of all sizes.

Actions

- ☐ Unify your data across sources.

- ☐ Invest in data quality through infrastructure, technology, and governance.

- ☐ Leverage AI and machine learning to analyze and uncover opportunities.

- ☐ Identify and interface with new customer behaviors to improve your data.

07

Mapping Multi-Faceted Customer Journeys

Connecting personalization with persuasion is powerful because it speaks to the underlying motivations of the customer. That's why mapping your opportunities for persuasion to ethos, pathos, logos, and kairos—as discussed in Chapter 5—is a valuable exercise, as well as a novel way of thinking about identifying key areas for personalization. But as we saw with the two modes of thinking—fast and slow—there's often a multi-step process of decision-making that happens for our customers. It doesn't usually happen in one single interaction with a brand. For products/services that are low involvement (like the groceries we talked about in Chapter 5), that consideration process may be quite short. For bigger, more involved purchases (such as a car or a software platform), the buying process may be significantly lengthier, with more steps, and may even involve multiple parties.

At the same time, our customers' willingness to research has increased as access to information has become easier with the internet. Think about the last time you discussed a new restaurant in your neighborhood with a loved one. Did you look up the restaurant's hours? Did you check its social media to see how the food looked? Did you look at Google reviews to get a sense of the ambiance? Did you open their menu on their website? If you're anything like my mother, you may have gone as far as looking at the wine menu to make sure it suited your tastes. Understanding what steps go into the consideration and conversion process of our customers allows you to deliver the right information at the right time—integrating kairos into everything you do.

To understand this decision-making process—and to turn it into an actionable framework for your company across marketing, sales, and other customer experience teams—many organizations use purchase journey maps or customer journey maps. Your organization may already have customer journey maps created, but often these maps don't go far enough in offering the frameworks that help your marketing team plan meaningfully. So even if you already have customer journey maps, let's look at how we can improve upon them together.

What a Customer Journey Map Is—and Isn't

Your customer journey maps break down your audience's decision-making process into steps or stages, so that you can better map out both how the customer thinks and how the company/brand can intervene at these times. You may be familiar with the AIDA model—representing attention, interest, desire, and action—which is one of the most common of the hierarchy of effects models of behavior. Or you may have seen one that includes stages such as awareness, interest, consideration, action, and loyalty (representing the post-purchase experience). These are just basic frameworks; what your customer segments' journey stages are called are up to you—in fact, I encourage teams to eschew set models and define the journey stages in a way that's highly specific to your customers' behaviors.

Customer journey maps are often represented in linear fashion, but in many industries buyer behavior isn't linear. Customer journey maps can and should represent these circular—or even circuitous—buying processes. For instance, there are subscriptions—think Netflix or HBO—which are circular buying processes, simply requiring re-upping each year. As long as the value is justified in your review of those subscriptions, customers keep the status quo. But consider the client of a consultancy, where one large project is followed by another engagement, but with another team. This new team won't follow the same customer journey as the first, since they bypass awareness and interest and move straight to consideration—but they may also need to move to request for proposal (RFP) or do additional research, essentially expanding from consideration back out to exploring their options, before moving back into consideration and to decision-making.

Whatever model you use, and however the model represents your customers' experiences, keep in mind that a customer journey map is *not* the same as a sales funnel. Whereas a sales funnel represents a winnowing of a large number of customers into a smaller and more qualified pool of customers at each stage, the customer journey map represents one individual's

FIGURE 7.1 Sample visualizations of a customer journey map and a sales funnel

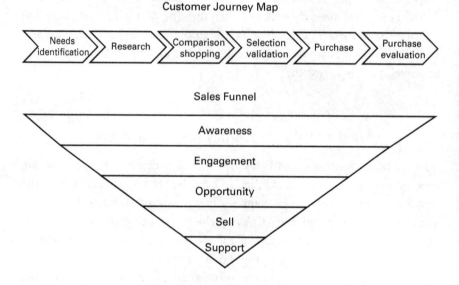

experience of the purchase process (see Figure 7.1) It's an amalgamated model of a likely or idealized customer experience as they proceed towards a purchase decision (and beyond). Furthermore, whereas a sales funnel is usually written from the company or brand's point of view, representing the stages of the process based on how the company categorizes its activities, the customer journey map should be based on how your customers research and engage. Sales funnels are important for understanding the volume, speed, and conversion ratios of the different stages of interaction with customers, but that will not tell you what matters to customers, only what matters to the company.

Rightsizing Your Customer Journey Maps

The objective of customer journey maps is to bring to life the experiences of the customer in a way that allows your team to better prepare for their needs. Each individual customer segment can and should have a different map—and their lengths and shapes may not be the same.

To illustrate, let's think about two different kinds of shoe customer. One is a pragmatic customer; they are focused on getting shoes that are long-lasting, practical, and well-reviewed. The other is a fashion-oriented customer; they are focused on selecting a shoe that's on-trend and popular within the right circles of influence. For the pragmatic shoe customer, you might map the customer journey stages as:

- *Needs identification:* Recognizing that they need new shoes based on a specific need or use case.
- *Research:* Casting a wide net to find the right stores and brands that may provide good options.
- *Comparison shopping:* Whittling down the options by comparing similar options to each other.
- *Selection validation:* Using third-party and shopper reviews to validate their decisions on the top one or two products.
- *Purchase:* Making their final selection.
- *Purchase evaluation:* Receiving the product, trying them, and deciding whether or not to keep them.

Let's talk about the fashion-oriented customer. You might map their customer journey stages as:

- *Trend recognition:* Observing specific styles and/or brands being worn by influential figures, either in social media or in traditional publications.
- *Research:* Looking into the brands and/or sources that produce the product they're interested in, as well as similar options.
- *Mulling:* Weighing the purchase of their ideal selection against the option of purchasing similar look-alike products.
- *Purchase:* Making their final selection.
- *Purchase evaluation and sharing:* Receiving the product, trying them, and deciding whether or not to keep them, as well as sharing their experience on social media.

Whereas the pragmatic customer did more research and needed more validation to purchase the shoes, the fashion-oriented customer was more decisive. How they decided to start their journeys was very different: The pragmatic customer was motivated by an internal need, while the fashion-oriented customer was swayed by external pressure. In both cases, there are many opportunities for shoe brands to engage with these customers in meaningful, personalized ways that would help to sway them on their journeys.

For organizations, it's important that your customer journey maps represent the unique considerations of your audience, because your time and resources are limited. Understanding what the audience is convinced by, why, and how much time they spend engaging with information at each stage before moving onto the next helps your organization to deploy resources wisely.

MAKING YOUR CUSTOMER JOURNEY MAPS WORK FOR YOU

In my friend Jeanne Bliss's book, *Chief Customer Officer 2.0*—which shaped the discipline of customer experience—she shares the story of Samir Bitar, who was the Director of the Office of Visitor Services at the Smithsonian Institution, the world's largest museum, education, and research complex. Charged with their inaugural visitor experience strategy, Bitar and his team created four visitor journey maps, for their four key personas, that helped to inform 19 museums and galleries, nine research centers, and the National Zoo. Once they completed these maps, they began using the maps as tools to audit their experiences and identify opportunities. They created a list of improvements to make and started rolling them out across the entire organization (2015).

The lesson here is: Don't be afraid of your customer journeys being big and unwieldy. They need to be detailed to capture the nuances and challenges of your specific audiences. To make them even more tangible, Bliss even describes the benefits of building literal a "customer journey room" in your office to show the journey physically on your walls and make it something your team can reference and use to plan. If it takes creating posters to make customer journeys an integral part of your organization's planning process, so be it!

Adding Dimension to Your Customer Journey Maps

Beyond the stages of the customer journey itself, a well-designed customer journey map should summarize the organization's knowledge about the customer. For instance, a detailed customer journey map might include the emotional needs (not just the rational needs) and the barriers or challenges that might keep the customer from moving to the next stage (in other words, what we have to help them overcome). This allows marketers and other teams to get specific when crafting messaging for each stage.

In addition, the company's opportunities should be mapped out. For an organization that is using the customer journey map across teams, each team's roles should be identified. While maps often include the channels or touchpoints that the company may engage in, I think it's also important for organizations to identify which teams are responsible for what at each stage. For instance, at purchase and post-purchase, there are responsibilities that may fall on customer service, marketing, as well as customer experience or market research teams—and all teams should be coordinated and have transparency across communications touchpoints. For small teams, this may be relatively intuitive, but for large organizations, these touchpoints can quickly become unwieldy. When I work with universities' central marketing teams, the number of communications touchpoints that a student or alumnus/alumna receives in the course of a year spans many different departments and teams—there is often no line of sight across these teams. As one of our goals with data-driven personalization is to demonstrate a holistic and deep knowledge of each individual customer, mapping these responsibilities is a valuable—if often overlooked—step.

Using Your Customer Journey Map as a Blueprint for Learning

Up to this point, hopefully the recommendations on creating an effective customer journey map are not entirely new to you. Your organization may or may not have every element in place, but hopefully you have the bones of an effective customer journey map available to you. The ideal customer journey map is, as with everything in this book, going to be based on collected customer data and research. But where you don't have all the pieces, it's okay to identify hypotheses and test to learn. In fact, that's one way that you can use your customer journey maps: Use them as a tool to audit what gaps you have in your understanding of your customer data.

In addition, your team may choose to use the customer journey as an opportunity to put the types of persuasion that have the most impact into your planning framework. Layer in persuasion, identify the data to collect, brainstorm personalization opportunities. These additional dimensions take your customer journey map from an understanding of what customers need and when the company interfaces with them to how the company can persuade them.

Identify the following for each journey stage:

- *Description or name:* What's the customer journey stage?
- *Emotional need:* What emotional need is the customer trying to fulfill?

- *Barrier/challenge:* What would keep them from moving forward from this stage of the customer journey?

- *Company opportunity:* What can the company provide to address their challenge(s) or concerns?

- *Persuasive appeal type:* Based on the above, which of the persuasive appeals—ethos, pathos, logos, kairos (or a combination thereof)—should the company focus on?

- *Data to collect:* What should we learn about them at this stage that will help us deliver on the company opportunity?

- *Personalization opportunity:* What individualized information will be most relevant/valuable to them at this stage to help them overcome the barrier or address the emotional need?

Example in Action: Identifying Opportunities

While it's becoming more difficult to track behavior across websites, it's vital to track customer behavior on your owned platforms (i.e., your website) and deanonymize your customers when possible. Doing so allows you to deliver and refine the personalized experience for your customers. Not only can you serve messaging, content, and offers that are specific to the needs or attitudes of your customers, but you can provide the right resources to address their customer journey stages. Using the customer journey map as a tool, we can identify the best ways that the company can interface with them. For instance, for the fashion-oriented shoe customer we discussed earlier, there may be an opportunity to ask them to review the product and upload their own photos of wearing their new shoes the next time they log into the brand's website post-purchase. Since customer reviews and photos increase sales on websites, activating this post-purchase behavior not only makes this fashion-oriented customer feel valued, but also helps other customers in the future.

Now let's explore an example of a customer journey stage for the pragmatic shoe buyer, written out based on the framework we've just looked at:

- *Description or name:* Comparison shopping (this is the third of the six stages we identified earlier in this chapter).

- *Emotional need:* Wants to get clarity on the best choices for them and feel confident they're identifying options that suit their criteria.

- *Barrier/challenge:* Feeling overwhelmed by the options or feeling confused by how they compare.

- *Company opportunity:* Create clearly curated lists based on priority criteria, and provide third-party validation and/or reviews to increase their confidence.

- *Persuasive appeal type:* Ethos and kairos—this customer is driven by pragmatism, so the right information is important, and getting the timing right is important to winning their business.

- *Data to collect:* Which products/categories they spent the most time on.

- *Personalization opportunity:* Providing additional sources of credibility/ trustworthiness to help them make their decision.

Based on our journey map work, here's how we might personalize their website experience: On the pragmatic shoe customer's return visit to the website, we could first show them "Editor's Picks" with third-party reviews from *GQ Magazine* or *Wirecutter* (owned by *The New York Times*) within the category of shoes they reviewed previously. On their next visit, we show them the top customer reviews of the product whose product page they spent the most time on during the previous visit. In fact, it surprises me how few websites use their product reviews as part of what is displayed on subsequent visits. You know as well as I do that when you log into your favorite ecommerce store, they have your browsing history and can display your recently viewed products. Why not connect the dots?

EXERCISE

Workshop Your Customer Journey Maps

Now that we've reviewed the opportunities to use customer journey maps to better identify opportunities to convince your customers in meaningful ways, let's talk about how to put it into action:

1 First, review and revise your existing customer journey maps. What information is missing? Are they lacking specificity? Do you need additional customer journey information? Are you clear on the differences between the customer segments and their needs? Review Chapters 2 and 3 to bring in the research and data you need to understand the overall customer journeys.

2 Get buy-in from all stakeholders. Present and agree upon these revised customer journey maps to make sure that you've integrated all key information and consideration for each map.

3 Identify and brainstorm based on the company opportunities, persuasive appeals, data to collect, and personalization opportunities.

4 Establish what resources it will take to collect this data and personalize the experience for the customer, based on the opportunities identified.

5 Prioritize the most valuable opportunities based on the company's resources and its sales funnel—what will move the needle? Volume, speed, or conversion ratio? And at which stage(s)?

CASE STUDY

How Trust Insights Drives its Customers to High-Impact Content

Trust Insights is a marketing and management consulting firm that helps their clients get more out of their data (read as: make more money with their data) through improving their people, processes, and platforms. They also create a ton of useful resources—articles, podcast, newsletter, webinars—about how marketers can use data effectively. Not only do they advise on data, they also practice what they preach. I spoke to co-founder and Chief Data Scientist Christopher S Penn about how they use behavioral data to impact the customer journey on their own website. Just as Target identified pregnant customers in the example we looked at in the previous chapter, Penn's team wanted to look at high-value customers to understand what set them apart. He described their line of questioning as, "What pages do converting customers visit—and in what order—that non-converting customers do not?"

They dug into their own data. And once they identified these pages, Penn said that they began to cross-promote those pages on their blog posts, because "Guess what? Those are always the pages that get people on the conversion train" (2023).

RESOURCES RELATED TO THIS CHAPTER

Chief Customer Officer 2.0: How to build your customer-driven growth engine by Jeanne Bliss—The sequel to her pioneering book, *Chief Customer Officer*, Bliss provides a roadmap to uniting leadership around customer experience.

TrustInsights.ai—The team at Trust Insights have a wealth of knowledge when it comes to data in marketing. To learn more from them, be sure to check out the resources on their website.

CHAPTER 7 SUMMARY

To add dimension and clarity to your marketing planning process, integrate detailed, thoughtful, and data-informed customer journey maps. Don't be afraid to tailor your customer journey maps to the unique customer segments that your business has, rather than using common models. Furthermore, use the customer journey maps to specifically inform personalization planning by integrating information such as the relevant persuasive appeals, the data to collect, and the personalization opportunities.

Actions

- Rightsize your customer journey maps based on your unique audience segments.
- Add detailed dimensions to your customer journey map to make them more actionable for marketing planning.
- Workshop your customer journey maps to identify the most valuable opportunities and get buy-in.

08

Creating Content That Feels Personal

Does it feel like it takes more effort than ever before to convince a customer to say yes? Your brand doesn't just need to offer the most useful features, but you also need great customer reviews. Plus you have to make sure you have influencers sharing great reviews or tips. And customers want to see comparisons between your brand and competitors. Then they still want to see a demonstration of your product or service in action, and they want to read a couple of articles to make sure that your brand is to be trusted.

It's not just a feeling. In the average minute, over 230 million emails are sent, over 5.9 million searches are conducted on Google, and over 1.7 million pieces of content are shared on Facebook (Dixon, 2023). In other words, your customers are both inundated with information *and* they are proactively searching out more information than ever.

For the vast majority of marketers, content marketing is an integral part of our remit. In other words, to win over customers, you need to be providing the resources that capture their attention and generate desire—whether that's educational content, inspirational content, or content that builds community. In fact, the importance of content marketing continues to grow within organizations, with 71 percent of marketers saying that content marketing has increased in importance over the previous year (Content Marketing Institute/MarketingProfs, 2022). Yet, in such a noisy landscape, what we need to help our customers do is sort through the junk and get to the questions that matter to them.

Using data to determine what content will resonate with our customers based on their personal preferences gives you an edge in this environment. But we still need to create the right content for our audience that delivers on the promise of personal relevance.

Treating Content as a Dialogue

To deliver the right content to our customers, we need to treat content not as a one-way medium, in which customers consume whatever we publish, but rather a two-way conversation in which we're using data to create things that resonate with them, getting their feedback, and then refining our offerings. Think about Netflix and other streaming platforms. Not only does Netflix recommend shows to viewers based on their past viewing habits, but it also uses the data generated by their behaviors and consumption to understand what directors, producers, writers, or genres resonate with its audiences. It then uses that data to inform its pipeline for new shows. For example, when Netflix developed the American version of *House of Cards* with director David Fincher, it was touted as an example of Netflix's usage of big data to identify overlapping circles of interest to create a winning formula for the development of a new series (Carr, 2013). Netflix continues to use data to determine not only which shows should be developed or renewed, based on its audiences' engagement (browsing, viewing, returning), but also which shows to cancel.

For many B2B and B2C brands, identifying what content is highly relevant to their audience (and what content isn't resonating) is also an opportunity to go back and edit or append content. For instance, a B2B software company with a popular article on industry trends might go back and update that article with new information or link to an updated version. Or the company could use that information to plan an annual trends report based on that popularity, redirecting older URLs each year to this newer, updated report.

Dynamically Serving Relevant Content

We can also learn from the home page experience of Netflix, which dynamically changes based on the interests and past behaviors of customers. Whether you're in a B2B or B2C industry, giving your customers the option to choose their own adventure—self-identifying traits that allow you to better understand what they're looking for, serving content relevant to that use case, and then refining that content based on what they engage with—is the best way to improve your content through data.

While the tools to serve content dynamically are more accessible than ever before—even platforms aimed at small businesses, like Shopify and

WordPress, integrate with plugins that make it easy—serving this content requires your content to be tagged in a way that makes it usable. If your organization's content is not tagged or organized in a way that allows you to specifically serve content based on audiences, interest categories, use cases, etc., consider this an exhortation to review your content and append this information. Keep in mind that this data doesn't need to be visible to your audiences (it may only exist on the back-end or in the metadata), but it must exist so that you can build these rules.

Starting Simple: Creating Content Based on Your Key Audiences

Of course, in order to show your customers content that's relevant based on their interests, you must first create that content. To determine what content we should create, we again go back to our key audiences and what we know about them. Think of your content planning process as a matrix (see Figure 8.1 for a simple example), with your key audiences on one axis and their journey stages on the other axis. As we discussed in Chapter 7 on

FIGURE 8.1 Planning matrix for identifying content opportunities aligned to the needs of each audience and each of their customer journey stages

		Customer Journey Stages				
		Awareness	Interest	Consideration	Action	Loyalty
Key Audiences	Audience 1	1. Content opportunity 2. Content opportunity 3. Content opportunity				
	Audience 2					
	Audience 3					
	Audience 4					

customer journeys, you should identify the company opportunities and personalization opportunities that your brand can address at each customer journey stage for each audience. With those in hand, you can audit your existing content to identify the gaps in your current library. You can also audit your current content's performance, based on engagement data (webpage visits, time on page, conversions, etc.), to identify areas for improvement.

Building Content Based on Shared Attitudes or Use Cases

Attitudinal and use case surveys and research—as discussed in Chapter 2—are particularly valuable for creating content, because they help frame the editorial approach of your content. For example, a museum might have local members who join because they want to visit the museum often, as well as members who rarely visit but are engaged in the mission of the museum. For the first audience, the museum might create monthly "hidden gem" audio tours to suggest self-guided experiences that allow frequent visitors to get more out of their visits and continue to be engaged. For the second audience, the museum might host monthly streaming talks with various curators about their current conservation projects or new acquisitions. But to get the most value out of this content, the museum needs to ensure that it's delivered to the right audiences. This is where segmentation of the audience would allow the museum to email the content to the right audience, with a personalized call to action based on their unique experiences. Or they could make sure that each type of content is on the home page of the members for whom it's relevant.

Showcasing content developed based on attitudinal and use case research is not only valuable for nurturing existing customers (or members, as in the museum example), but also for getting better results with top-of-funnel, awareness advertising. Your organization can and should use this information to create content that addresses your key audiences, refine it based on engagement, and then use the top-performing content within this awareness-oriented advertising to address similar prospects. Whether you're targeting based on third-party data, building lookalike audiences, or using custom audiences based on owned data, content that has a proven record with your existing audience will be more effective for these similar prospects—and therefore waste fewer ad dollars than content that has not been tested against your existing audiences.

CASE STUDY

How Kizik's Content Makes Use Cases Personal

If you have limited range of motion, you're a healthcare worker, or a new mother, you may have seen advertisements for direct-to-consumer shoe brand Kizik's products online. Their shoes don't require you to untie and retie them, but rather allow wearers to step directly into their casual and sporty sneakers (or tennis shoes), no hands necessary. The first time I saw them, I thought of my uncle, whose stroke has left him unable to tie his shoes independently.

Kizik is an example of a brand that has identified some very specific target audiences for whom the use cases of their products are clear and beneficial (trust me, as a mom on the go, being able to step into my shoes with a baby in my arms is definitely valuable). And they've created not only landing pages and articles, but also social media videos, user-generated content campaigns, and influencer campaigns to help showcase the benefits and address the needs and questions of each of these key audience.

They've recognized the benefits of telling authentic, specific stories about how these products benefit these specific audiences and demonstrating that through content. For prospective customers, many of which may not even be aware of the existence of this type of shoe, seeing others who share their needs and concerns using the product quickly moves them from awareness to affinity or even desire.

Building Content Based on Buying Behavior

MKTG Rhythm is a digital marketing agency that works with ecommerce businesses to leverage content and email automations to nurture their leads and their existing customers. What they recognize is the value of capturing segmentation early to truly customize the content received by the customers to help them make the most of the products. I spoke with Robbie Fitzwater, MKTG Rhythm's founder, and he shared with me the example of Methodical Coffee, a coffee roaster out of Greenville, South Carolina that not only sells direct to consumer, but also wholesales their products. Fitzwater described how they send different kinds of transactional emails to first-time buyers, their repeat buyers, and their subscribers. First-time buyers receive information, such as guides on how to brew their coffee beans using different methods. Repeat buyers get content written for coffee aficionados, such as comparisons of burr grinders. Subscribers get funny content that entertains them and showcases the brand's personality. In addition, MKTG Rhythm uses the engagement with this content to further learn about these audiences and serve up additional, relevant content the next time around. Fitzwater said, "From the marketing perspective, it's kind of a Trojan horse too because these emails get opened at about an 80 percent rate and they perform well. So it's a way that we start to add value through this [program], but, again, segment them differently" (2023).

USING AI TO DRAW ATTENTION TO THE RIGHT CONTENT

Sometimes making content feel personal to your audience can be as simple as switching out the headline and using language that speaks to the concerns (or benefits) identified in their customer journey. This is a space where AI tools are able to simplify the process. Not only are platforms including Google and Meta adding AI-suggested ad copy generation to their ad creation tools, but tools like Persado and Mutiny allow brands to add dynamic customization of messaging to their websites with little to no coding.

Lest you think that these types of tools are only useful to B2C brands, companies like Carta—an equity management platform used by public and private companies, investors, law firms, and more to manage their valuations, investments, and equity plans—saw an 80 percent increase in seed stage signups using the targeted messaging powered by Mutiny (Mutiny, 2023).

Infusing the Element of Time Into Content

Let's take a minute to revisit Aristotle's rhetorical appeals. We examined how they should shape the data you collect for personalization in Chapter 5, but they can also be extremely valuable in thinking through how you frame your content. It may be intuitive to create content that demonstrates credibility and expertise (ethos), acknowledges emotional needs (pathos), or provides logical arguments and information (logos), but infusing content with timeliness (kairos) is an opportunity to personalize as well.

Ask any parent with a child under the age of 20 if they've Googled something age-related having to do with their child before, and I promise you the answer is yes. Whether you're looking for the best toys for 7-year-olds or looking for books appropriate for 14-year-olds or trying to find acting camps for 16-year-olds, you are looking for information based on timing. And there are brands that have developed blog posts, listicles, videos, and guides based on every one of these topics. It's not only in the B2C space that your customers are looking for content based on timing—just in this last section, we looked at an example relating to seed stage start-ups. Timing impacts the relevance of information.

Furthermore, identifying when to deliver content (using data) can make content not only feel relevant, but uncanny. If you've ever seen an article, video, or ad online and thought, "I was *just* talking about that," you have experienced this effect: When we are primed for certain information, we pay more attention to it the next time it comes up. In addition, your customers feel more positively toward your brand when they feel taken care of, and content that is what the French call *prévenant*—or anticipating of another's needs in a thoughtful way—allows you to extend goodwill from your content to your brand.

With all of this in mind, you must ensure that your customer journey map takes into account real-world data on the critical inflection points of your customers' decision-making processes. Then use that customer journey map to plan content that addresses those needs.

EXERCISE
Consider Time in Your Content

In your industry, what factors of time matter to decision-making? Is there a specific timeline or season that is critical to your customers? Are there scenarios where your customers might need abbreviated timelines? Are there life stages they need to consider? Each one of these is an opportunity to develop content that resonates. Let's look at each of these scenarios and some examples:

Type of Timing	Scenario	Industry/Brand Opportunity	Content Title
Specific timeline	Home buying/ closing	Real estate	The first-time home-buyer's timeline
Seasonal	Tax season	Accountant	Your action checklist for tax season
Abbreviated timeline	Wedding elopement	Wedding vendor	How to plan your wedding in 30 days
Life stage	Retirement	Investing	Series: How to retire in 10 years, 20 years, 30 years

Identify the ways your audiences are impacted by time within their customer journey and brainstorm content ideas that address these time-driven needs. Using your search keyword tool or even just Google or Bing, search to see what competitive content exists around each of these topics. Identify the content gaps that exist in the market and use them as part of your next round of content development.

Creating Content at Scale

The challenge that most teams face is that there are not enough hours in the day to create the content to serve every customer need. And even if we focus only on our key audiences, it can still feel daunting to develop enough content to address the key questions that our customers have at each customer journey stage. In fact, I was talking to my friend Chris Johnson, CEO of LaneTerralever, a full-service digital marketing agency and sister company to Convince & Convert, about this challenge, which he has seen first-hand with many of his clients.

Johnson's team builds enterprise websites that have personalization capabilities, leveraging user behavior and media targeting to associate personas with users, with the goal of delivering a more personalized experience. "But post-implementation, the client rarely creates the content needed to deliver on those capabilities," Johnson told me. "Without the content to support the system, they really never were able to realize the benefit of what was created." Where Johnson sees opportunity is in AI-driven systems that personalize content and experiences without the creative and management overhead associated with older approaches.

Using generative AI tools programmed with the specific parameters of your audience segments' needs, considerations, and pain points can help to speed up the content creation process. On one hand, the opportunity is to introduce a direct chatbot (as with ChatGPT) that can answer common questions on the fly. As AI tools built on LLMs (which we discussed in Chapter 4) become more sophisticated and accurate in understanding customer requests, they become significantly more useful to both customers, as well as to customer service agents and salespeople, who can use them to generate highly relevant content specific to the customers' needs.

Yet, it takes a ton of computing power to generate these unique responses—and these responses don't necessarily allow marketers to control the overall content marketing strategy. Therefore, as we think about the future of content, the approach to generating customization may be a hybrid approach. Rather than generating content specific to the individual *à la minute*, we may use these generative tools to build a large (but finite) database of content that is cached and then use a chat interface to serve up these content pieces to customers with personalized context. Think of an FAQ that's delivered in a personalized, relevant manner.

No matter how you create the content, it's safe to say that it is an essential part of the marketing landscape in the digital age. But the expectations of customers for their digital experience go beyond content to encompass their overall experience with brands. In the next chapter, we'll explore how these expectations continue to expand the boundaries of content outside of marketing.

RESOURCES RELATED TO THIS CHAPTER

Content Marketing Strategy by Robert Rose—Rose is the Chief Strategy Advisor for the Content Marketing Institute (CMI) and CEO and Chief Strategy Officer for The Content Advisory. He is one of the voices that has defined content marketing strategy over the last two decades, and this book showcases his scalable, strategic approach to content marketing.

Youtility: Why smart marketing is about help not hype by Jay Baer—This essential guide to content marketing is filled with funny, engaging, and helpful examples of how brands can provide value across all different industries.

CHAPTER 8 SUMMARY

Ultimately, it's not enough to simply deliver personalized messages. Brands must also provide resources that speak to the customer's unique needs, challenges, or identity. To do so, brands must create content that serves the customer. To do this, you must create feedback loops between the content and the customer, using data to inform content planning and to drive informative engagement.

Actions

- ☐ Treat content as a dialogue by serving relevant content and providing mechanisms for feedback.

- ☐ Focus on your key audiences with content that's built specifically to address their unique needs, challenges, or identity.

- ☐ Identify opportunities to infuse the element of time into content to breed a sense of urgency or relevance.

- ☐ Implement mechanisms to create content at scale, while preserving quality.

09

Delivering Seamless Omnichannel Experiences

Do you have a favorite bar, pub, restaurant, or café where they know you? They know your favorite menu item or how you take your coffee. Maybe they know your preferred table, and they ask about your dog. It probably feels good to be known in that way—it makes you feel recognized and validated. You probably frequent that bar or restaurant regularly because it makes you feel at ease and appreciated. When it comes to customer expectations, that kind of recognition is what customers want from their brand experiences. This is backed up by research: When Salesforce surveyed nearly 17,000 consumers and business buyers for the 5th edition of their "State of the connected customer" report, 83 percent of those surveyed said that they're more loyal to companies that provide consistency across departments (Salesforce, 2022).

It should be no surprise that customers want a seamless experience and to be recognized by the companies they engage with. However, because customers engage with brands on so many platforms now—social media, email, apps, in-store, etc.—it can be difficult for brands to deliver those expectations. Furthermore, a seamless experience isn't just about being known and receiving personalized experiences, it's also about consistency across touchpoints, as well as increased convenience and efficiency.

As we saw in Chapter 7, the customer journey map is useful not only for marketing teams, but also for uniting customer experience across all points of your organization. By understanding where data can inform your organization throughout the customer journey and learning from that data, you can better deliver on a seamless omnichannel experience. After all, one of the goals of this book is to help you know your customer better than your competition does, *and* to be more relevant to them.

Who Sets the Bar for Seamless Experiences?

I asked my friend Christopher S Penn, whom we heard from in Chapter 7 and is co-founder and Chief Data Scientist of Trust Insights—a data and technology consultancy—which brands or companies he thinks are setting the bar for customer experience. What he told me is that he doesn't think of a particular brand, but rather the technology we all have in our hands and in our homes, saying, "You can—with your finger—have a car dropped off at your house. You can have wine dropped at your house. You can have a date dropped off at your house, right? The expectation is a zero-friction purchase process, and it is done with your finger or now just yelling into the air, 'Hey, device, order me another six pack of paper towels.' It is a zero-friction world" (2023).

Penn is right; customers' expectations are being shaped by the technology they use every day, as well as big players like Amazon and Google, which understand the importance of making it easy for customers to get what they want, when they want it. I asked him to share his advice, and he told me: Every company needs to identify where the friction points are in their own customer journeys and address those pain points to improve the customer experience and win customers. This point is proven by research: Half of all consumers said they have left a business's website and completed their purchase elsewhere because the website was poorly curated (Zoghby et al., 2018).

UNDERSTANDING WHERE YOU LOSE CUSTOMERS

From a data perspective, we should be actively collecting information that allows us to identify where customers drop out of the sales funnel or don't move forward with their customer journeys. For instance, you might look at your website and review the top exit pages (web pages from which customers leave your website).

Ask yourself: Which of those pages *should* keep driving customers forward, but clearly don't?

Using website heat map tools (such as Crazy Egg or Hotjar) or user experience testing tools (such as Optimizely), you can track not only where people click and where people leave a page, but also what calls-to-action work to keep them on-site. The easier you make it for customers to find exactly what they're looking for —before they get frustrated, bored, or distracted—the more likely it is that they will say yes to you.

Disrupting Through Better Experiences and Data

I often work with brands in regulated industries such as healthcare, financial services, and insurance, where marketing is limited due to legal and regulatory constraints. The pace of change is slow in these industries, partly because the companies don't feel competitive pressure—their competitors face the same constraints, so nobody feels a lot of urgency around improving. And yet, as we've discussed in Chapter 7, your customers' experiences aren't shaped only by your industry. If someone else is doing it better in *any* industry your customers engage with regularly, they will wonder why you (or your industry) aren't doing a better job. These dissatisfied customers are ripe for the picking by disrupter brands who often focus on the points of friction that exist in legacy industries.

Take Lemonade Insurance Company in the US, which is known for their simple (read as: painless) shopping and intake process and their unique marketing approach aimed at Millennials and younger renters, homeowners, pet-owners, and other insurance customers. Perhaps you've seen their "oddly satisfying" Instagram posts or the rave reviews from YouTubers. As a customer myself (first purchasing renters' insurance, then homeowners' insurance from Lemonade), I can tell you that it is extremely easy to use the Lemonade website, get onboarded, and get support. In addition, their terms of service are designed to be easy-to-read and extremely human.

According to an article from Digiday (Monllos, 2019), not only has Lemonade built an in-house creative team to shape their direct response and programmatic marketing so that they can focus on high-quality marketing that capitalizes on their audience insights, they have also invested in their data attribution and tracking. Their approach focuses on channels where they can test and learn through iteration and tracking. In the same article, Shai Wininger, co-founder and co-CEO of Lemonade, stated that they're leveraging their data and they're even able to serve 10,000 variations of an advertisement to 10,000 different people or segments.

It's both their investment in the customer experience as well as their support of marketing through data and technology that allows them to win against traditional insurance brands.

Why Must You Adapt?

Here's the thing—the expectation for consistent omnichannel experiences isn't new. We've been trending in this direction for several years now.

Research by Accenture Interactive found that 91 percent of consumers are more likely to shop with brands that recognize/remember them and provide offers and recommendations that are relevant to them (Zoghby et al., 2018). If your brand hasn't adapted to these expectations, know that you risk losing customers. This threat is real, and it continues to grow.

WHAT WILL SEAMLESSNESS LOOK LIKE IN THE (NEAR) FUTURE?

Have you noticed that, in the last few years, Google search results are more informative than ever? If you look up a local business, you don't even need to leave the results screen to get their hours, photos of their interior, and even a summary of reviews. If you look up a celebrity, the Google results page might include their birthday, their children, and even their known associates. Google is implementing what's known as a "zero-click". approach—they don't want you to click through and leave the search engine. They want you to stay on their results page. To achieve this, they are pulling content—from top questions to images—right in their search engine interface, so that users don't need to go to specific websites to feel like they got the information they need.

Of course, Google is a search engine, so it's naturally a place where people search for answers. But what could this kind of zero-click experience look like for most businesses? Imagine if someone could get all their answers from your home page, without leaving. This might feel daunting, as you would need a heck of a lot of information to live on one page. Or perhaps instead your page could respond to the specific needs of the customer. Again, I turned to Chris Penn of Trust Insights, for perspective. He said: "The smart, forward-thinking places will figure out how to integrate a large language model in that process so that the customer can ask the question, and get a real generated answer by machine, that doesn't require them to click anywhere."

In other words, a chatbot (or even voice-enabled assistant) that is AI-driven and that has all the information that your customer needs could serve up the right information, in the right order, and even include personalized offers. This kind of frictionless experience is valuable to brands in all kinds of industries. I've even had early-stage conversations with a major university about how these kinds of tools could improve the experience for prospective students through a more personalized experience.

What Data Drives Seamlessness?

If you travel a lot, whether for business or leisure, you probably belong to at least one loyalty/points program. For large hotel groups like IHG or Marriott, that means that there is one customer profile that's shared across brands—if I stay at a Westin one time and a Marriott the next time, my preferences and needs should be on record. In fact, I once checked into a hotel and was asked if I still preferred an accessible room, a note that had been put into my records from a trip two years prior, when I was recovering from a broken ankle. It's vital to make sure that your customer records are clean (i.e., duplicates removed, so that customers have single records), unified across systems (as we discussed in Chapter 6), and that they are shared across teams (e.g., marketing, sales, customer service) as well as brands within the confines of applicable regulations and local laws (such as Europe's GDPR, which we'll discuss in Chapter 10).

Ultimately, seamlessness is about consistency of experience. For customers, it's feeling like a brand knows them and the shared history between the brand and the customer, no matter the location. Beyond making sure that your records are unified and clean, it's important to make sure that your organization owns the data that allows you to deliver on customer expectations. Owned data that is specific to the behaviors, interests, and timing of customers' needs allows brands to create customized messages across platforms. Beyond being able to segment your audience and/or tailor account-specific website, app, or email offers, integrating your owned data into third-party advertising platforms using custom audiences allows you to then tailor ad experiences based on this same data. It's this owned data that allowed Amazon to target me with baby items on Instagram, as I described in Chapter 5.

Collecting Data That Improves Customers' Experiences Across Channels

Understanding why customers are engaging with your brand allows you not only to better personalize on your owned channels, but also to serve up better advertising on third-party platforms (and be more efficient with your ad budget) by providing them more relevant messaging and content. On your website, collecting owned data might look like customer surveys when customers and prospects set up their user accounts. For instance, auction website 1st Dibs asks first-time users what kind of shopper they are (designer versus individual). Shoe brand Cole Haan has a short intake survey when users set up their account, which asks about style preferences. Collecting owned data might also look like using cookies on your website to track the main pages that the visitor selects. For instance, New York University's website (nyu.edu) has long had a menu bar that allows users to choose their experience based on their affiliation—students, faculty, alumni, employees, or community.

Again, the goal is to make the data usable across touchpoints. For instance, you may have noticed that when you make a reservation at a fine dining restaurant—via their website or a third-party app—you're asked about dietary restrictions or special events; proactive restaurant managers take that information and input it into their CRMs for reference when you come in, so that you feel taken care of.

While your customer data may not always be complete, being able to collect data to determine what messages *not* to show is as important as determining what messages might resonate. We've all seen an ad for a product we've already purchased or a membership we already subscribe to. You might feel slighted by the brand—don't they know we're *already* a customer? And, more importantly for the brand, it's a waste of ad dollars and resources.

CASE STUDY
How Nike Apps Immerse Users in Nike's World

In 2010, Nike launched its first Nike+ app for iOS, providing free running programming to runners of all skill levels (Chartier, 2010). Today, Nike's suite of apps includes Run Club, Training Club (multi-disciplinary exercise app), and SNKRS (app aimed at sneaker enthusiasts and collectors). All of these apps are free to use and high-quality. They provide free instruction, community, and loyalty points. And while Nike's products are integrated into the apps, the apps provide a lot of content that have nothing to do with the products themselves.

These apps keep customers engaging with the Nike brand—creating a surround-sound experience of Nike's expertise whenever they open the apps. Plus the apps build loyalty through what my friend, marketing and customer experience expert and author Jay Baer, calls "Youtility", or content so valuable that you would pay for it, but that a brand provides for free.

Of course, these apps are integrated with Nike's customer accounts as well. And because of the data that Nike collects in the app on how much you're exercising, what kinds of exercise you prefer, and/or what style sneakers you tend to buy, they are able to serve highly targeted messages and offers to users of their apps. The data collected across these apps and their websites also gives the Nike team the ability to parse out their highest value customers, so they can focus on those brand loyalists rather than spending time marketing to customers who are just there for the free content and unlikely to spend money. Because of this deep trove of customer data, Nike was able to weather the global Covid-19 pandemic by investing heavily in its direct-to-consumer business at a time when it was forced to close its 900 stores, alongside its retail partners. Not only did Nike successfully withstand this setback during the global lockdowns, but it thrived, and its stock price hit an all-time high (Fernandez, 2020).

Why Customer Experience is a Vital Part of Your Toolkit

So why am I including a seamless omnichannel experience in Part Two of this book, "Building the Toolkit for Personalization"? It's simply this: Marketing can only go so far alone. Marketers can tell a compelling story and showcase relevant messages in the right places to bring in a customer— but if the customer doesn't get personalized service, isn't delivered personalized recommendations, and doesn't feel that their needs for convenience, efficiency, and recognition are being met, then the brand will not keep the customer for long. Improving customer experience across the organization should be one of the goals that data-driven personalization serves—and, ultimately, it's a cross-disciplinary exercise that will require teams to come together, as we will look at in Part Six of this book.

EXERCISE
Uncover Points of Friction

Do you know what stops your customers from moving forward throughout their customer journeys? Using your customer journey maps, identify and review the touchpoints that customers typically engage with to make a purchase decision with your brand. Essentially, "secret shop" your experience.

You can even divide up your customer segments or personas amongst your team to each review a segment/persona. Then come together to review the findings and build an action checklist for areas to address.

Identify points of friction based on these questions:

- How relevant or personalized is the information at each step?
- What vital information takes more than one step to find?

- What vital information is missing?

- Where are the key resources? Are they available where the customer will need them?

- How easy is it to request more information?

- Is information made available at the right times?

- Are the touchpoints consistent?

- Are the touchpoints clear?

- Is choice given where appropriate, based on the customers' preferences or needs?

Food for thought: Not all of the information will need to live on every single channel. For example, you may find that some information is best served by being delivered piecemeal via email or SMS, because it's more useful to customers who are already in the sales process when delivered directly to them. The goal is to improve the experience of customers where they truly interact with the brand, based on their needs.

RESOURCES RELATED TO THIS CHAPTER

The Experience Maker: How to create remarkable experiences that your customers can't wait to share by Dan Gingiss—Leveraging his many years of designing customer experiences at organizations from McDonald's to Humana to Discover, Gingiss shares his framework for helping your organization to put customer experience (CX) at the heart of its competitive approach. Since we don't have time to consider all aspects of CX in this book and only touch upon the communications aspect of omnichannel experiences, I encourage you to pick up this book and the books by Jeanne Bliss mentioned in earlier chapters as resources if you're interested in learning more about this topic.

CHAPTER 9 SUMMARY

Our opportunity for using data goes well beyond marketing. Integrating data into how brands deliver on customer experience across touchpoints is a game-changer—one about consistency and quality. We must understand what customers believe seamlessness should look like and also use data to deliver on that seamless experience.

Actions

- ☐ Align your decision-makers around the current state of your customers' expectations.

- ☐ Improve data collection by integrating feedback mechanisms and data unification across your marketing and customer experience ecosystem.

- ☐ Uncover points of friction within your customer experience and identify the data needed to address these challenges.

10

Balancing Privacy and Personalization

If you have friends like mine, they will enjoy sharing examples of marketing messages and advertising they've received with you, on the assumption that you—as a marketer—will have an opinion or be able to commiserate. For instance, my good friend Liz recently texted me about two video ads that she was shown on YouTube. The first was for a hair serum that she was definitely going to buy—they truly understood her needs as a curly-haired woman! The ad was just one of several she had seen recently that made her feel like the YouTube algorithm was incredibly accurate. She'd bought several products based on ads on the platform, and she was starting to feel like it knew too much about her. But several days later, she texted me about a new ad she was shown: One for an American chain restaurant with a heavy focus on burgers and ribs, which Liz—as a health-focused vegetarian—would not be going to anytime soon. Although she was previously concerned about YouTube knowing too much about her, she now felt like they'd let her down with this latest ad.

What Liz's texts demonstrated to me is the duality of customers' expectations around personalization. On one hand, customers want marketing messages to speak to their specific needs and to be relevant to their specific lives, just as we discussed in Chapter 8. On the other, there's also discomfort, as customers' concerns around privacy continue to grow. In the last several years we've seen the roll out of the General Data Protection Regulation (GDPR) by the European Union, moves by Apple and other companies to limit tracking on devices, and the phasing out of third-party cookies on web browsers like Google Chrome.

As marketers, especially ones who are looking to capitalize on the opportunities that data and personalization bring to better serve our customers and therefore make more sales, we have to consider both the pros and cons of personalization for our customers. Not only is this important from an ethical point of view, but it's important in building strong relationships with our customers that lead to loyalty. In this chapter we'll not only look at the concerns with how technology and data are being leveraged, but also at brands that are making transparency a part of their messaging approach.

Understanding the Discomfort With Personalization

Have you ever browsed online using incognito mode or cleared your browser cookies after you looked something up because you didn't want it to be in your search history or you didn't want to be targeted by brands based on something you bought for a friend? Or perhaps you're trying to avoid being tracked when you're browsing airplane tickets to avoid dynamic pricing? You know that brands are there lurking, waiting to target you—and there's something a little disquieting about them making assumptions based on your behaviors. Of course, customers do understand that data is being leveraged to offer more targeted, more personal experiences—like those YouTube ads that Liz experienced—still, they experience some discomfort in being followed around the internet, even if there is an upside. In fact, more than a third of consumers find it creepy when they get ads on social media sites for items they've browsed on a brand website, according to a survey by Accenture Interactive (Zoghby et al., 2018). Yet, retargeting ads such as these are some of the most basic ways that marketers aim to reengage prospective customers and keep them interested.

For more than a decade, the idea of personalized content online has been inextricably tied with debates about privacy and ethics. Back in 2014, Kate Crawford, a research professor at USC Annenberg and leading scholar in the implications of AI, described "surveillance anxiety" as a part of the reality of living with big data. She described this anxiety as a fear that the data trail we leave is too revealing and also may misrepresent us. At the same time, Sara M Watson, a technology critic and fellow at the Berkman Center for Internet and Society at Harvard University, wrote about how targeted advertising felt creepy even when the ads weren't relevant, simply because of what they seemed to identify as *possibly* relevant to a person. She outlined how our digital footprint is a doppelgänger that allows for both self-observation as well as self-criticism.

I believe it's this very human element of self-criticism that elicits strong feelings in our audience and causes them to experience ambivalence about the very idea of personalization. In Watson's article, she shares an example of an advertisement for an anorexia research study, which—while targeted broadly and only on demographics—made the viewer question the assumptions of the organization (2014). And, of course, there was the famous example of the father of a teenager who was livid when his daughter received a circular from Target aimed at new moms—part of the campaign we discussed in Chapter 6—until he realized sometime later that his daughter was, in fact, pregnant (Duhigg, 2012). Customers ask themselves, "Is this what they think of me?" And it may upset them to think the answer is yes.

Provide Feedback Mechanisms for Personalization

As we think about how our brands should navigate the balance between personalization and privacy, understanding *why* our customers feel uncomfortable allows us to address their discomfort and build trust. Customers want to be known, but they want to be known accurately. My friend Liz was happy to be known as someone with curly hair, but she was disappointed by the thought that YouTube thought of her as the kind of person who would go to a burgers and ribs restaurant.

Giving customers the power to give feedback based on our assumptions not only allows them to mitigate their discomfort by providing a response mechanism to our assumptions, it also improves our data so we can provide better recommendations in the future. For instance, you may have seen the menu in the corner of ads from Google and Meta that allows you to hide ads and share feedback. In addition, both Google and Meta also do occasional surveys to improve their ad experience for users. Similarly, platforms ranging from Netflix to Zendesk (a provider of customer service and knowledge base tools) provide feedback mechanisms on every recommendation with their thumbs-up/thumbs-down buttons. Each of these touchpoints allows customers to improve the data that the brands have, providing a better experience for the customers and improving future conversion rates for the brand.

For brands that deal with sensitive information such as health-related topics, going a step further to allow customers to filter out certain keywords, categories, or topics can also go a long way to building trust. For example, with all of the emotions that can come with a holiday like Mother's Day (including the loss of a family member, infertility, and estrangement), brands including Levi's, DoorDash, Ancestry, and Kay Jewelers have allowed their customers to opt out of marketing messages related to Mother's Day (Hawkins and Tyko, 2023). These brands presented options via email, as well as in customer accounts, to allow them to proactively avoid receiving messages that would upset them, thereby avoiding turning off existing customers or having prospects unsubscribe entirely from all marketing messages during this period. In Chapter 1 we saw that the majority of companies do collect customer preferences when it comes to data, and yet customers aren't always clear on what is and isn't collected. Being transparent and proactive in communicating with your audiences about how you collect data and how you use data is a powerful way to build trust.

Confusion About Data and Privacy

79 percent of US adults are very or somewhat concerned about how companies use their data, according to Pew Research Center (Auxier et al., 2019). It's no surprise, what with high-profile data security leaks, increases in the exploitation of data (such as email and SMS scams), and accelerating complexity of where and how data is being collected. This concern isn't just about the usage of data, but also about issues around lack of control, transparency, and security.

That same study found:

- 81 percent of US adults said they have very little or no control over the data that companies collect.
- 59 percent said they have very little or no understanding about what companies do or don't do with the data collected.
- 70 percent said their personal data is less secure than it was five years prior.

In order to be good stewards of data and to build trust while taking a data-driven approach to personalization and marketing, brands need to reckon with this reality: There is a huge disconnect between what brands and marketers believe should be done with data and what their customers believe. How can we address this disconnect as marketers?

The Ethical Responsibilities of Data Stewardship

First, we must collect data ethically. We must then make data security and hygiene paramount to our foundation of success (as discussed in Chapter 6). Not only do we need to make sure that customers' data is protected from bad actors (cybercrime and scams are major concerns the world over), but we also need to make sure we're treating their data and their usage with care. This goes beyond cultivating trust between our customers and our brand; it goes to respecting them. In Watson's article that we discussed earlier in this chapter, she shared a shocking example: A man who discovered that the death of his daughter was part of data brokers' profile of him, when he received a piece of direct mail that said "Daughter killed in car crash" between his name and his address (2014).

Make Policies Around Privacy and Data Usage Clear

Next, we must be transparent about how we are using data and what customers should expect from us. This might seem obvious, and yet, there's a large divide between what businesses disclose and what customers actually understand. In fact, according to the 5th edition of the "State of the connected customer" report from Salesforce, 64 percent of consumers said that most companies aren't transparent about how they use personal information (2022). Furthermore, as we saw from the Pew Research Center study discussed previously, more than half of adults said they don't understand what companies do or don't do with the data they collect. You might respond that this information is described by your company's privacy policy, but that same study found that less than a quarter of adults say they always or often read a company's privacy policy before agreeing to it and 36 percent say that they *never* read a company's privacy policy before agreeing to it (Auxier et al., 2019). It's not enough to have the information disclosed in an opaque wall of text; if we are to truly make our policies around data and privacy truly usable, we must make them easy for our customers to find, read, and understand—as we'll see in the upcoming case study.

In addition, this work isn't just about doing the right thing for our customers—there are benefits for our organizations as well. The Salesforce report also found that 79 percent of consumers said they would more likely trust a company with their information if how they were going to use it was clearly explained. In other words, we have the opportunity to increase the amount of data we receive and get more out of its usage if we make it clear to our customers how it will benefit them and how we will safeguard their data (2022).

CASE STUDY

Lemonade Insurance Makes Transparency a Differentiator

How transparent is your insurance company? If you're with Lemonade Insurance Company, the answer is "very transparent." The company has an entire category on its corporate blog called, "Transparency" and over the years it has shared everything from growth numbers to strategy on its website. The company has also taken this same approach to its privacy policy, which is entitled "Lemonade's Data Privacy Pledge." Not only does it start with a "TL;DR" statement (that's "too long; didn't read" or a summary statement to provide the gist of a longer passage of copy), but it has simple, human paragraphs that explain its policies around data in plain English. Each section of the policy is short and easy to read. It covers everything from how data is used to how they fight fraud to pricing to data tracking. And it includes a table of what data they do and don't collect. It truly reflects the company's philosophies around transparency, and that pays dividends.

In fact, a study by J D Power found that among homeowners not currently insured by Lemonade but aware of the brand, 34 percent said they definitely or probably will purchase from Lemonade if it is available in their state—at a time when the same survey found that overall satisfaction with insurance declined across the board (J D Power, 2022). That's significant brand affinity.

Go Beyond Compliance

What Lemonade demonstrates is that compliance is only a starting point. Of course, brands need to make sure to collect and store data in compliance with relevant regulations, including GDPR and the California Consumer Privacy Act (CCPA). But those laws and regulations are often a lagging indicator of customers' concerns. They have been passed in response to growing discourse; they're not necessarily thinking ahead. Here, too, we can learn from Lemonade, which has a proactive approach to cybersecurity and preventing attacks on their data. Beyond preparing for breaches, the company has even invested in a ransomware readiness assessment and an in-house developed security data lake, according to an article in *ITPro Today* (Schwartz, 2023).

Here's the thing: Staying compliant does come with costs. Not only is it expensive to implement new tools to obtain explicit consent, but regulatory costs caused many firms to struggle in these early years. Furthermore, because of the associated costs, many smaller firms collected less data for targeted services and advertising, giving an edge to large firms like Google which could gather data across more product offerings. A two-year look back at the implementation of GDPR found that these high compliance costs largely affected small and medium businesses (Prasad, 2020).

Yet, these challenges also push us towards best practices. To stand above the competition, you must think holistically about how your brand can and should leverage data, collect data across a unified ecosystem, and be explicit with your audience about how data will be used to benefit them.

RESOURCES RELATED TO THIS CHAPTER

Tech Humanist: How you can make technology better for business and better for humans by Kate O'Neill—In this clear, engaging book, O'Neill explores the implications of technology and data for businesses against the implications for all people. It's a relevant read for the world we live in.

CHAPTER 10 SUMMARY

Customers are confused about how data is collected, and they're afraid about how it's used and safeguarded. But they also trust brands that do a good job being transparent more than the competition. Good data stewardship isn't just the right thing to do, but it can also be a brand differentiator.

Actions

- □ Audit your current touchpoints to identify places for customers to give feedback on incorrect or irrelevant recommendations.
- □ Review data and privacy policies and aim to present information in plain English.
- □ Plan beyond meeting legal and compliance obligations to truly address what's best for your customers.

PART THREE

Fostering Emotional Resonance

11

Uncovering What Drives Your Customers

Back in Chapter 5 we talked about how emotion is essential to decision-making. Without it—when that part of the brain is damaged—a person literally isn't able to make decisions. Emotions are that essential to how people decide, and therefore how they buy. Part Three of this book is all about how brands can foster emotional resonance. You might be wondering: What does this have to do with data-driven personalization? Well, the goal of our work with data-driven personalization is to convince our customers to choose us, to decide that our brand is the right fit for them. So understanding how to appeal to their emotions, what motivates them, and how they say yes allows us to be strategic in how we collect and deploy data.

In Part Two, we laid out the tool kit for personalization; we focused on building the systems that will serve as the foundation of our data-driven work. Now, in Parts Three and Four, we will explore how to tap into what resonates with our audience. We'll explore how data can help us identify stories that drive our customers to act, how data can help us measure the messages that move the needle, and how building communities can help us to collect more data that informs our brands and benefits our customers.

Understanding Customer Motivations

In his revealing book *Drive*, Daniel H Pink lays out three levels of motivation that drive people. Motivation 1.0 he describes as our basic biological drives—the things necessary for survival like food, water, and shelter. Motivation 2.0 he describes as what's traditionally known as the "carrot and stick" model: Incentives and punishments. Motivation 3.0 he describes as intrinsic motivators, which he identifies as autonomy, mastery, and purpose (2011). In the book, he posits that, as our society has continued to evolve and become more complex, external motivators like incentives and punishments no longer hold sway. Therefore, these intrinsic motivations are crucial to driving personal performance and achieving fulfilllment.

This isn't just true of personal performance; it's also something that we see in marketing and motivating our customers. The internet has made it so easy to put incentives in front of our customers, to the point where customers expect it. Yes, coupon codes can work as a "carrot" by incentivizing new customers to give you their email address, but it doesn't make them loyal to your brand—and it certainly doesn't stop them from immediately unsubscribing from your emails when you start marketing to them. Similarly, limited time offers can help to move people who are on the fence but interested to buy, but it doesn't move them down the sales funnel.

So what works to build longer-term relationships with customers then? Let's take a look at those higher level, intrinsic forms of motivation: Autonomy, mastery, and purpose. Pink defines autonomy as the desire to control one's own work and decisions, mastery as the pursuit of skills in a particular area, and purpose as the yearning to connect one's actions to a greater cause or to make meaningful contributions. Many brands can tell stories that align to these areas. Whether your company is a fashion brand that helps people express their autonomy through creative dressing or a brand like Blue Apron whose meal boxes help people not only to save time in preparing meals but also to learn new cooking skills, you can tap into motivation 3.0 to tell more engaging stories to your customers.

But why do autonomy, mastery, and purpose drive modern people? I believe it's because they align with self-actualization—what influential psychologist Abraham Maslow described in his hierarchy of needs (which you may have learned about in college/university) as the highest level of psychological development and fulfillment one can achieve, where a person seeks to fulfill their potential (1943). In other words, motivation 3.0 matters because customers want their shopping behavior to reflect their overall sense of self and their values—they want to demonstrate through their shopping actions what matters to them. In fact, a study by the World Economic Forum found that an average of 70 percent of respondents, across the 25 countries surveyed, said that they buy from brands that they believe reflect their own principles. Furthermore, the World Economic Forum found that the share of respondents in the UK, France, and the USA who tended to buy based on shared principles rose by about a fifth between 2013 and 2021 (Willige, 2021).

Throughout this book, we've already seen examples of brands that tell stories about what their values are: Patagonia, Nike, Lemonade Insurance. But, more than that, these brands allow their customers to participate in showcasing these shared values through their actions. Whether they take part in Patagonia's clothing recycling program or Nike Run Club challenges, customers are empowered not only to engage with the brand, but also to demonstrate their own values and showcase their own identity.

Of course, corporations are driven by their own intrinsic goals and values. This chapter does not suggest that your brand should adapt to the values of your customers, but rather to lean into those values when they align with your core audiences' motivations. When your messaging taps into these desires, they will stick in the minds of your customers and drive buying behaviors, because customers connect on an emotional level.

INFLUENCE AND IDENTITY IN THE AGE OF SOCIAL MEDIA

For those who remember a time before social media, you may remember when "keeping up with the Joneses" was a phrase that referred to comparing your lifestyle with your neighbors or colleagues. Now with the ability to peek into the lives of people around the world, customers experience fear of missing out (FOMO) when they see how others live. The ability not only to showcase one's life but to be judged by how one lives is perhaps why we see this increase in desire to buy from brands that reflect one's principles—we know it's something that might be seen and judged by a broader audience. Moreover, we as a society are more readily sharing what we buy and why we buy them; in fact, *The New York Times* published an article in 2023 exploring how even individuals with modest followings are behaving as if they were tastemakers or influencers, posting recommendations videos and curating affiliate stores (Maheshwari). But it's not just an assumption that others are paying attention to our buying behaviors; 72 percent of 18- to 29-year-old social media users say that they follow influencers or content creators, and 44 percent of those ages 30 to 49 say they do as well, according to Pew Research Center (Faverio and Anderson, 2022). Now more than ever, our actions—buying, participating, and showing—speak louder than our words.

Analyzing What Matters and What Motivates

So how do we know what matters to our customers? As we've discussed in Part Two, using behavioral data across your brand's owned digital channels can help you to develop hypotheses and identify areas to explore further. Look at what content and messages get the most engagement and/or drive key actions. Or identify topics, tone, and persuasive appeals that have impact. But to truly understand what drives our audiences and/or how they see themselves, we have to look beyond their preferences to what they believe and how they speak about their beliefs. We can do this in a number of ways, such as surveys, focus groups, pulling in third-party data, and using social listening tools, each of which can help round out our understanding of our customers.

Zooming Out With Surveys

Surveys are a powerful tool for understanding customers that are, in my opinion, often underleveraged by marketing teams. They're usually inexpensive to develop and conduct, and they allow you to specifically target. Beyond asking questions about your product or service, it's important to zoom out your questions and make sure that you're asking about the industry at large as well as your specific product or services. Here, just as with what data to collect (Chapter 5) and how to frame our content (Chapter 8), I want to ground us in Aristotle's rhetorical appeals as a starting point.

For example, let's say that you're a travel or hospitality brand, looking to understand what drives customers. You could develop your lines of survey questions based on our four appeals as follows:

Ethos (credibility, expertise) questions:

- Whose opinions do you trust when making travel decisions?
- What makes a brand trustworthy when it comes to travel?
- How do you share your travel recommendations with others?

Pathos (emotional) questions:

- Why is travel important to you?
- When you travel for leisure, what does it provide you on an emotional level?

- What do you want to convey to others when you share your travel recommendations?
- How important is it to select travel brands that align with your beliefs?

Logos (information-oriented) questions:

- What's most important to you when selecting a travel brand?
- How important is sustainability to your travel decisions?
- What are your top three priorities when selecting a travel destination?

Kairos (timing) questions:

- How far in advance do you plan travel?
- Would you try a new experience on the spur of the moment?

While these types of surveys are not necessarily the in-depth attitudinal studies that we discussed in Part One of the book, they provide color and specificity when it comes to how your marketing team crafts its messages, based on your audiences' beliefs. By allowing your team to identify specific priorities by the numbers, these surveys can concretely give you direction in terms of what messaging to craft and test further. But, of course, testing is still essential to proving out your hypotheses, as we'll see in the coming chapters.

CASE STUDY
How Methodical Coffee Uses Customer Insights to Make its Products Easier to Understand

Methodical Coffee in Greenville, South Carolina is a small batch coffee roaster that focuses on bringing out the natural characteristics of the coffee bean. Not only do they have several cafes, but they also sell direct to consumers online, a business that grew during the Covid-19 pandemic. I spoke to CEO Marco Suarez about how he and his team leverage different tools, from ad hoc conversations with customers in their cafes to customer reviews to customer surveys a few times a year to foster that emotional connection between the brand and the customer.

One insight that they gained in using surveys was that there was a disconnect between how their customers were used to describing coffee—terms like light, medium, and dark roast—and how Methodical develops its coffees, which don't necessarily fit neatly into those buckets. He and his team explored how they could better tell the story of their coffees in terms that their customers would understand intuitively, "So we developed a categorization of our coffees—classic, contemporary, avant-garde—which has been hugely successful." Their classic coffees are dark, but not bitter. Their contemporary coffees feature lots of red fruit and baking spice characteristics. Their avant-garde coffees feature unusual flavor notes. Suarez continued, "Not only that, [the categorization] has become terminology that we can even use to describe our customer base." In other words, the terminology isn't just shorthand for the taste profiles, but also for the type of person who those profiles might appeal to.

It may seem like a small thing, but people who buy coffee aren't buying it to quench their thirst (motivation 1.0). Choosing to buy specialty coffee from a local roaster is a small act of autonomy that allows the customer to demonstrate not only their values (buying local, supporting small businesses, trying new and unusual flavors), but also to showcase their identity. By making it easier for customers to understand exactly how its products align with their sense of self, Methodical Coffee taps into these unconscious drivers.

Getting Real With Focus Groups

What do you think of when you picture focus groups? Perhaps it's the focus groups that we've all seen in films and television: A group of five to eight people being led in brainstorming and word association games at a conference table in a room with one-way glass, while a team of researchers take notes on the other side of the glass.

Nowadays, it's as likely for these focus groups to take place online, with live participants sharing their opinions using their mouse and keyboard, rather than sharing them aloud. The benefits of online focus groups is that it can eliminate some of the "group think" and biases that can occur during in-person sessions. Online focus groups also allow brands to broaden their reach and number of participants more easily to collect qualitative data at scale. For instance, at Convince & Convert, we worked with Converge LLC, an Arizona-based research platform company, to conduct online focus groups for one of our higher education clients to understand the motivations, beliefs, and concerns that their stakeholders had around public safety.

Conducting focus groups allows your brand to dialogue with real customers. They allow your brand to identify strong areas of emotion and understand the positive and negative associations around them. These kinds of online focus groups can also be a testing ground for messaging, before rolling them out to a broader audience. For example, if you're working on a political campaign or work in an industry like healthcare, it may be extremely important to be able to do your message testing within a closed environment. Because of the larger scale of these online focus groups, you're also able to pull out a mix of qualitative and quantitative data, allowing your team to cut sentiment and key topics by specific audience demographics or even motivational or attitudinal information.

Incorporating Third-Party Data

In Chapter 4 we explored some of the third-party tools available to marketers to integrate additional insights into your customer profiles. When it comes to understanding customer motivations and drivers, incorporating third-party data allows you to expand your concrete knowledge of your customer. After all, it shouldn't surprise you that customers are more open and vocal about their beliefs on their own personal social media channels than they are on your brand's channels. Using audience analysis tools allows you to identify sentiment, relationships between topics, and even perform cluster analysis (grouping individuals who are more similar to each other than they are to others in your community).

Social listening tools from companies like Meltwater or Sprinklr can help you to identify the conversations by keywords. There are also tools like Audiense Insights and SparkToro that can help you to dig into your audiences— by the brands they engage with, the websites they frequent, or how they describe themselves—to understand their interests, their politics, their community affiliations, and even their mindsets.

This data can help you to refine your customer personas or archetypes, identify hypotheses for testing, and also more clearly make the case for how your brand or products may connect with the higher-level motivations of your customers.

When You Can't Connect The Dots... Directly

You may be thinking that some of the concepts in this chapter go against earlier recommendations. After all, in Chapter 6 I exhort you to try to unify as much of your data as possible. But, as we saw in Chapter 10, there are good reasons that customers might not want their individual records to be associated with their specific opinions, beliefs, or political affiliations—and there are legal considerations for companies in terms of collecting *too much* personal data without clear use cases. Furthermore, methods like surveys and focus groups work best when customers don't feel that their responses will directly impact their future relationships with the brand.

Again, we have the opportunity to use this data as a springboard for adding dimension to what we know about what motivates our customers. We can also use it to develop messages and creative to test. And we can also use it to develop further lines of questioning and content to help our customers choose the right resources that then allow us to collect deanonymized data that gives us more clarity on what matters most. For brands developing AI models, marketers could go as far as training an AI bot to respond as if it has the motivations and beliefs of our customers, giving you a real-time message-testing tool. Ultimately, understanding what motivates our customers is an important exercise for all businesses. Although the research methods that we've looked at in this chapter are not free from bias, they are tools that allow us to be more thoughtful and precise about what our customers truly care about—rather than relying on assumption or conjecture.

RESOURCES RELATED TO THIS CHAPTER

Drive: The surprising truth about what motivates us by Daniel H Pink—A book I've
   often assigned to my graduate students, *Drive* is an engaging read. While
   we talk about it from a marketing perspective in this chapter, the book itself
   focuses more on how motivations move individuals. Side note: I also
   recommend Pink's other excellent book, *When: The scientific secrets of perfect
   timing*, as another interesting read that's completely unrelated to the topic
   at hand.

CHAPTER 11 SUMMARY

To build longer-term, more deep-seated relationships with our customers,
brands need to understand what motivates them. Learning what matters, using
research techniques including surveys, focus groups, and third-party data

platforms, can give dimension and specificity to the brand's knowledge and inform future testing.

Actions

- Identify the tools that your team can leverage to understand your customers' motivations.
- Develop questions based on your hypotheses around their motivations, as well as open-ended questions that allow them to give honest feedback.
- Use ethos, pathos, logos, and kairos to round out your lines of questioning.

12

Data and the Desire to Understand How We Compare

In my work as a strategic marketing advisor to organizations, I'm often asked by marketing teams how they compare to their peers. "What's the average open rate in our industry?" "How much traffic should our social media channels be driving to our website?" "How much engagement is typically seen from a campaign like this?" Let's be honest: You've probably asked yourself something along these lines.

As a matter of fact, start typing in an industry (say, "financial services") and an area of marketing (like "social media") and you'll find that the autofill tool in Google or your preferred search engine will suggest "benchmarks" as one of the next options. It's no surprise that, especially in a rapidly changing digital landscape, what we marketers want to know is: How are we doing compared to others? Are we doing all right? Are our results typical? Perhaps that's why my friends at Content Marketing Institute and MarketingProfs (full disclosure: I've spoken at events by both organizations and advised MarketingProfs on their social media strategy) have been producing their annual B2B and B2C content marketing benchmarks reports for more than 13 years. They recognize this very human desire to understand what our peers are doing and what "normal" looks like for others like us.

Brands that help customers understand what these benchmarks look like in their own lives and situations, as well as brands that help customers track their own data, are well positioned to build stronger relationships with their customers. Not only do brands have the opportunity to build stronger customer experiences through making sense of this data for customers, but they also have the opportunity to use this data in messaging to persuade customers.

Providing Reassurance and Driving Progress

Of course, it's not just marketers who love a good benchmark. Across all industries and across all areas of life, we want to understand how we compare to others. That might sound like we're driven specifically by competitiveness, but I believe that what we desire is more. often about fitting in than standing out. We want to know that we're doing okay, and we want to know what that looks like in our situation. For instance, as a mother of a young child, I often refer to the American Centers for Disease Control and Prevention (CDC) Milestone Tracker app, which allows parents to keep track of standardized milestones for developmental progress. In addition, I've had many a conversation with other parents about anxiety or questions around whether our children are reaching their milestones as they should. In fact, sometimes I envy our parents' generation, during which you could only compare with people you knew and had conversations with, rather than having the entire internet at your fingertips.

In a world in which it's so easy to compare to others on social media and using search engines, both we and our customers are likely to search for what "typical" looks like in a situation, looking for benchmarks. Our opportunity—and why this chapter is in Part Three, which focuses on emotional resonance—is to tap into our customers' desire for understanding by providing the data that helps them make sense of their world and how they compare to their peers.

Driving Improvement and Participation Through Gamification

Beyond just reassuring your customers, giving them mechanisms to track their progress and understand how they measure up to their peers (okay, yes, a little competitiveness may come into play) can help facilitate their quest for self-actualization or self-improvement—ideas we explored in the prior chapter. And in so doing, your brand can strengthen your customers' perception of the brand's role in achieving those goals.

Have you ever seen those three rings on an Apple Watch? Whether you own one or you just know someone who has one, you are probably familiar with the idea of "closing the rings," shorthand for achieving one's health goals as set in the Activity app on the Apple Watch. The Activity app also suggests new goals each week based on past performance, making the experience dynamic (2023). This kind of quantitative data provides feedback to your customers, making it more obvious as they improve with your brand. Similarly, American medical spa chain Skin Laundry takes progress photos (qualitative data) as repeat customers continue their laser treatments to help make improvements to skin texture and coloration clear. For customers, this tangible, quantifiable progress feels good and demonstrates value.

Or consider the fitness brand Peloton, which offers a wide variety of statistics and data to users, both personal and in the context of others. When participants in live classes are exercising, they can see their output as compared to everyone else who is in that live class on a leader board. Peloton's customers can push themselves based on their own progress, or they can push themselves based on their virtual neighbor's achievements. Either way, they're leveraging data to help customers chase after their goals.

Even if you're not a wellness brand like these examples, there are many opportunities to help your customers understand their own progress as compared to others. For instance, if your product or service has an onboarding period, giving your customers a sense of not only how long the process typically takes, but also where they are in that progression can drive a sense of urgency. Ultimately, aggregating our customer data and analyzing it to understand what "normal" looks like is valuable not only to help us serve customers better but also to help us message more effectively to them.

Helping Customers Make the Argument on Our Behalf

As I mentioned at the beginning of this chapter, benchmarks are all the rage, whether it's for social media, email, search, influencer marketing, direct mail, etc. Yet, there are often still benchmarks that aren't available in these various areas of marketing. It's something I experience routinely; in my work, I frequently look for benchmarks to help make the case to my clients, and industry-specific data can be particularly tough to find. And, of course, it's not only in marketing; every industry will have some benchmarks about a topic or use case that doesn't currently exist. But this can be an opportunity for content marketing.

Enter what my friend Andy Crestodina calls the "missing stat," or a piece of information that people in your industry often say but rarely support with a specific data point. Crestodina suggests that there's a huge opportunity to leverage our brands' data to find these missing stats, publish them, and generate more visibility for our brands and more marketing qualified leads (Crestodina and Hou, 2022). And he would know; as the co-founder of Orbit Media Studios, a web design company, he has developed numerous articles for their website, featuring these valuable and highly sought-after numbers such as the average bounce rate for websites that drive high levels of traffic to his company's website and that rank highly in search engines. Then for visitors who realize that their company's website, indeed, has an unusually high bounce rate, Orbit is well positioned as the expert firm that's ready to help them solve this particular issue. Similarly, content production firm ClearVoice conducted research that found that the top challenges faced by marketers included time, creating content, content quality, writing, and consistency—all the kinds of things that a firm like ClearVoice can help with (2019).

For us as marketers, the key is to pinpoint these "missing stat" opportunities and identify the data that we might have to generate the statistic or benchmark, such as in the upcoming case study. Orbit Media Studios, as a web design company, had access to hundreds of customer websites, allowing them to generate aggregate numbers on average bounce rates. But surveys can also be a useful tool for marketers to generate data that not only informs your organization but is worth publication. Likewise, this data can often be a valuable draw for not only search rankings, but also backlinks and public relations opportunities.

CASE STUDY
How RivalIQ Has Established Itself as a Go-To
Source for Social Media Benchmarks

Social media software company RivalIQ offers a powerful tool that allows its customers to track their own social media metrics, as well as their competitor's social media metrics, allowing for easy benchmarking and analysis. They're also a stellar example of a brand that has identified the data that their customers are looking for—and generated a publicly accessible report based on that data.

RivalIQ has published the definitive guide to benchmarks across social media platforms including Facebook, Instagram, Twitter, YouTube, and TikTok, using the aggregate data they have in their system (which you can find at www.rivaliq.com/blog/social-media-industry-benchmark-report). They've further parsed the data by industry, making it possible to look at average metrics around engagement, audience size, and medium by industries including alcohol, fashion, financial services, food and beverage, health and beauty, higher education, home décor, influencers, media, non-profits, retail, sports teams, tech and software, and travel (Feehan, 2023).

Their report not only comes up within the first few results on Google for "social media benchmarks" but it is often cited by other publications, providing backlinks and improving the search rankings of the RivalIQ website, while also elevating the brand's visibility in the industry.

Benchmarks Go Beyond Progress

It may seem like benchmarks are most useful in a B2B setting, but even among consumer product brands we can see the opportunities to generate data that establishes norms. For instance, if you've ever gone shoe or clothing shopping online, you may have noticed that the reviews often feature fit information. Did the reviewer find that the item fit as described or was it larger or smaller? Many brands also roll up that data and offer a fit rating on the products themselves. For a prospective customer, knowing that a shirt fits as expected or has a looser fit is valuable in setting expectations and helping them understand how it should be worn.

Data can also be used as social proof and set expectations or norms. Take a look at prescription skincare brand Curology, which lists the following numbers on its website: 93 percent report effective and over four million treated (2023). By proactively collecting data on the opinions of its customers on the efficacy of its products, Curology has been able to generate credible numbers (ethos appeal). Or consider one of my firm Media Volery's clients, Brooklyn Creative League. One of the first coworking spaces to open in Brooklyn in 2009, Brooklyn Creative League is an independently owned and operated office space that has built a strong community of friendly professionals; in its 2020 annual survey, the team asked members if they would recommend the space to a colleague and 100 percent said "yes." Talk about a resounding word of support to share in the sales process!

Want another example? Think about the impact of norms and social proof on fundraising. Having worked with universities and alumni associations across North America, I know competition between individual colleges within a university, participation rates across the university, and average donation sizes by class can make a big difference in driving behaviors. We'll talk more about the impact of social proof in the next chapter, but in the meantime, ask yourself: How can your brand generate data that helps tell the story of customers' experience with your product?

EVEN ARBITRARY DATA MAKES MESSAGES MORE CREDIBLE

Here's the thing: Countless studies in behavioral economics and behavioral psychology have demonstrated that people are influenced even by information that has nothing to do with anything. For example, in an experiment by two Cornell researchers, two groups of subjects were shown advertising about made-up pharmaceutical drugs. One group was shown text about the drug only and the other group was shown both text and a graph. An incredible 97 percent of those who saw the text and graph said they believed the drug worked, compared with 68 percent of the people who saw only the text. Here's the kicker: The graphs weren't relevant to the information presented, and yet their mere presence made the information more credible (Tal and Wansink, 2016).

My goal here isn't to encourage you to include fake numbers in your marketing messaging—far from it—but rather to recognize the power of generating real and relevant data to help make your argument. As we'll see in this next passage, we are all susceptible to biases and the right numbers can be used to sway our audiences.

Benchmarks, Anchors, and Bias

The term "benchmark" comes to us from the field of land surveying. Historically, surveyors would mark a permanent feature (e.g., stone, wall, pillar) to use as a reference point for other measures—the benchmark. All other measurements of the site were made based on this first mark, so this mark was essential to get right and create a strong foundation. As we discussed in Chapter 5, our brains rely on heuristics (mental shortcuts) to help us process information more quickly. One such heuristic is the usage of anchors, and just like the traditional benchmarks of old, this refers to the initial information that is received, which establishes a reference point for the subsequent information.

In the influential book *Nudge: Improving decisions about health, wealth, and happiness* (2009), Professors Richard R Thaler and Cass R Sunstein describe how anchors bias our thinking, even when they are completely irrelevant to the conversation. For instance, imagine that I asked you to estimate the price of your personal computer. If just prior to that question, you had heard the number 2.5 million, your estimate would likely be significantly higher than if you had just heard the number nine, even though those numbers had nothing to do with the question at hand. This would be what

Thaler and Sunstein call an "arbitrary anchor." Anchors can be used delib-erately, however, to set expectations or to influence decision-making; this would be what the authors call "suggested anchors."

Suggested Anchors and the Effect of Multiple Options

Think about the most recent subscription you paid for online. It's likely that there was a pricing table that showcased a few different levels of pricing. More than likely, there was a pricing level in the middle that was highlighted in a brighter color that was marked "our most popular option," or some-thing to that effect. Offering several different price points creates a reference range for your audience's minds. Knowing what the range is allows them to guess at what might be high or low—it's why restaurants often include a few higher priced items that don't sell frequently but create more demand for the second-most expensive item, or perhaps it's why if you're like me and prefer a "cheap and cheerful" drink, you often find yourself ordering the second least expensive glass of wine (that's still dry, of course).

Price, in particular, is often used as a heuristic for quality—rightly or wrongly. In fact, the "Chivas Regal effect" is a term based on the apocryphal story that in the 1940s, Scotch Whiskey brand Chivas Regal doubled its prices in the US and saw a large jump in popularity (Frane, 2016). Or consider the impact of higher tuition at small liberal arts institutions like Ursinus College in eastern Pennsylvania; in early 2000, its board voted to raise its tuition nearly 18 percent and it received nearly 200 more applica-tions than the year before. (It also increased student aid to offset the real impact on students.) Private universities and colleges across the US have done the same in pursuit of status, creating a bit of an "arms race" in higher education (Glater and Finder, 2006). This is a place where universities should use data to tell a compelling story about what factors might justify their tuition and how they actually offset the real costs for what percentage of their students through scholarships and other monies.

Here's the takeaway: To take advantage of suggested anchors, we have to understand our customers' needs and perceptions. This is another area where thoughtful research should be leveraged to not only identify what the norms are for our customers and their peers, but also to understand what factors impact their decision-making, and therefore what anchors might be valuable in swaying them.

Providing Data to Give Confidence

As you've seen in this chapter, when it comes to providing data for our audiences, it's often about giving them the confidence to say yes. Whether that's about reassuring them that they are well within the norms of their peers, incentivizing them to improve based on tangible and specific goals, driving action by giving them credibility to make the argument, or guiding the selection process by providing frames of reference, the data we use to drive messaging must be rooted in the very human needs and motivations of our audiences.

RESOURCES RELATED TO THIS CHAPTER

Nudge: Improving decisions about health, wealth, and happiness by Richard H Thaler and Cass B Sunstein—Featuring tons of interesting psychological experiments and real-world examples of the good that can be done through tapping into people's inherent cognitive biases, this is a fascinating book. It's one that I have always assigned to my Consumer Behavior graduate students.

Content Chemistry, 6th Edition: The illustrated handbook for content marketing by Andy Crestodina—If you're looking for an extremely hands-on resource on all things related to content marketing, be sure to check out Crestodina's book, which features lots of screenshots, examples, and use cases. It's a great resource, particularly for members of your team who may be newer to the field of marketing.

CHAPTER 12 SUMMARY

Data can help you paint a more concrete and convincing picture to your customers by providing them with reference points for the norms within their specific space, metrics on their own performance or progress, as well as proof of what others value or believe. Understanding how to identify these opportunities, as well as the cognitive biases that impact how this data is interpreted, is key to taking full advantage on behalf of your organization.

Actions

- Identify "norms" or benchmarks that your customer would benefit from understanding.

- Identify areas where data would help your brand to drive participation, activity, or progress.

- Review how this data is presented in your messaging to enhance trustworthiness and/or take advantage of suggested anchors.

13

Harnessing the Power of Social Proof

Let's face it—we all rely on recommendations from others. We put more credence in the experience of people we are familiar with because we trust that the information that they're sharing with us is reliable. But barring the availability of first-person recommendations, we'll take second-hand or "overheard" recommendations. In other words, we've all given or received recommendations on products or services that we've "heard good things" about, even if we don't have experience with that product or service ourselves. The data backs this up: In my friends Jay Baer and Daniel Lemin's report, "Chatter Matters," their survey found that nearly half of Gen Z have made a recommendation based on second-hand knowledge and about one in four Millennials, Gen Xers, and Boomers have done so as well (2018a).

And if we can't get recommendations from our own network, we'll rely on the recommendations of strangers on the internet. Between the proliferation of review sites like Wirecutter (now owned by *The New York Times*), "haul" videos on social media (featuring the purchases and product reviews of influencers and normal people alike), and the ubiquity of reviews on every kind of website—from healthcare to employers to plant seeds—we are surrounded by the opinions of others.

Why does this matter? First of all, these various forms of social proof are powerful (see the upcoming box for more on social proof). Word of mouth is not only directly responsible for nearly one-fifth of all purchases, but it influences as much as 90 percent of purchases, according to Baer and Lemin's related book, *Talk Triggers* (2018b). Customers treat word-of-mouth, reviews and other forms of social proof as shorthand for trustworthiness, as well as for relevance. When your customers hear how others like them benefit from your products or services, they can quickly gauge whether or not they want to move forward in their customer journeys.

Second, what people say about your brand—the specific words, the sentiments, and the imagery they use (part of the voice-of-customer data we discussed in Chapter 3)—is an opportunity for your organization to learn. Now, more than ever, it's easy for brands to find and listen to the conversations that are happening out in the world about their products and brands. And it's not just for B2C organizations selling products. From airlines to investment banks, companies are actively investing their time and energy into understanding the conversations around their brands.

In this chapter we'll look at the opportunities to create more relevant and more personalized marketing messages by leveraging this information. Then we'll examine the data gathering and research opportunities. Then, finally, we'll look at ways to feed the virtuous cycle of generating social proof that benefits our brands.

WHAT IS SOCIAL PROOF?

It's no surprise that in new situations we look to others for guidance—their actions, opinions, and words. People perceive the behaviors of others as a good guide for what is correct or acceptable. They observe the behaviors and words of others to know what is desirable and what is undesirable. In his seminal book *Influence: The psychology of persuasion*, psychologist and professor Robert Cialdini describes this principle as "social proof." Social proof can take the form of following the actions of influential individuals, taking into considerations the opinions of experts, and also relying on testimonials or reviews (2006).

In the internet age, the "social" part of social proof has become particularly powerful. In this chapter we'll take a look at how the number of reviews can impact the believability and relevance of what's being said in aggregate; for instance, we may think a product with one thousand four-and-a-half-star reviews is more reliable or proven than a product with three five-star reviews. And we'll also look at situations where the believability of certain people—such as influencers—is tied to their social media footprint.

Whose Voices Are Credible?

As we discussed in Chapter 5, ethos-based persuasion appeals focus on credibility to build trustworthiness. Brands can demonstrate credibility through their experience, their associations (such as their clientele, their experts, their partners, their organizational partnerships), their longevity, their proliferation (the number of customers they touch or their global footprint), and/or their track record of success, among other factors. In other words, these associations or facts allow customers to feel comfortable with doing business with a brand, even if they themselves don't have experience with the brand.

What does this look like in real life? If you've ever considered participating in a crowdfunding campaign on a platform such as Kickstarter or Indiegogo (where entrepreneurs can pitch products and projects to raise the funds to actually produce or scale their product), you may have noted that the track record, credentials, and experience of the team pitching the project are vital parts of the storytelling. How much they make you believe they can deliver on the project plays an essential part in your decision-making on whether or not to back the project, because—after all—there are no guarantees that any crowdfunding campaign organizer will deliver on a project. Companies that have proven track records of success, such as Pela Case (which produces compostable phone cases among its products already on the market), are more successful at launching new products like their Lomi composter, which raised over $7 million on Indiegogo (Indiegogo, 2021).

Or consider the iconic Dyson ads of the 2000s and 2010s, which featured James Dyson himself explaining the technology and innovation that has gone into his company's signature vacuum and home appliance products (Hanlon, 2012). By showcasing the expertise of the inventor and revealing some of the aspects of the work that went into the products, the Dyson brand looked to build trust among its prospective customers by leveraging the credibility of the inventor as an engineer with a track record for building unique and innovative products. For many brands, revealing the experts behind the work can be a powerful opportunity. Think of financial services brands that feature their chief economics officers in thought leadership emails or videos, or real estate development firms that showcase their star architects in their social media or in advertising. Identifying the voices within your organization that are trusted by your customers can be a huge opportunity to build trust, especially for new brands or even established brands that are new entrants into a specific marketplace.

Proof From People Like Us

However, this doesn't mean that all credibility is based on expertise. Indeed, year after year, the Edelman Trust barometer finds that, globally, people trust people like themselves more than they trust CEOs of companies or journalists. In 2023, 61 percent trusted people in their local community and 63 percent trusted their neighbors, compared to 48 percent who trusted CEOs (Ries, 2023). And of course, at the beginning of this chapter, we looked at all of the ways that word of mouth, and even second-hand word of mouth, can provide credibility to brands. This is why encouraging word of mouth, referrals, and reviews on your company's website(s), on social media, and on third-party websites is so important.

Why do people trust others like themselves? Perhaps it's because they assume that the feedback given is less likely to be biased and more likely to take into consideration the use cases of real people. Even if they don't know anything about those individuals, their words—especially in aggregate— carry weight. Furthermore, now with the advent of video reviews and video demonstrations, it's easier than ever to see these people showcase products in action.

Reviews aren't just impactful for products; they're also extremely impactful within service industries. The healthcare booking and review website Zocdoc found in analysis of behavioral data on their website that overall star score is hugely impactful on healthcare providers' success on the platform. In fact, they found that by driving up overall rating by half of a star (such as from three and a half to four stars), the average provider will increase their number of monthly appointments by 37 percent. But it isn't just about the overall score; it's also about the quantity of reviews. (Remember when I said that the number of reviews impacts believability?) Zocdoc's analysis also found that the top quartile of doctors with the most patient reviews received *five times* more appointments than the bottom quartile—in other words, professionals with more ratings are more appealing to those booking on the website (Kharraz, 2013).

Influencers and Their Role

In addition to generating more reviews (which we'll talk about later in this chapter), brands should solicit testimonials from their best customers and also identify trusted voices within the customers' industries or areas of interest to collaborate with—whether through PR efforts or through paid campaigns. In other words, influencers are an opportunity that businesses should leverage in many industries—and identifying them is an opportunity to leverage research and data about your customers.

Identifying influencers can happen in a few ways. As we saw in Chapter 11, surveys and focus groups are useful tools in the quest to understand ethos appeals. Whose opinions do customers trust and/or seek out to make decisions about specific types of purchases? What resources do they leverage to learn and reassure themselves about what brands are trustworthy? We also saw that leveraging social listening and third-party data is a valuable resource, particularly in uncovering influencers, because it allows your company to identify those who your customers already follow online and within social media to understand whose voices they find credible.

Let's look at these two in tandem. A few years ago, my team at Convince & Convert was working with marketing automation company SharpSpring to help them reach marketing agency owners and decision-makers who might choose to use their email products on behalf of customers. Their assumptions were that these prospective customers would be interested in learning from marketing-specific thought leaders and well-known figures since they ran marketing agencies. But in conducting audience survey research on their behalf, we found that these agency owners were more focused on learning from experts who could help them scale their business and grow their teams. In other words, they weren't solely interested in marketing thought leaders, but rather on agency growth and organizational experts. We then leveraged social listening tools to identify the marketing experts that these prospects *were* engaging with to build a list of influencers that combined these interest areas and built the SharpSpring Agency Acceleration Series, featuring 13 macro (large footprint) and topical influencers. Within 60 days of the launch of the campaign, we saw more than 4,000 registrations to attend this virtual webinar series and more than 2,500 marketing qualified leads from this program (Convince & Convert, 2020).

It's important to recognize that the survey research challenged our assumptions about what the prospects valued and who they were interested in learning from. Not only did it help us to redirect our client's efforts and resources to more relevant influencers to work with, but it actually allowed the client to be more effective with their budget, because many of these agency growth experts were topical influencers with modest followings, rather than big-name marketing gurus with large but broad audiences.

HOW TO IDENTIFY INFLUENCERS THAT MATTER TO YOUR AUDIENCE

There are many tools on the market that allow you to search for influencers by topic, by region, by audience affinities, etc. But just because they talk about the topics your customers engage with doesn't mean that they are engaged with or trusted by your customers. In addition to searching for influencers in these ways, it can be extremely valuable to understand who your audience is already following and engaging with. Consider instead combining those tools with ones like SparkToro—which allows you to see what customers who interact with a specific website, social media account, or topic are following in terms of websites, social media accounts, media resources, and even podcasts—to build a list of potential influencers. Or create a survey that you can send to a small, representative segment of your audience to get real feedback. Use a Likert scale (those three-point or five-point scales that range from "strongly agree" to "strongly disagree") or a multiple rating matrix (where users rate many items in one grid) to help you identify the influencers that your audience likes, trusts, and actually follows. This method of pulling in third-party data and then validating with your own research will save you time and resources in the long run.

Analyze Social Proof to Learn

Why is it important to identify the credible voices that are trusted by our customers? In the end, it helps us to create more relevant and personalized marketing messages. Industries from makeup to fashion to parenting products already leverage the voices of regular people and influencers in their digital advertising to showcase their products, but the more refined your organization can make the pairing of spokesperson and prospective customer, the more efficient you can be in your results. The applications go beyond advertising, however. For instance, search is now an ingrained part of the buying process. We all search to see what other people say about the new restaurant in our neighborhood or the dentist we're considering going to. So understanding not only who our audience trusts but what these voices are saying is also important.

Understanding What Customers Say Out in the World

Every day, conversations and interactions that are about your brand are happening. When these conversations happen online in public forums, they can be captured and analyzed using social listening tools. These tools not only monitor for brand or product mentions, but also for related hashtags, keywords, or topics. Most of these tools provide some level of sentiment analysis, and you can use them to identify trending topics, frequently asked questions, and the terminology that real people use within their discussions. Many of these tools can even pull in images, using AI to analyze when your brand logo appears in the public photos of customers.

This data can be useful to help you understand the language and lexicon of your customers, allowing you to reflect that language back to customers in your copy and creative. It can also help you to identify opportunities to reach out to customers to create user-generated campaigns that feature the best of their images, their stories, and their use cases. Think about the last time you saw an ad, blog post, or video that leveraged customers' words and images— did it help you feel more connected to those real customers? When brands like Dove (the well-known American soaps and skincare brand) showcase videos, stories, and images from their actual customers in their "Real Beauty" campaign, it adds a level of depth to their messages, providing social proof and adding credibility to their commitment to customers' experiences of beauty and skin-care products. But, now more than ever, you don't have to be a large company to use your customers' words in your messaging; as we'll see in Part Five of this book, communities are built on shared vernacular, jokes, and imagery.

Parsing Reviews as Feedback

Beyond social listening, using the tools available to analyze and understand the reviews on your own brand's website is another important way to not only improve your customer experience, but also to identify the resources customers need (in other words, gaps in your current content marketing or product marketing efforts), and the language that they specifically use when making buying decisions. Identifying common threads and/or helpful termi-nology can help you to build better prompts for collecting useful reviews (which we'll talk about in just a bit). Furthermore, built-in tools now allow customers themselves to rate reviews based on their helpfulness (you may have seen this mechanism on Yelp or Amazon) and actually sort the reviews based on these ratings.

I want to note that customers do, of course, leave reviews to share positive feedback and to help others like them, but they also use reviews as a space to complain or express displeasure to the company. In his book *Hug Your Haters*, my friend Jay Baer and Edison Research surveyed people who had complained to businesses and found that, when complaining via review, 53 percent of them expect a response from the company (2016). Reviews aren't only an opportunity to learn what customers say, but also how your company can effectively mitigate complaints for the benefit of others considering purchasing. Identifying trends over time within the reviews can help your company to address product or marketing flaws, as well as customer service issues.

How to Garner More Social Proof

To encourage customers to share more stories about your products and brand, you have to create the impetus for them to share those stories. That can come in the form of incentivizing reviews such as gamification or rewards for customers who review on your website; for instance, review site Yelp has used badges over the years to identify their "elite" power reviewers (full disclosure: I was a "Yelp Elite" user back in 2010). It can be in the form of identifying your long-time clients and appealing to their sense of community to share their experiences. It can also be about designing smart user experiences that drive customers to review, using prompts to ask them to share their specific feedback on common issues. You may see this on apparel websites, with prompts about size, fit, and quality, for example.

Beyond reviews, we've discussed the value of customers sharing their photos and videos of brands in this chapter, and using hashtags to encourage photo sharing is just one example of simple ways that brands can activate customers. Brands like furniture company West Elm showcase customer photos both on their website and in their social media using #mywestelm, and big box store Target has an entire Instagram account (@targetstyle) dedicated to showcasing user-generated content. Contests that ask customers to share their experiences with a product or service can also be valuable. The travel and hospitality industry has been particularly effective at using contests to generate buzz about places.

But more than that, sometimes, harnessing the power of social proof comes back to the idea of shared cultural moments. If you've ever watched a trending dance on TikTok or participated in the Instagram "top nine" posts at the end of the year (featuring your nine top-most liked images for the year in a grid), you've participated in these cultural moments. Let's take a look at this case study for one such example.

CASE STUDY

Spotify Wrapped Offers Users a Must-Share Reflection on Their Year

Since 2016, Spotify has showcased an automated year-in-review called "Spotify Wrapped" to users. This recap not only highlights their most-streamed songs, favorite genres, and other fun facts about their listening behaviors, but it is designed to make it easy for users to share these eye-catching graphics in social media. Among my music-loving friends and family, seeing others' posts makes it irresistible to share your own, creating a viral effect. In fact, tweets about Spotify Wrapped increased 461 percent between 2020 and 2021, according to social media analytics company Sprout Social (Woods, 2022).

Ultimately, why the Spotify Wrapped campaign works well is that it goes beyond social proof. It's not *just* about the norms of sharing this particular recap. It comes back to what we discussed in Chapter 11: Sharing one's Spotify Wrapped is really an opportunity for Spotify users to showcase their identity and their sense of self. That's the optimal method of garnering social proof—tapping into the underlying motivations that make someone want to talk about your brand.

What your customers say about your products, services, and brand is the best way for your brand to learn not only about what matters to them, but also how to personalize communications to them. Making sure you have a proactive plan to integrate listening to, learning from, and generating social proof is key to a well-rounded, data-driven marketing approach.

RESOURCES RELATED TO THIS CHAPTER

Talk Triggers: The complete guide to creating customers with word of mouth by Jay Baer & Daniel Lemin—This is a great, practical resource for learning how to generate more word of mouth within your organization, going beyond marketing to making operational and customer experience decisions that are worthy of discussion, much like the Spotify Wrapped example.

Influence: The psychology of persuasion by Robert B. Cialdini—This classic in the world of marketing and psychology is a valuable resource for any marketer and one that I often include on the reading list for my graduate students.

CHAPTER 13 SUMMARY

What others like us say, do, and act like impacts our expectations. And particularly, when it comes to brands, products, and services, the behaviors of others can build trust. Brands have to proactively listen to, learn from, and generate social proof.

Actions

- Identify the voices that matter to your customers through research (surveys, focus groups, third-party data analysis, social listening).
- Analyze the kinds of language and imagery that impact your customers.
- Proactively develop touchpoints and triggers for your customers to generate social proof on your behalf.

14

Developing and Testing More Relevant Messaging

Throughout Part Three we've focused on fostering emotional resonance. If you've been using the action checklists in each chapter, you've now done the work to identify what motivates your customers, you've identified the data that helps to persuade your customers, and you've identified the voices to leverage to be trusted by your customers. But what about the specific messages to put in front of them? How do you effectively identify the messages that connect with your customers? And once you craft those messages, how do you test them for effectiveness? And how do you learn and refine them to improve performance? In this chapter we'll take a hands-on approach to working through these questions.

Producing Marketing Messaging Based on Your Customer Knowledge

Here again, I want to come back to our foundation of persuasive appeals: Ethos, pathos, logos, and kairos. Back in Chapter 7 we discussed how to build a powerful customer journey map, each of which should identify the key stages of each of your customer segments' purchase processes. I also encouraged you to map the type of persuasive appeal(s) that would be most powerful at each customer journey stage. For instance, early in the customer journey, we often see that pathos—that emotional connection—is important to get someone to stop and say, "Yes, I relate to that. Maybe I should consider this product or service." Take this information (the persuasive appeal), the motivations of your customer (see Chapter 11 if you need a refresher), and the lexicon of your customer (see Chapter 13, where we used data to identify the language and imagery of our customers), and use that as the base for brainstorming.

EXERCISE
Message Brainstorming

Let's work through this together with an example from the travel and hospitality brand:

- *The brand:* Let's pretend we're developing messaging for a small boutique hotel chain whose properties are in scenic, beautiful locations in nature, within driving distance of major metropolitan areas. Think of the Hudson Valley outside of New York City or Joshua Tree outside of Los Angeles. The brand's value proposition is that it offers a variety of experiences from guided stargazing to goat yoga to barbecuing by the water, but they take care of the itinerary, the directions, and the planning (lending equipment and providing the food and beverages) on behalf of the guest.

- *The customer:* The segment we are focusing on comprises highly driven individuals who wants to make the most of their limited vacation time. Age isn't a driving factor as the brand has customers ranging from the those in their early twenties to those in their fifties, but what they have in common is attitudinal: they are strivers, control-oriented, and, furthermore, our research shows that they feel that they work hard and they deserve an experience that is both memorable for themselves and just a little bit enviable to their friends. Their experiences reflect their sense of self, and they want to set the agenda, but at the same time they have limited bandwidth to plan.

Grab a piece of paper, and start brainstorming against each category and see what you come up with. (Working with a team? Work individually and then come back together for the next part of the exercise.) See if you can develop one or two of each that keep the persuasive appeal, motivations, and lexicon in mind:

- ad campaign headline
- landing page headline and introductory copy (100 words)
- Instagram organic post

Perhaps you've focused on the aspects of building memories. Or perhaps you've highlighted the joys of letting someone else take care of the details, while the guest reaps all the benefits. No matter how you've approached the copy, the goal is to truly develop the messaging based on the insights. When you're finished, review what you've written and reflect on how well the copy aligns with what you know about the customers. Make adjustments as needed, based on the following questions:

- Have you positioned the messages to focus on the emotional needs of the customer—their desire to have an experience aligned with their sense of self and to make the most out of their time off?

- Do you address the motivations and pain points they experience—their desire for control, but also their limited bandwidth?

- Are you using the language that they would use day-to-day, whether it's on social media or with their friends?

Of course, sometimes more than one persuasive appeal will be important at a specific customer journey stage. For example, in the late consideration stages, when a customer is close to making a final decision, often customers value both ethos (to build trust in the brand and product/service) and logos (key information and specifics). And there may be multiple motivations to consider, and of course there are many different elements of lexicon that you may want to leverage. So how do you know when you've chosen the right messages? That's where testing comes in.

Testing Your Messaging

I'm a firm believer in the scientific method: Identifying a question, researching that topic, developing a hypothesis, testing with experiments, analyzing the data, and reporting the conclusions. That's what we're doing throughout this chapter and throughout this book. When it comes to testing our messaging, there are many different ways to collect data and see what works, so that we can learn, conclude, and iterate.

Testing in the Field

For small businesses and businesses that need to move fast, testing messaging live is the best way to learn without slowing down the momentum of the everyday operations. In our digital-first marketing ecosystem, it's easier than ever to conduct A/B testing (testing a variation against a control) and multivariate testing (testing multiple components at one time) across channels. Whether you're testing messaging on your website, in email, in SMS, or in advertising, there are a variety of tools that can help you to build, run, and analyze your live tests. Furthermore, as more tools integrate AI into their technologies, it is easier than ever to match messaging to target audiences and even get suggested copy. Tools like Optimizely, Adobe Target, and Google Optimize are extremely valuable in setting up tests on your websites and landing pages so that you can identify the messages that work. They allow you to test headlines, imagery, calls-to-action, and body copy. They also allow you to test different page layouts and how information is prioritized when presented to the customer, so that you can better understand which navigational experiences are optimal.

On advertising platforms, the technologies to run multivariate testing continue to improve as well. You're now able to run many versions of ads within single campaigns, allowing the advertising platform to display the strongest performers more frequently, optimizing against your campaign budget. Note that Meta (parent company of Facebook, Instagram, WhatsApp, etc.) can even enable automated optimization against multiple versions of copy and creative. However, using this automated tool doesn't give you the data back; in other words, Meta simply shows the best copy or headline more frequently, but not which copy or headline works best. Because there's no output from this particular optimization tool, you can't truly learn from its usage. Therefore, while it can be a time-saver for some businesses, if your goal is to improve your strategic approach to messaging I still recommend setting up multiple ad versions within your campaigns so that you can analyze the performance data and learn from the results of your ads.

Testing Before Launch

For organizations addressing sensitive topics or industries, testing messaging before roll-out can be critical. In those situations, there are two approaches to testing. The first set of approaches include some of the methods we discussed in Chapter 11, such as surveys and focus groups that leverage current customers or prospects. For instance, during the early days of the Covid-19 pandemic, my team at Convince & Convert worked with the University of Arizona to build the strategy for the launch of their Covid Watch Arizona app, an exposure alert app to help stop the spread of the virus among the university's stakeholders. To make sure that the roll-out of the app was sensitive to the issues around health, privacy, and data security—all of great importance to the university and its stakeholders—we developed the messaging based on attitudinal research that we worked with the university to conduct. Then, once we had developed the messaging, we used surveys to test the messages in front of various stakeholder groups on campus including students, faculty, and community members (who would also be able to use the app), so that we could identify the messages that resonated most strongly and those that would cause friction. This methodical approach paid off with strong results for the university. According to an interview with NPR, more than 15,000 people downloaded the app within just a few days, far exceeding the estimates (Garcia-Navarro, 2020).

The second set of approaches is to use survey panels, who are people specifically recruited as a representative sample of a particular target audience. This approach can be particularly useful for a new company that doesn't have an existing audience, a new product or service that a company is still in the process of developing, and/or a product or service aimed at a niche audience that is not well represented within a company's current customer base. Companies such as SurveyMonkey, the survey software company, offer research panels recruited based on the parameters that you set. There are even panel testing companies specifically for the B2B space, such as Wynter; for B2B businesses, understanding how decision-makers within organizations behave, react to messages, and perceive information can truly make the difference in developing smart messaging.

Testing your messaging before launching doesn't mean that you don't have to revise your messaging once it's out in the world. After all, surveys aren't representative of the broader context that your customers will experience in the real world, which can color their perceptions of your messages. Whether you test before or during launch, keep in mind that the testing process is ongoing. In every marketing campaign, we need to continue to iterate based on learnings. That's one of the biggest values of a data-driven approach to marketing: The marketing becomes part of our learning process and, now more than ever, we are collecting the feedback in real-time, allowing us to continue to evolve our marketing approach and refine our marketing strategy.

Strategic Marketing and the Scientific Method

Here's the thing: You may not be developing creative briefs or copy in your day-to-day job; you might even be one of the lucky marketers whose tool stack already involves AI-augmented tools that can do a lot of this message writing and testing automatically. So you might be wondering: What are the benefits of exercises like the one in this chapter? Furthermore, you may wonder: Why change how we are doing things now? What are the benefits of building testing into your marketing processes, instead of running campaigns and reporting after the fact?

Of course, as the marketing industry continues to leverage AI and machine learning technologies, many types of testing will become easier to implement, but strategic thinking will always be required to design the marketing approach, identify the best course of action based on knowledge of the customer, and also to thoughtfully assess the learnings from the implemented tests. Ultimately, using the scientific method goes hand-in-hand with a well-rounded marketing strategy, because it assumes that there is always room to learn and get better. Building your testing into your marketing approach not only acknowledges that there is room for improvement, but it is a more agile approach in terms of deploying your resources and budget in the long run. If there's one lesson you should take from Part Three, it's the need to treat testing as part of your fundamental marketing operations.

LETTING AI TAKE THE DRIVER'S SEAT

It's no secret that AI technologies have been transforming the marketing landscape in the last few years and will continue to transform the industry as the technologies become less expensive and more accessible. In this chapter, we've discussed at length the methodologies to develop tests and identify storytelling and messaging components to test. But, much like how your Accounting 101 in college/university taught you the theories behind reading profit and loss statements and organizing journal entries while recognizing that most of the mechanics would be done by software, I want to acknowledge that much of this messaging work will be done using software, whether now or in the near future. Companies like Persado, which deploys what they call "Motivation AI," offer tools that allow you to take your knowledge of your customers and automatically generate personalized headlines and copy that speak to the specific motivations and attitudes of your customers at scale (Persado, 2023).

While not every company will have the resources to implement tools like this into their customer experience today, as we've seen throughout this book this rising tide impacts the expectations of all of our customers. And it means that we all need to be aware of the necessity of integrating more data-driven personalization into our customer experiences.

Why You Must Shore Up and Document Your Marketing Strategy

In Parts Two and Three of this book we've explored the tools we need not only to build the data repositories that we need to personalize our messages, but also to carry out the research about our customers, and the intrinsic strategic thinking that's needed to use this data well. To take a strategic marketing approach, especially one that leverages data and personalization to drive results, we must not only take the time to understand what messages will resonate with our customers, but also why.

Being able to connect the dots between what the customer cares about and how they react to specific campaigns and executions allows your team to move forward in a more deliberate and proven method that is, therefore, more efficient and cost-effective than using your gut. Even in this technologically advanced period, I often speak with marketers whose strategies aren't based in research or a documented, essential understanding of their customers. In a recent report, 63 percent of marketers said that they either did not have a content marketing strategy or that they had a strategy but it was not documented (Content Marketing Institute/MarketingProfs, 2023). That's nearly two-thirds of marketers. At a time when all industries face stiffer competition, it is absolutely vital to take the time to incorporate the work you've done based on Parts One, Two, and Three of this book into your marketing strategy to create clarity across your team and organization on how marketing will serve both your customers and your organization.

RESOURCES RELATED TO THIS CHAPTER

Made to Stick: Why some ideas survive and others die by Chip Heath and Dan Heath—While it goes well beyond messaging, Chip and Dan Heath's book is a useful resource on how to craft stories and narratives that stick in your customers' minds.

CHAPTER 14 SUMMARY

Let's pull it all together: Take the persuasive appeals that will convince your audience, the motivations that drive them, and the lexicon that they use every day when thinking about your industry/category and use those as the strategic foundation for your messaging and creative. Once you've developed messages, don't rest on your laurels. It's time to test, iterate, and test some more to refine your marketing messages for optimal performance.

Actions

- Lay out the strategic foundation for building your messaging and creative.

- Develop marketing messages to test, based on your hypotheses.

- Build testing opportunities into your marketing timelines.

- Test, learn, and iterate—then adjust your hypotheses and continue the cycle of improvement.

PART FOUR

Tapping Into Community

Tapping Into Creativity

15

The Sway of Belonging

How do you think about your identity? What are the words that you use to describe yourself? Do you think about your company or job? Do you think about your family? Your alma mater or school affiliations? Your hobbies? When I think about my own identity, I think of myself as a mother, a New Yorker, a marketer, and a knitter—among many identities—in no particular order. For me, each of these identities comes with a community of people that I turn to for support, connection, and camaraderie. For most of us (and our customers), who we are is reflected in the company we keep.

Our identities, which are of course essential to the premise of personalization, are inextricably tied to the people who are like us. Leveraging these communities allows brands to build credibility, to address emotional resonance, and to showcase relevance. All of these ideas we've seen throughout the book to deepen our brands' relationships with our customers are also reflected here in our exploration of communities.

Why are communities an additional tool beyond the types of persuasive appeals that we've explored in Parts Two and Three? Communities amplify the beliefs of their members. They create stronger affinities than messaging alone. They provide support, not just agreement. And they are natural networks that spread the word. Up to now, we've looked at how we target and speak to our customers as individuals, but in Part Four we'll explore how we can speak to them in groups. We'll look not only at why communities matter to our customers, but also what brands should learn from these communities, and how to activate the network power of communities to spread brand affinity, build trust, and cultivate brand loyalty.

The Power of Belonging

In Chapter 11 I referred to influential psychologist Abraham Maslow and his oft-cited hierarchy of needs. His writings described a progression of needs that people seek to fulfill. Once the basic physiological and safety needs are fulfilled, Maslow wrote that social needs or "love and belonging" needs are the next that people seek to address (1943). Communities don't just provide support and safety, they also align with the higher-level motivations that drive people (also discussed in Chapter 11): Giving them purpose, allowing them to express autonomy, and promoting mastery of new skills. Belonging to a community is, therefore, not just essential to how we survive in the world but also how we achieve self-fulfillment and growth. Furthermore, harnessing the power of belonging is a highly impactful tactic for marketers because it influences such a wide variety of motivations.

Culture and Community

What makes a community? It isn't just the shared interests or traits; it's the shared culture: Values, traditions, language, and norms. For instance, my good friend, Alex, has been a runner for about twenty years. She's been part of a Team in Training (TNT) group—a charity-driven running group associated with the Leukemia & Lymphoma Society that has local clubs across America—for most of that time. TNT community members can be recognized by their signature purple jerseys at races throughout the US. They have a shared language and shared semiotics (or symbols) like the signature purple, the recognizable blood drop logo, and the TNT shield logo, that helps make it easy to signal to others who belong to this community that they are part of the same inner circle.

In addition, TNT members have a shared purpose around curing cancer and participating in endurance sports. Belonging to a group gives members a shared identity, and purpose creates a virtuous cycle that helps keep people engaged in the community. This purpose also provides a shortcut to building trust among members because there are shared values and because belonging to the same group provides a halo effect.

Furthermore, belonging to a group speeds up one's ability to build a network. When Alex moved from New York to a new state some years ago, she immediately joined the local TNT group near her and was able to form relationships with new people, despite being new in town. This is a familiar story to most of us who have ever moved to a new place or started a new job. Tapping into your university alumni network, a fraternity or sorority you belong to, your new colleagues, and/or the local group of people who share your hobby (sports, crafts, video gaming, reading, etc.) gives us a starting point.

When brands tap into communities, they are also tapping into the shared culture, extending that same trust and halo effect to the brand. Much like the benefits of social proof, the benefits of leveraging communities for brands are many.

Identifying Communities

All the way back in Chapter 5 we discussed the different categories of data that brands can collect about customers, which included identifiers that might indicate potential communities, such as industry, affiliations, roles, and even life stage. By analyzing the data available to us about our audiences—including disclosed data, survey data, and social listening data—you can identify opportunities to speak to our audience's community affiliations. In some cases, the communities are built right into the industries you represent. For instance, as a knitter, crocheter, and weaver, I often enjoy content online that speaks to the unique quirks, inside jokes, and preferences of these communities. It's no surprise that brands that serve crafters like me will try to use signifiers of shared understanding (like how one can never own too much yarn) to build trust and camaraderie among their customers.

Let's take a look at another example, this time in the B2B space. At Convince & Convert, we work with many associations, most of which are aimed at professionals in different industries, such as the Professional Convention Management Association (PCMA). Associations are often focused on the furtherment of a specific trade; therefore, they focus on the community of people who work in the specific industry and are building their skills in that industry. By speaking about the shared challenges, needs, interests, and responsibilities of the professionals they serve, they can not only grow their own brand affinities, but also leverage the pride, relatedness, and even fellowship that people who have similar experiences undergo.

In fact, shared experiences are probably the key to identifying communities to speak to. Communities aren't just built on shared interests or shared work experience/industry. They can be built around values, generation (think about all the content specifically aimed at Millennials or Boomers that speaks to nostalgia or shared experience), even personality type (for instance, you've probably seen all the content that addresses the various Myers-Briggs personalities). If you explore the social network Reddit, with its hundreds of thousands of communities or "subreddits," you'll find people convening around industries like user experience or information technologies, but also people who just love specific breeds of dogs—or even more general topics like "oddly satisfying" internet videos.

The wide range of shared interests and shared values that can be tapped into also means that brands can build communities based on loose affiliations, rather than only tapping into existing communities. We'll take a look at those opportunities later in this chapter, but first, let's take a look at how brands can tap into existing communities using their language.

Integrating Voice-of-Customer Data

It's no revelation that shared language—slang, tropes, memes, hashtags, etc.—demonstrate that you're part of the in-crowd. It's one of the reasons that leveraging the unique vernacular of a people can lend an air of authenticity. Think about John Steinbeck's classic American novel *Of Mice and Men*, or the well-known coming-of-age novel *The Outsiders* by S E Hinton, both of which use the dialect and argot of their characters (farm hands during the Great Depression and teens in the 1960s respectively) to demonstrate how they stand out among others in their world. It's one of the reasons that the fans of musicians like Taylor Swift often spend hours debating their word choices and references in online forums.

But nowadays language changes particularly rapidly. Ask the parent of any teenager if they know what the latest slang is and they'll tell you it seems to change almost weekly. Social media has accelerated the speed at which ideas are disseminated, which means that it can be more difficult for brands to keep up with what's relevant to their audiences. How should marketers build mechanisms for identifying what's in? How do you find the microtrends, burning questions, and slang of your customers? In other words, how do you collect voice-of-customer data?

Of course, tools like social listening are an important part of your toolbox, but more than listening for sentiment or topic, brand marketers must listen for the verbiage of their customers. In addition to passive listening mechanisms, brands should also deploy tools that spawn feedback in customers' own words:

- Analyze open-ended responses in customer service feedback.
- Scour customer reviews on owned and third-party channels.
- Implement pulse surveys (short one- to two-question surveys designed to elicit a snapshot of customers' thinking, sent to a smaller percentage of your audience).
- Engage in polls and "ask me anything" sessions (AMAs) on official social media channels.

Once you've identified that shared language, pull it into your marketing messaging. And if possible make sure it's targeted to the unique customer segments that you serve. How you might speak to a Gen Z buyer is different from how you might speak to a Boomer. How you might sell to a tech company buyer is different from how you might speak to a financial services buyer. Planning for the nuances of each audience should be part of both how you listen and how you speak to your audiences.

Collecting the Unique Data of Your Customers' Community

Are you a pet owner or do you know a pet owner well? Pet ownership undoubtedly opens the door to a community with its own language, community tropes, and its own resources. Monthly subscription dog-toy-box company, Bark Box, knows this audience. Its website declares, "Dog people get it" (2023) and it features mostly user-generated content showing off pets, shared jokes and memes, as well as experiences that other pet owners will relate to.

Beyond just catering to the way its customers relate to others like them, Bark Box also collects its data to reflect the unique considerations of its customers. It collects the dogs' names, breeds, size, gender, allergies, as well as their toy needs (i.e., durability). This data is leveraged—perhaps even more so that the human customers' data—to tell stories that are highly relevant to their customers. When there's an opportunity to structure your data to include key information that's unique to the community that your customers belong to, do so. You can then use this information to target content, messages, and offers specific to their needs, like the brand in this next case study.

CASE STUDY
How Farm House Tack Makes Riders Feel Understood

Founded in 2005, Farm House Tack in Landrum, South Carolina, serves horseback riders of all kinds. Whether you're a serious competitive rider or you have a child who is just starting to take lessons, Farm House Tack has the equipment that you need. From the first touch-point on the website—a pop-up box that asks, "What type of rider are you?" in exchange for a discount code—this small business is thinking about how to collect information that will help them customize the content, products, and experience of their prospective customers (2023).

I spoke with Farm House Tack's ecommerce manager Michelle Drum, who told me that her focus is on making sure to put the right products in front of the right customers. Based on what type of rider the customer is or is shopping for, the team uses email automations to showcase content that's highly relevant to each customer segment. That could be blog posts like "Top 5 things your child needs for horseback riding summer camp" for new riders, or in-depth skills for more serious riders like "How to wrap a horse's foot and why you need to know." The company also showcases specific product brands and categories to customers based on their buying behaviors, making sure that serious riders are shown the right apparel for competition and parents of new riders are shown brands that are good value. No matter the category, customers are given messages that speak to their unique needs.

But one of their biggest hits, when it comes to custom messaging, is a simple birthday wish—for the horses. Owners/riders get a fun birthday card for their horses' birthdays, addressed to the horse, featuring a photo—originally staged by Michelle—featuring her two horses with a birthday banner and cupcakes. They see that the brand is just as devoted to their horses as the customers are to their own, and they see the brand celebrate their horses by name. Michelle says that it's a message they see consistently shared on social media with the brand tagged and that they get responses via direct message as well (2023). Sometimes it's the simplest things that can make our customers feel welcome in our community.

Building Owned Communities

As we saw in Chapter 9, building your own communities—as Nike has done with its popular exercise and sneaker apps, which we've previously discussed—can be an extremely efficient and effective way to collect more data about your customers' behaviors and preferences. But building owned communities can also be a part of your value proposition.

Take LEGO Ideas, LEGO's online community for avid makers and fans to showcase their creations, participate in challenges (for prizes), and submit their proposals for future LEGO sets. LEGO recognized that part of the appeal of the blocks is customers' ability to develop sculptures, sets, and art—to demonstrate their own creativity. Instead of only letting those outlets exist on third-party websites, LEGO decided to empower its biggest fans through officially sanctioned community events and its own website. This online community features member profiles, allows fans to connect with each other, and gamifies the experience of participating in the community. It also deepens the relationship between the brand and its most avid fans—making them feel supported, seen, and heard by the brand.

Here's another example from the B2B space: Rosenfeld Media is a publishing house and user experience conference company in New York City, as well as one of our clients at Media Volery. Focused on the user experience industry, they go above and beyond the typical business conference to ensure that their conference attendees get a great experience. During the Covid-19 lockdowns (and continuing to today), they started offering free cohorts—small, organized groups led by a facilitator—to help attendees of virtual events get the benefits of networking and building connections. They also offer free communities by topic that have dedicated emails and even community calls—open forum discussions on Zoom on the hot industry topics of the moment—each month. In addition to all of that, Rosenfeld Media offers a free Slack channel to conference attendees that facilitates attendees' abilities to connect with each other, share information such as job listings, and learn from the community. These free experiences connect their customers and prospects to each other in a way that isn't necessarily facilitated by other resources within the user experience space, which elevates Rosenfeld Media's perception and presence in the industry.

Not every company will have the opportunity or the bandwidth to build a community for its customers, but they can be a powerful resource to deepen the relationship between the brand and the customer, identify the most avid of fans, provide a competitive advantage to the brand, and offer up learnings that can shape personalization. In the next chapter, we'll look at some more examples of the ways that brands can leverage communities.

RESOURCES RELATED TO THIS CHAPTER

Design for Belonging: How to build inclusion and collaboration in your communities by Susie Wise—This charmingly illustrated guide takes a hands-on approach to helping readers think through the choices that foster belonging. It focuses on the very human experiences at the nexus of belonging and design.

CHAPTER 15 SUMMARY

Belonging to communities is psychologically powerful, providing safety, support, and identity. When brands can tap into the culture of communities— their shared language, shared purpose, experiences, values, and networks—they can easily build credibility. But more than just ethos, community-building can help brands to collect more data about their customers and also cultivate loyalty.

Actions

- Determine the key identifiers that indicate potential communities for your brand to tap into.
- Prioritize those identifiers that have the most impact.
- Identify the mechanisms that need to exist to build a community/ communities based on those identifiers; does one already exist (i.e., on a third-party platform) that your organization can tap into? Or is there an opportunity to own that community?
- Develop a pilot program to roll out a test community.

16

Getting the Most Out
of Communities

In the previous chapter we explored why communities can be a powerful medium for building customer loyalty through shared identity, shared culture, and social connectedness. We also looked at some examples of companies like LEGO that recognized the desire of their customers to connect and, therefore, facilitated the building of communities through owned forums or platforms. In this chapter we'll continue to explore four ways brands can improve these communities through research and data and benefit from these communities as opportunities to build more robust owned data about customers and their behaviors.

Shaping the Community Conversation

As we've seen, communities are often a metaphorical resonance space allowing ideas to echo and reverberate among community members. They can facilitate collaboration between members, as well as enable participants to inspire each other. But when it comes to building a community from scratch, it's not a given that the right people will come together to create a sustainable, engaging, and valuable space. For brands, there's a huge opportunity—and, perhaps, necessity—to seed communities with content and individuals who will further the mission of the community, as well as provide value and inspiration to others. Brands must use the techniques we discussed in Chapter 13 to research the influential voices who will inspire their audiences and leverage them to guide the conversations.

Take Adobe Creative Cloud, which is a suite of tools including Photoshop, Illustrator, Premiere, and many others that are staples of creatives like photographers, graphic designers, and filmmakers. Over the years, Adobe's marketing teams have recruited a wide variety of content creators to not only showcase their art, but also their behind-the-scenes processes, as well as to create tutorials. But beyond just showcasing the possibilities of Adobe's tools, the diverse and varied backgrounds of the individuals that they feature demonstrate that the tools aren't just for "traditional" pros. Content creators like director Karen X Cheng, whose viral social media videos and unique behind-the-scenes demonstrations have propelled her career, are among the voices that Adobe has purposefully elevated to shape their community to include hobbyists and creatives outside of the mainstream. By curating community contributors, brands like Adobe are matchmaking between their audiences and their contributors by leveraging their knowledge of their customers.

Similarly, to make inroads in its key market segments such as salespeople, marketers, and educators, presentation and video software company Prezi has taken a proactive approach to identifying content creators that not only represent its ideal customer profiles, but also who create content that speaks to the specific challenges of those customers. Prezi users not only see that collaborator content in emails and in their resource library, but can also browse the Prezi gallery for inspiration from these and other Prezi users (full disclosure: I have created content for Prezi in the past). While platforms like Prezi may work with creators directly to seed their libraries, they also have the opportunity to test and adjust whose content rises to the top over time. They can highlight the voices whose content has performed well in the past, and/or develop more individuals whose content both appeals to the community while furthering the company's goals. In other words, brands must use audience data to inform how they shape their communities throughout their lifecycles—it's an ongoing process of input and feedback.

Leveraging Data to Improve Community Engagement

Now let's talk about an industry where cultivating community comes with the territory. If you went to college/university, especially in the US, chances are that you were contacted by your institution's alumni office or association shortly before graduating to encourage you to join. It's common wisdom in the higher education space that getting students to enroll in their alumni organization before they graduate can increase the likelihood that they will stay actively engaged (and donate to the institution) once they've completed their degree, so there's a drive within this space to get students involved early.

Universities have a vested interest in their alumni, because they make up a large part of their donor base, act as referrers for future students, and behave as ambassadors for the university and its reputation out in the job market, among other reasons. And yet, many universities collect limited data about their alumni. Sure, they might have their updated contact information and perhaps they collect some employer or industry data, but often times they don't do the work of understanding what they care about, how they engage with other alumni, or where they go in terms of their career. And, more importantly, they don't necessarily centralize this data in a way that allows them to deepen their connections with these alumni, instead leaving it up to the departments and schools/colleges within the university to maintain their own records.

Many universities also focus on life stage or stakeholder type when looking at alumni, such as "recent grads" or "PhD grads," rather than attitudes or behaviors. This misses out on the opportunity to activate their alumni based on their interests and attitudes in a way that creates value for the community. When our team at Convince & Convert worked with Texas Exes, the alumni association for the University of Texas at Austin and one of the largest alumni associations in the world, they were like many other alumni organizations. But they recognized that their content wasn't resonating with alumni and that there was an opportunity to better understand their community. We worked with them to conduct attitudinal research that identified three key attitudinal archetypes (Convince & Convert, 2022).

These groups, based on their attitudes and behaviors, each included people who were five years out of school, as well as fifty years out. While some groups skewed a little younger or older, they each represented a large portion of the overall community. These insights also helped us better understand how these people engaged with others in the group, giving Texas Exes more clarity in terms of how to create meaningful opportunities for them to get involved. For instance, perhaps Group A could be activated through social opportunities like "Homecoming" (the traditional annual event that welcomes alumni back to campus) or local meetups, while Group

B might prefer structured opportunities focused on topical interests or professional pursuits like a forum on new technologies or alumni arts fair. Finally, Group C wasn't interested in connecting with other alumni on a social level, but they could potentially be engaged through activities that were designed around projects or initiatives with impact, like leading a mentorship group or judging a business competition. Understanding how these archetypes wanted to engage within the community is important because alumni organizations like Texas Exes are charged with keeping alumni involved.

The lesson here is that data and research can help us better understand how we can get the most of our communities—how to activate our communities better, how to keep community members engaged, and therefore how to keep those community members' satisfaction with our brands high. But data doesn't just inform how organizations can improve communities. Communities can also help organizations better understand their audiences by giving them more opportunities to collect meaningful data, as we'll see in this next example.

Expanding the Conversation to Collect More Data

There are some large global companies that are so well-known that their former employees will mention them for years after they've left those organizations. You may have even seen these descriptors in your colleagues' LinkedIn summaries or Twitter bios, like "ex-Googler" or "previously at McKinsey." In fact, some of these companies have recognized the power of this alumni network, hosting official platforms for their former employees to connect, learn, and contribute. Organizations like Blackrock, Deloitte, Nestlé, and Goldman Sachs have developed robust communities that allow them to continue to build brand affinity among former employees, which cultivates opportunities for referral both for business development and hiring. For example, in an article for *Harvard Business Review*, professors Alison Dachner and Erin Makarius note that these companies see higher ratings on career review website Glassdoor (brand affinity) and that they tap alumni for contract work, paid mentoring, and even rehiring (referral). Furthermore, they suggest that more companies should organize formal alumni networks, since only 15 percent of companies surveyed had them, but in 67 percent former employees organized their own informal groups (2021).

Using their communities, these companies are able to collect a variety of data about their alumni, which they can leverage. In the same article, the authors share an example of Booz Allen Hamilton, the management consulting company, which uses its alumni databases to fill short-term, temporary, and project-based staffing needs (2021). But this data can also help them understand the career trajectories of their alumni, the opportunities they may have for business development (ostensibly, many of these alumni may end up in related companies or start their own firms that might do business with these companies), and also the strengths and weaknesses of their own organizational hiring and employee development (useful for diversity, equity, and inclusion [DE&I] initiatives). By extending their relationship with their alumni, they expand their own opportunities to collect and learn from that data.

When Data is Part of the Competitive Advantage

Of course, in the internet age there are also many organizations that cultivate community to collect customers' behavioral and interest data as a means to sell advertising—that's basically the model of every social media platform. But building communities with a deep understanding of a unique niche can truly set an organization apart competitively. Let's look at an example from the parenting space. One of the best-known American parenting books is *What to Expect When You're Expecting*, first published in 1984; it's so well-known that it's often gifted to expectant parents, and it even inspired a 2012 romantic comedy starring Cameron Diaz and Jennifer Lopez. The company that grew out of that book, What to Expect, now offers a wide variety of content for parents and soon-to-be parents, from due date calculators and baby registry tools to videos and articles, on its website and app. It also offers a robust forum community that allows users to talk about whatever is on their minds.

When you visit the forum page on the website, the first thing you see is an option to "find moms who share your birth month" (What to Expect, 2023). These due-date groups allow users to connect with others on their exact timelines, from pregnancy all the way into raising their children, for learning, commiserating, and gaining support. These segmented groups also allows What to Expect and its advertising partners to be extremely precise about learning what users care about at different stages of their pregnancies and child-rearing (both experiences that are very much tied to developmental age), as well as serving up the right messages to those users based on needs.

The precision of its understanding of its audiences gives What to Expect a strong ability to market both its own and partners' content and products to its audiences. But lest you think that all community-building opportunities are online, let's take a look at an example that combines offline and online data in our next case study.

CASE STUDY

How Netline Leverages Offline and Online Data to Match Content to the Right Audiences

Netline is one of the largest B2B lead generation platforms online, helping B2B brands get their assets in front of the right audiences to build brand affinity and connect with prospective clients. According to its Chief Strategy Officer, David Fortino, they typically process about 700,000 gated asset registrations per month for B2B marketers around the world, featuring around 15,000 gated pieces of content (ebooks, white papers, case studies, analyst reports, etc.) being shown to businesspeople. Owned by Informa and powering the gated content of publications like the *Wall Street Journal*, *Fortune*, and *Fast Company*, Netline's platform collects and analyses a broad pool of content consumption behavior and demographic data as part of its services.

Because of its deep database that factors in at least 18 different characteristics or points of data about each individual, Netline's customers (the marketers who want their content served to prospective leads) are able to reach individuals not only based on industry and job title, but also based on their behaviors and interests across hundreds of different websites. "We are converting not only all of the kind of transparent online intent signals at the person level, but also, uniquely, we're the only intent platform that's weaving in offline intent," Fortino explained to me (2023). By leveraging the hundreds of industry events organized by parent company Informa (a British publishing, business intelligence, and exhibitions group), Netline also understands what conference sessions, events, and webinars individuals actually attend. So, for instance, Netline knows when three people from an organization have attended offline sessions about how to better integrate analytics tools into their operations. Therefore, Netline can serve content from its advertising partners on this topic to those individuals *or*, through their Intentive platform, they can facilitate account-based-marketing by a partner to reach out to these individuals. In other words, the communities that Informa has cultivated within these industries powers Netline's abilities to connect advertising partners with customers based on the actual problems they're trying to solve.

Fostering Community Conversations to Build Knowledge

Beyond collecting user data from communities to inform your models, communities can be a powerful source of informational content—which can be leveraged as data as well. For instance, look at the Microsoft Support Community, a robust and wide-ranging forum website that supports Microsoft products including Windows, Skype, Xbox, Office, and much more. This Microsoft-owned community allows users to ask questions of each other, get support from power users, and also search for questions from others who may have the same issues. But for a company like Microsoft, the opportunity isn't just in having customers help each other (and thereby save time and effort from their own support staff), this data may also be useful to (a) identify common questions that require official support documentation, (b) identify technical issues its teams need to address, and (c) create information that can train its AI-driven systems to support both its customer support teams and its customer-facing technologies in the future (as we'll discuss shortly). Other tech companies, such as the popular open-source website platform WordPress, also have these robust knowledge bases that offer both the opportunity to support their communities while also offering the companies a wide variety of information to analyze and use to improve.

In a world where search is a default manner of discovering content online, having a deep repository of resources makes it likely that your brand comes up as a resource. Think of forum websites like Reddit or Quora, which often rank highly in search results in a wide variety of obscure topics—as well as brands like QuickBooks, whose forums cover both topics about their products and services, as well as general accounting questions. The wide range of topics asked and discussed on these platforms are resources for users with similar questions. Ask yourself whether your brand has an opportunity to host the conversations about your particular industry—to build a community of people who are discussing their challenges in your space—so that you can leverage that content as a learning opportunity and a source of knowledge.

Finally, building a content bank of questions and answers is also an opportunity when it comes to building your own generative AI engines—for customer service and customer experience. In the next few years, we'll see companies and governments grapple with the legalities of training AI models on data without explicit permission, so building an owned knowledge base now that your company could leverage to train its own AI tools (with proper permission from your users) is a smart way to prepare for the future.

Communities as Self-Sustaining Spaces

Have you ever joined a group only for it to peter out over time? Whether virtual or live and in-person, groups can lose momentum because they don't have the qualities that make them self-sustaining: Ongoing value to the community members, consistency, strong shared culture. Building owned communities has a lot of benefits for brands, as we've seen in these last two chapters, but without putting the customer experience at the center of how they are designed they will not be sustainable. In the next chapter we'll look more at how community members can become sources for referral and networking, promoting the kind of longevity that pays dividends.

RESOURCES RELATED TO THIS CHAPTER

Building Brand Communities: How organizations succeed by creating belonging by Carrie Melissa Jones and Charles Vogl—With deep experience building communities with brands like Google, Patreon, and Coursera, the authors explore a framework for developing resilient communities.

CHAPTER 16 SUMMARY

This chapter builds on the frameworks of Chapter 15 and its action checklist should be used in tandem with that of the previous chapter. Communities present both an opportunity to deepen relationships with customers through the leveraging of customer data and research, as well as a method for brands to collect ownable data and learnings. By thinking of communities as spaces to foster conversations and exchanges between customers, users, and/or community members, brands can extend their impact and their insights.

Actions

- Define the types of data that will help improve the community experience for users/customers.
- Identify the insights that could be leveraged to increase or shape the conversations and engagement within the community.
- Determine the ways in which the community's conversations should be studied to improve the brand's insights.
- Review the ways in which the brand can get more value out of the content and data created by the community.

17

Cultivating Community-Builders

In just about every industry, there are brands that use referral codes to incentivize word of mouth. That's because, as we discussed in Chapter 13, word of mouth has an outsize impact on purchase behaviors. In fact, 83 percent of Americans agree that a word-of-mouth recommendation from friends or family makes them more likely to purchase the product or service discussed (Baer and Lemin, 2018). Many of these brands use simple incentives like discounts or credits for the referrer to motivate their fans. For instance, the HR software company Gusto offers a referral fee when a new company sets up an account with the referrer's code or link. Those brands that are more advanced will also use data to identify their strongest referrers and incentivize them using an affiliate program. Companies like Amazon even offer their affiliates special bonus periods or tiered incentives to spur them on further. Other companies (like those we explored in the last chapter) may encourage participation in these programs through gamification or insider benefits.

Referral programs and affiliate programs exist on a spectrum of different types of network and community-building tools that companies tap into. On one end, you have these simple programs aimed at simply bringing in more customers. At the other end, you have programs that are aimed at enriching customers' experiences, so that they become brand loyalists.

There are of course lessons to be learned from referral programs—especially those that leverage data and research to better understand what drives their participants, who their best participants are, and how to increase their rate of participation. However, we'll want to look more closely at the brands that understand the power of identifying the individuals who go further than spreading the word through other, more engaging vehicles. We particularly want to look at how brands activate those community members who invest time and energy into their communities.

Identifying Power Networkers

Think about your circle of friends or your colleagues. Is there someone who always seems to be introducing you to someone new? They are natural connectors or networkers, who make you feel welcome in new situations, introducing you to someone with similar interests. Personally, I think of someone like my friend Jodi. She's the kind of person who, if she's five minutes early to a bar where we're meeting up, will manage to chat up the owner, get their entire life story, and get invited to some cool event that they're hosting. Or I think of someone like Cait, a speaker and volunteer at my local speakers' association chapter, who proactively reached out to prospective members like me to make sure that we knew someone at the upcoming mixer and made us not only feel welcome, but also informed of the ways we could engage with the organization.

Natural community-builders like Jodi and Cait are valuable people to have in your own personal networks, and also for brands to identify and engage with when building communities. They add value to the community through building connectivity, which deepens the relationships within the community, and they are ambassadors of insider knowledge. Building communities is more art than science; by using the tools available to us, we can better research, identify and empower these community-builders to multiply the impacts of our brand communities.

Activating Customers Who Engage

To identify these naturally prolific networkers, brand marketers may start with identifying the customers in their existing communities who engage the most, such as the power-users within a forum who answer dozens of questions or keep conversations going. Take a look at participation data within your knowledge base, your blog, your social media, and/or your company's events (virtual or in-person)—there are likely customers who go above and beyond. And they may even already be known to your social media, social customer service, or events teams. Activating these individuals by inviting them to participate in more formalized roles is a great way for brands to build on top of their existing brand loyalty.

In Chapter 15 I mentioned Rosenfeld Media, a publishing house and conference organizer in the user experience space. Rosenfeld Media has been smart and strategic in identifying the enthusiastic engagers in their communities and given them roles as curators and community facilitators—

asking them to help build the programming for the next cohort of the community. Not only do these facilitators help shape programming that resonates with the broader community, but their involvement incentivizes these individuals to further engage with the brand. As we'll see later in this chapter, this approach is highly effective because it aligns the goals of the brand with the motivations of the individual.

Brands may also dig into those referral programs we discussed earlier. While there are many referral programs out there, often these programs miss out on the opportunity to use this owned data and identify the patterns within their strongest referrers: Are they a certain size of organization? Have they been a customer for a specific range of time? Do they engage with customer service more than the average customer? By identifying the characteristics of your most engaged customers, you can use those parameters to identify others like them.

Spotting Those Who Spread the Word

We've previously looked at some of the benefits of using social listening as a tool to understand and identify trusted voices among your brand fans. When it comes to identifying power networkers, brands should use social listening tools to identify those not just with large audiences, but with high engagement rates among their audiences. In fact, it may be more effective to identify micro-influencers with smaller, more engaged audiences—those audiences are more likely to trust the personal recommendations of these micro-influencers and more interested to engage with their content.

To take a different approach, many brands use net promoter scores (NPS) as part of their measure of customer satisfaction and customer loyalty. Since the question centers around how likely the customer is to recommend a brand to someone else, it's another useful tool to leverage, when it comes to identifying customers who may be strong advocates of the brand. Consider segmenting your brand's audience by NPS score to identify brand promoters, those who give the highest scores to your brand.

In addition, customers who are consistently creating user-generated content about your brand, high-frequency reviewers, and/or high-engagement participants in your brand's content are also extremely influential voices to elevate. As we saw in Chapter 13 with review website Yelp's "Elite" program, creating events and giving status to people based on their activity can be a smart way to further activate these customers and community members, encouraging them to further spread the word.

Exploring Interest Through Surveys and Questionnaires

Just because someone is a brand fan doesn't necessarily mean that they want to play a more active role in building the community. By starting with the criteria we've discussed in this chapter, marketers and brands can identify strong candidates for community-builders. Then, by using tools such as surveys, questionnaires and even focus groups you can dig into their desire to participate in more active ways. Brands can also build programs that encourage these power networkers to raise their hands. But to do so, they must be thoughtful in building programs that align with the personal motivations of those individuals, as we'll soon examine.

EXERCISE
Pinpoint the Data That Reveals Community-Builders

Take a look at your audience data. What data do you currently collect or intend on collecting that can support you identifying members of your community that are high engagers? Go through the following list and determine the most useful data sources to utilize.

Behavioral:

- Writes reviews on-site frequently.
- Submits their own photos/content to the brand frequently (such as for reviews or customer features).
- Comments on brand social media frequently.
- Participates in knowledge base or support forums actively.
- Has high scores or rankings within owned user communities.
- Gives high scores on NPS surveys.
- Proactively gives (helpful) unsolicited feedback to customer service or support.
- Frequently attends online or in-person events.

Customer relationship:

- Long-time customer.
- Has previously provided testimonials for the brand.
- Identified by sales team as a trusted customer.

- Social media
- Creates posts about the brand on their own social media accounts
- Creates posts about the brand on their own website
- Frequently uses the brand's hashtags or tags the brand (in positive posts)
- Active as moderators or users in brand-related (but not necessarily brand-led) social media groups (such as LinkedIn, Facebook, or Reddit groups)

Consent and preference:

- Has opted in to participating in early feedback initiatives (such as survey groups or beta testing)

Empowering Your Community-Builders

As we discussed in Chapter 11, to truly drive behaviors, we must tap into customers' motivations from a behavioral psychology perspective, providing them the tools to fulfill their own desire for autonomy, mastery, and purpose. While we can identify potential community-builders, we also need to support them through programs that allow them to do what they do best: Be natural connectors of people. Let's take a look at some examples in each category.

Supporting Community-Builders' Autonomy

Referral programs and affiliate programs often rely on their community-builders telling the story of the brand or products in a way that's relevant and tailored to their audiences. For instance, perhaps you've seen TikTok videos or Instagram Reels that talk about must-have products from Amazon. Another example from an entirely different industry is email platform ActiveCampaign, which recognizes the power of its affiliate network to share the virtues of its products with other like-minded people, such as small business owners or agency owners sharing their business lessons and favored tools with others like them. When it comes to these kinds of community-based referral programs, most brands understand that it doesn't make sense to dictate an approach—since each of these affiliates' networks are very different—but, rather, facilitate their abilities to tell the stories that make sense for them.

ActiveCampaign's affiliate program includes a starter pack with resources to help new affiliates jump start their program, including graphics, video assets, webinars, and business papers that they think will be helpful. They also have a closed community specifically for affiliates, where influencers can share their best practices to help new affiliates learn along the way (2023).

To tap into the autonomy of your community-builders, support them with the tools that they need to succeed, but give them room to exercise their own creativity. Then, provide them with a space to trade knowledge with each other. Whether you're building an affiliate program or a learning community, giving space to these community-builders to make the programs their own is essential. After all, they don't have to be there. They're choosing to be a part of your brand's community because they believe in the brand and what it stands for.

Developing Community-Builders' Mastery

Some products or services require a certain level of skill or mastery to get the most out of them. For brands in these kinds of spaces, developing communities to support their users is part of a smart strategy to increase benefit for customers and build brand loyalty. For instance, sales and marketing software-as-a-service platform HubSpot offers educational programming to help customers become experts in their platform and even earn certifications to demonstrate their proficiency in the tools. Similarly, they organize HubSpot user groups or "HUGs," which are local groups each led by a HUG leader (HubSpot, 2023), who are knowledge experts that have raised their hands to start a local group and applied through HubSpot. HUGs may be organized around specific skills, industries, and/or products, so that like-minded individuals can connect and learn from each other.

Similarly, Fiverr—the freelancer marketplace—also offers a similar program for its millions of freelancers. In addition to local events and clubs, there are specific opportunities for those individuals who are interested in getting more involved to apply for leadership positions within the community and to enroll as mentors to support other freelancers who are looking to build their businesses (Fiverr Forum, 2023).

Brands like these can take a data-driven approach to uncovering the interests, learning goals, and key questions that their community members have. But to facilitate their community actually getting the answers and support they need, they must turn to these community-builders. By combining data with the human driver of a desire for mastery, these brands can activate their communities in meaningful ways that increase customer satisfaction and the likelihood of these community members to spread the word.

Rallying Community-Builders Through Purpose

While I share the examples of HubSpot and Fiverr to talk about the opportunities to cultivate community-builders that want to master skills or share their skills, these are also good examples of brands that have rallied their community-builders through a shared purpose: Helping others build businesses like themselves. Of course, we see organizations in the non-profit space rally their top volunteers to grow through the ranks of the organization through their devotion to the cause. Think of organizations like Habitat for Humanity that not only encourage individual volunteerism, but also build chapters on college campuses by cultivating local leaders for their Women Build program, as well as developing young volunteers through their Habitat Young Professionals program. These programs not only activate passionate members of their community, but also build the skills of these members with an eye towards leadership and further activation (Habitat for Humanity, 2023).

Learn From Your Community-Builders

These community-builders represent the most devoted of your customers, and therefore it's important not only to pay attention to what they're saying, but also to actively seek out their feedback and input. For brands and marketers, it's not only about identifying these individuals in your system to understand their passive behaviors engaging with your website or implementing robust social listening to understand what they're saying out in the world, but also using them as a laboratory for experimentation and feedback. Incentivizing these community-builders to give feedback via focus groups, preview emails, and surveys are just a few ways that you can learn from these individuals who are embedded in your broader community and have their ear to the ground.

Throughout Part Four we've explored the ways that communities can add value to a brand, improve customer loyalty, and serve as engines for brands to extract further insights. They are critical to how people seek out experiences and seek to engage in the world because, as we learned from Maslow, belonging is such a fundamental part of what people seek out and need in order to thrive. In Part Five we'll explore another level of Maslow's hierarchy of need—self-esteem—and how brands can tap into the effects of this behavioral driver while leveraging data and insights.

RESOURCES RELATED TO THIS CHAPTER

Belonging to the Brand: Why community is the last great marketing strategy by Mark Schaefer—In this clear and engaging book, marketer and futurist Mark Schaefer explores the ways in which brands should build communities and tap into community-builders.

CHAPTER 17 SUMMARY

In this chapter we went deeper into communities to focus on the power networkers or community-builders who serve as the glue for these communities. To build successful, prolific, and self-sustaining community programming, brands must identify these community-builders, empower them, and learn from them.

Actions

- Review available data to identify methodologies (such as social listening, website activity, or NPS) to identify potential community-builders.
- Develop programs that support community-builders' motivations to engage with the brand and spread the word.
- Develop the tools to support these programs.
- Create and utilize feedback mechanisms to learn from community-builders.
- Track the impact of your community-builders over time to adjust and iterate upon the program.

PART FIVE

Deepening Customer Profiles

18

The Appeal of Status

Throughout this book we've looked at the different ways that we can tap into behavioral psychology to understand our customers, connect with them in relevant ways, and identify the data that will allow our brands to deliver these messages meaningfully. In Part Five we'll explore how we can use the mechanisms at our disposal to increase our knowledge of our customers—first looking at status and loyalty programs and then looking at customer relationship data. Then we'll explore how to bring together all aspects of customers' data into the ideal customer profile for your organization.

Why We Love a Loyalty Program

Do you belong to a loyalty program or membership program? If so, you may enjoy the ways that you're recognized because of that status. Maybe you're greeted as a long-time member when you call the customer service line or you get special bonus gifts when you check in at the front desk. Perhaps it's an online membership, and you get special perks when you're shopping online. Why do we enroll in loyalty programs and willingly give brands more data about ourselves?

The simple truth is that we all aspire to be known or acknowledged in our lives—and brands certainly recognize the power of this longing. Furthermore, this desire for status is distinct from the need for belonging, which we talked about in Part Four of this book. Whereas belonging focuses on harmony within the group and fitting in, status is about standing apart (Anderson et al., 2015).

It's this universal desire for status and special treatment that has so many credit cards offerings rewards programs that promise you elite entry to airport lounges, concierge services, and other markers of prestige. Brands recognize that this desire can be leveraged to create brand loyalty—moreover, building towards this status allows brands to collect more data and knowledge about each individual customer.

But status isn't just about being elevated. In his 2015 research on status and prestige, Professor Cameron Anderson of the Haas School of Business at the University of California, Berkeley, and his team define status as having three components: First, individuals with high status are given respect and admiration; second, others defer to these individuals' wishes, desires, and suggestions willingly; third, these individuals are seen as having social value to others. These different components come into play as brands develop programs that appeal to customers, and they also point to different ways that we as marketers can personalize our messaging to our customers.

Making Customers Feel Appreciated

As we just discussed, the first component of status is that the person is given respect and admiration. This is demonstrated through both words and actions. For brands, this kind of appreciation or care can come in simple forms of personalization—for instance, if you're a Citi customer, you may have logged into your account and seen a note that thanks you on the anniversary of your account (Gingiss, 2023). Whether it's one year or twenty-one, Citi chooses to use space in its account experience to acknowledge customers' loyalty.

Or it can come in grand gestures: For instance, in the second season of the television program *The Bear*, which focuses on a group of people opening a fine dining restaurant in Chicago, one of the main characters is training at a fine dining restaurant, when he witnesses the maître d' explain that they have researched each of their customers for the evening via social media. He highlights a couple that has been saving up to eat at this fine dining restaurant, and he exhorts his team to give them an experience they'll never forget and not to send them a bill at all (Russell, 2023). While this scene is a work of fiction, it reflects a reality in the fine dining world. Many of these top tier restaurants specifically research their customers, who are spending hundreds of dollars to dine in their venues, to give them a personalized experience designed to demonstrate next-level care (Settembre, 2023).

Know More About Your Customers, So You Can Go the Extra Mile

Just about every company should be able to harness data like a customer's account age for an anniversary email campaign. Many years ago, I worked at a company where we introduced an anniversary campaign that gave big discounts to our most loyal email subscribers. In fact, we offered coupons of 50 percent off orders (yes, 50!) of up to $200 to customers who had been on our email list for over 10 years (the email list was 14 years old at the time), because we knew it would generate word of mouth, and we wanted to truly reward these most loyal customers. Because we had been building a robust customer database with online data since 1998, we had this kind of data to leverage, even in the early days of email marketing and social media.

Anniversaries are something that just about any brand can capitalize on. But keep in mind that one of the goals of this book is to get you to think about the competitive advantages of knowing your customers *better* than your competition. So don't just stop at anniversaries. Ask yourself: What data does your brand have that can help you make grand gestures that set your brand apart? Perhaps you're a cosmetics company or clothing brand and, based on order history, you can determine the color palette that resonates most with your customers to create a personal inspiration board in their account or even a custom phone background to send to them. Perhaps you're a car company and you can send road trip playlists based on your customers' self-identified use cases (family trip versus business trip) that you send out just in time for summer trips. And if you don't have the right data, ask: How could you go seek it out?

Back in Chapter 6 I shared a story about my husband frequenting the botanic garden where we're members. As a reminder, he was frustrated because he had received a letter in the mail that encouraged him, as a neighbor of the garden, to become a member—despite the fact that he was regularly going to the garden at least twice a week. This disconnect came from the fact that the garden didn't track which members entered the garden, generating member tickets only based on the fact that a member showed their membership card and asking for a zip code (postal code). Let's imagine that, instead, the botanic garden kept track of which individual members frequented the garden. They could then generate a letter thanking my husband for his patronage, present him with a token of their appreciation (such as a self-guided tour of blooms for the upcoming months), and also upgrade his membership level for the year for free. Beyond building loyalty, this kind of gesture also increases the value of my husband's customer lifetime value: Since defaults are a powerful mechanism, this would then incentivize my husband to remain at this higher level of membership once this upgrade was over, once he had experienced the value in this higher tier of experiences.

Making Customers Feel Heard

Another aspect of status is the idea of voluntary deference—others value the wishes and opinions of the individual. How can brands make customers feel like their opinions matter? Look at brands that have beta tester communities or "insider" initiatives like Microsoft 365 Insiders. These individuals are given early access to tools and resources from the brand and are able to send feedback directly through these programs. In addition to these kinds of programs, social listening campaigns that focus on surprise and delight—going the extra mile to surprise customers—can be another approach, as we'll see in this next case study.

CASE STUDY
How Sam's Club Proactively Responds to its Brand Fans

The team at Sam's Club (the warehouse club chain owned by Walmart) has a robust social listening program that leverages social listening tools to uncover opportunities to provide next-level care to members. For instance, a mom shared a video of her child, Nathan, insisting on buying some Sam's Club cookies on her own social media channels; Sam's Club's team noted that video and immediately worked with their VP of Bakery to reach out to Nathan and his mom and make him their official cookie taster (Sam's Club, 2021).

Furthermore, the Sam's Club team built this two-way approach to engaging with their best customers, brand ambassadors, and influencers on social media as part of their social customer care initiatives (Baer and Brown, 2021). By taking a proactive approach to listening and engaging with high engagers, the brand makes these social media ambassadors and insiders feel like they have a direct line to the brand. And for the brand, they provide a valuable resource for feedback.

Deference to customers' opinions isn't limited to social listening. In 2008, international coffee chain Starbucks launched a platform called "My Starbucks Idea" that generated over 150,000 ideas from customers on how the company could improve its products and services, with hundreds of ideas implemented in the 10 years that the program was available. Not only did the brand allow other users to search the ideas and add their votes to their favorites, but they also used the platform to share updates on the progress of the ideas that it introduced. Ideas including free Wi-Fi, cake pops, and even flavors like hazelnut macchiato came from this program (Livescault, 2022). A program like this gives brands like Starbucks more than just a new way to innovate and learn from its customers, it also gives them the ability to reward their most loyal customers with status. Imagine if the creators of these successful ideas are acknowledged and thanked every time they purchase from Starbucks—it would not only increase loyalty, but also demonstrate to other nearby customers how seriously Starbucks takes the opinions of its customers.

Making Customers Feel Celebrated

The final component of status is that individuals with status are seen as having instrumental social value; others elevate them due to their qualities. How do we make our customers feel elevated or held in esteem? This goes beyond being heard or appreciated to being recognized as special or elite.

Online pet retailer Chewy invested in making customers (pet owners) truly feel recognized as individuals—or at least their *pets* are recognized as individuals. They send out more than 1,000 hand-painted portraits of pets each week, using pet photos that are on their Chewy accounts or shared via customer service interactions (a wonderful way to make the most out of these photos as data). Many of the customers who receive these paintings share these surprise gifts on social media, which generates exposure for the brand and loyalty from these customers (Pincombe, 2021).

Making customers feel elevated can also be as simple as early access to unreleased products, which sneaker and streetwear brand Kith offers to its app users. With an extremely loyal community of fans who often line up in front of Kith stores to be among the first to purchase new products released, it makes sense that Kith would prioritize those that make a commitment to engage with the brand further with special access. An even more exclusive example would be the American Express Centurion lounges, a perk designed to reward its most elite card holders with priority dining reservations and private dining, members-only events, and more (Griff, 2023).

Going Beyond the Dollars

Here's the thing: A lot of brands, particularly those with loyalty programs, tend to think about status as something that's granted based on dollars spent. We see that with airline miles and most retail programs. But there is a huge range of behaviors that brands can and should look to reward to build customer loyalty.

We've talked about rewarding customers who generate content (e.g., reviews, knowledge base articles, photos) on behalf of the brand in Part Four. But what about customers who are frequent site visitors or frequently consume your brand's content? For brands that offer tools or service subscriptions, such as software, what about celebrating frequent users?

The Pursuit of Maintaining Status

The desire for status may be universal, but so is the need to act to maintain it. This is no surprise to anyone who has ever received an email about their airline miles nearing their expiry and scrambled to act to keep them. This behavior is backed by the research by Professor Anderson and his team, which concluded that people engage in behaviors designed to attain or maintain their status and that they may react negatively when that status is threatened (2015). For brands, this desire to maintain status is another opportunity to expand their customer profile. Brands can harness this drive to maintain status by asking customers to share feedback, update their profile information, or to simply share their interests—focusing on collecting data that helps the brand to build stronger, more meaningful relationships with its customers.

Status isn't limited to one mode of engagement with customers. In fact, throughout this chapter we've examined brands that confer status on their customers, whether through loyalty programs, memberships, participation in specific channels (e.g., apps), and/or usage of specific products (e.g., the Centurion credit card). To best harness the power of status to drive customers and develop customer loyalty, brands must consider the ways that customers want to be held in esteem.

RESOURCES RELATED TO THIS CHAPTER

Creating Superfans: How to turn your customers into lifelong advocates by Brittany
 Hodak—Featuring stories from brands like Walmart and Disney, as well as
 artists like Taylor Swift and Dolly Parton, this book focuses on how to build
 brand loyalty in multiple ways.

CHAPTER 18 SUMMARY

As we entered Part Five of this book, we explored the ways that brands can
seek to deepen their knowledge of their customers. We looked at the behavioral
psychology of status and the ways that brands can recognize customers so that
they feel valued and heard. By conferring status onto their customers, they can
tap into customers' desires to be known and acknowledged. Leveraging data to
demonstrate this understanding of their customers is an opportunity for
brands, as is encouraging customers to share more personal details, where
relevant.

Actions

- Consider the three ways that brands can demonstrate special status to
  customers.
- Audit current loyalty efforts to determine ways to improve their relevance
  and personalization.
- Review opportunities to identify loyal customers beyond just dollars spent.
- Identify ways to leverage the desire to maintain status, to have customers
  improve the brand's profiles of them.

19

Increasing the Value
of Your Customers

When you go to the grocery store, do you ever fall for the siren song of the items near check-out? You know, the impulse items that are so irresistible when you're shopping hungry (this is why I try not to go to the market before I've eaten!). Or have you decided to buy something on an end-cap—the displays at the end of store aisles that face the main thoroughfares of the store—just to try something new? Over the last 100 years, retail stores have perfected the art of increasing the value of their customers by exploiting our behavioral psychology to drive additional sales.

Now imagine how much more effective those displays would be if they were tailored just for you: Specific products shown based on your tastes and preferences. In some ways, that's the reality that ecommerce platforms strive to deliver. But outside of a few large players like Amazon, most of the products that are being displayed to customers as cross-sells and up-sells are displayed based on rules of the relationships between the original product and the other products. They're *not* usually displayed based on what the customer prefers to buy, what they've bought before, and what they're likely to buy in the future.

But as the technology we have available to predict behavior continues to develop and we are able to better track our customers, their preferences, and their behaviors, we are able to improve in leaps and bounds. Particularly, as more AI-powered merchandising and customer profiling tools become widely available (as we'll talk about in Part Six of this book), more businesses will be able to profile customers accurately and predictively display the right products (and services) to each customer based on their unique needs. And, by doing so, brands can then increase the value of those customers.

Increasing the value of your existing customers can have an outsize effect on your bottom line. Why? Think of the Pareto principle, a rule of thumb coined by economist Vilfredo Pareto stating that 80 percent of outcomes come from just 20 percent of causes (Tardi, 2023). In other words, just a small portion of most businesses' customers are likely responsible for the majority of the revenue—as well as other value-driving behaviors like referrals and word-of-mouth. With that in mind, making sure that we are leveraging our data to increase the value of these current customers is a strategic imperative when it comes to data-driven personalization.

You probably learned in business school or economics that:

CLV = average purchase value × average purchase frequency × average customer lifespan

To increase customer lifetime value, you need to increase one of these factors. Let's talk about how you can use data to improve your ability to deliver persuasive messages or offers to the customer at the right times.

Improving Average Purchase Value

Just about every business understands the importance of cross-sells and upsells as mechanisms for increasing purchase value, but understanding how data can help you to make the case is a huge opportunity. When it comes to cross-sells or selling additional, sometimes complementary products to customers, businesses have traditionally thought about the opportunities in terms of relationships between products. Again, let's think about the local grocery store: Perhaps you've seen tortilla chips displayed with salsa, or lemons near the Dover sole. However, reviewing your existing customer data can identify the products or services that are most frequently associated with your high-value purchases—that might not be obvious based on the products themselves. In other words, you might find that certain products have a high correlation that wouldn't be obvious to a merchandiser. Perhaps someone who buys queso dip also tends to buy beer, for instance.

Alternately, you can identify products that similar customers tend to buy with the original product; you've probably seen an example of this on Amazon which shows you items "frequently bought together" on many product pages. As we saw in Chapter 12, social proof goes a long way when it comes to making the argument for why and how customers should behave—so these suggestions and anchors help to make the argument for why the customers should pick up an extra product while they're shopping.

Similarly, offering add-ons is a powerful way to increase average purchase value. Think about the way travel websites like Orbitz offer travel insurance *and* tell you how many other similar travelers have benefited from their policies recently. Brands can not only use data to help make the argument in terms of social proof, they can also use data to understand the most effective price points and timings to make these offers; in other words, actively experimenting against different customer profiles can help to make these incremental gains for brands.

Aligning to Customer Motivations

Throughout this book, we've seen the ways in which using personalization and tailored messaging can help to move the needle with customers—so it is with increasing average purchase value; making sure that the right offer with the most relevant products or services is displayed to your customer at the right time is our opportunity. When it comes to upsells or selling a more expensive product or service to the customer, it's particularly important to understand your customer motivations and align to their needs. By leveraging your customer profiles and owned or third-party motivation or behavioral data, you can identify what might make customers make a more expensive purchase: Is it social norms? Is it a desire to project status? Is it a need for reassurance? Addressing your messaging to these needs and providing proof (via more data) of the benefits of making a higher-value purchase can make the message more persuasive.

Furthermore, identifying customers who are just at the tipping point can make the messages more relevant. Using data to identify customers who spend above a particular threshold, but who aren't yet the most valuable customers, can give the brand an opportunity to turn loyal customers into brand fanatics. Think about the messages or offers you can put in front of those borderline customers to make them truly feel appreciated and like they're getting an offer they can't refuse. In the previous chapter, I shared the example of an anniversary campaign offering 50 percent off orders to our oldest accounts—that was a memorable campaign that won my employer lots of brand fans. What could you do that would have a similar effect?

Increasing Average Purchase Frequency

There are several ways to increase average purchase frequency, including memberships, subscriptions, and reengagement campaigns. Think about membership clubs like Costco or Sam's Club; the mere act of belonging to a club like this increases your likelihood to shop at the stores on a regular basis, because you've paid a fee to belong. Similarly, online brands like Amazon Prime and Public Goods get their members to treat them as a default source for their regular shopping by creating a paid membership that ostensibly pays for itself by giving members discounts and/or special perks, but in fact increases the lifetime value of the customer by increasing average purchase frequency. Data can be particularly helpful here for brands in identifying what are the perks that members use most and what are the ones that they rarely use, creating opportunities to improve the programs for both the customers and for the brands.

Leveraging Defaults Through Subscriptions

When it comes to subscriptions, you may think of brands like Netflix or even the Patreon accounts that support independent artists. The brands get recurring revenue while the customers get consistent access to content that they enjoy. But let's think outside the box: Brands like Who Gives a Crap toilet paper, Cora period products, or Dollar Shave Club shaving products offer essentials that people literally need on a consistent basis with a simple subscription model. But other brands that offer staples are also keeping customers coming back on a regular basis, even without a literal subscription; think of Misfits Markets—a grocery delivery company that reminds customers to get their grocery orders in each week and saves their credit card information and product preferences to speed up the purchase process.

These brands leverage the power of defaults as a valuable tool to keep their customers. But it's important for these brands not to rest on their laurels; it's easy to focus on delivering as frequently as possible, but it's also easy for customers who skip one or two deliveries to instead cancel their service until they catch up with their backstock. Instead, these brands should leverage their data to fine-tune their delivery service automatically, offering their customers the rightsized cadence for their lifestyles, rather than treating all customers as one and the same or putting the burden on customers to adjust their delivery schedules.

Reengaging Customers

Data is also extremely important when it comes to reengagement or "win-back" campaigns. When customers haven't bought in a while, it's important for brands to find ways to reconnect with them meaningfully. Figuring out which customers are ripe for reengagement is key since brands shouldn't try to reengage with customers who may have left due to unhappiness or dissatisfaction. Instead, brands should leverage their data to identify customers whose shopping behaviors have simply petered out. Social media and display advertising can be a powerful tool for retargeting these lapsed customers, but offering them messages that particularly acknowledge their preferences, interests, and past relationship with the brand—in other words, messages that make them feel recognized and known—can allow brands to successfully resonate with these customers. All of these are areas where data and good segmentation are particularly valuable to a brand. The more refined your targeting and the more relevant your messaging, the more impactful your efforts will be.

Extending Customer Lifespan

At every stage of the customer journey, there is room to improve by extending customer lifespan. For instance, at the beginning of the customer journey, it may take your customers a while to make a purchase; how can you speed up the purchase journey so they make their decisions more quickly? (Be sure to refer back to Chapter 7, where we discuss the customer journey.) First, identify places where there are barriers to customers getting the necessary information for them to move forward. What can your business do to address these barriers? Second, identify places where incentives may move the needle. Think about abandoned cart emails or exit intent pop-ups (those messages that pop up when you're on a website and your mouse moves off of the browser window, offering you a discount or special gift for finishing your purchase); they may be blunt instruments, but they're good examples of methods to improve the purchase behavior.

Enhancing the Brand's Perceived Value to Customers

When it comes to services and more complicated products, enthusiasm can be high when customers first make the decision to buy, but as time goes on and the complications of onboarding arise, enthusiasm may wane, and frustration or inertia sets in. Using data to identify the customers who haven't yet completed certain key steps to onboarding or setup is just one example of ways that brands can avoid attrition. By intervening when customers exhibit certain behaviors that indicate that they need a stronger hand, brands can improve customer experience. Similarly, identifying customers who underutilize certain key features and need additional training or education is another opportunity.

To increase the perceived value to the customer, brands must anticipate their frustrations and make it really clear that they care about the customer getting the most value out of the product or service. That may be as simple as having progress bars within their accounts to showcase how their accounts are set up or what they should do next. Similarly, increasing perceived value can take the form of gamification, showing how they compare to others like themselves. Consider fitness apps like MyFitnessPal that track and celebrate the progress that customers have made using their tools. Even if the progress had little to do with the tool itself, the perception that the app was a part of that progress makes it more likely that a customer will continue to engage with the tool.

Avoiding Churn

At some point or other, we've all experienced the annoyances of cancelling a subscription. The internet is littered with anecdotes about complicated breakups with brands. As much as brands want to avoid churn (or the loss of existing customers), making it hard to leave is definitely the wrong answer. Instead, companies need to, again, look at the customer journey. What are the behaviors that indicate that someone is unhappy and considering leaving? For instance, are they visiting pages to change their subscription level or cancel their membership? Are they looking at pages to return products or pages to complain about products? Are they leaving reviews on third-party sites or making comments on social media that indicate unhappiness? Before it gets to the point of your customers leaving, ask yourself: Are we using our data to understand the behaviors that indicate that someone is considering leaving? Just like we've all been in relationships in which, in hindsight, it was obvious that the other party was about to break up with us—the signs were all there—most companies have been in a position of denying the obvious. Instead, make sure that your brand is leveraging data to home into the warning signs and deploy interventions sooner rather than later.

WHO OWNS CHURN IN YOUR ORGANIZATION?

Back in Chapter 16, we took a look at lead generation company Netline, which allows B2B companies in a wide variety of industries to reach prospective customers. Chief Strategy Officer David Fortino also shared another interesting use case with me: Identifying potential churn (2023). Since the platform allows users to look at the content that's being consumed by their existing leads in the system, Fortino shared, "If you see one of your existing clients is consuming a lot of content around what you've already sold them, that should be a point of concern and alarm." Knowing your customers are shopping around should be an opportunity for you to step up your game, as we've seen in this chapter. After all, as Fortino said, extending customer lifespan is "more about customer sustenance" than anything else.

However, a challenge that many marketers might face is that churn is a muddy middle ground between sales, marketing, and account management. Or, as Fortino stated, "No one really owns churn identification, which is real concerning and something that, especially in this market, has been probably the largest point of risk for most organizations." So, with that in mind, be sure that as you're thinking about how to increase customer lifetime value, you look at how your organization analyses and handles churn.

Strengthening the Referral Engine

The final way to increase customer lifespan is by thinking about customers' value past their actual consumption. In Chapter 17 we explored the various ways that brands should identify and cultivate community-builders to increase word of mouth and generate more referrals. Here, brands should particularly think about how they can be detailed and effective in leveraging data to understand the best referral sources and power better sharing. Not only should you be using unique, tracked links for every individual customer, but you should make it infinitely easy for customers to share both product and content recommendations. In today's age, that means leveraging AI tools that can help scale their ability to share tailored messages to their audiences, particularly if you're sharing content in a B2B space where referrals are the lifeblood of customer decision-making.

Valuing Customers Long-Term

It should be obvious that long-term customers are essential to brands, and yet so much of marketing is aimed at the top of the funnel instead of at the bottom of the funnel. Understanding how to keep, nurture, and grow our relationships with our customers is essential to a robust marketing strategy. As my friend and "godmother" of customer experience Jeanne Bliss says in her many keynote speeches and four books, brands have to value their customers as assets, not cost centers.

RESOURCES RELATED TO THIS CHAPTER

Would You Do That To Your Mother? by Jeanne Bliss—In this book, Bliss explores how companies can build their relationships with their customers on a human level, by treating them the way you would want your mother to be treated by a brand. It goes beyond the numbers and the data and explores the ways that brands can and should leverage customer experience to improve customer lifetime value.

CHAPTER 19 SUMMARY

We explored the various elements of customer lifetime value—average purchase value, average purchase frequency, and customer lifetime—to better understand how brands can and should use data to identify the customers who are best candidates for intervention or engagement at each stage of the customer journey, investigate the ways to and places where the brand should intervene, and consider the most effective ways to sway them.

Actions

- Review customer data to make impactful recommendations for cross-sells and upsells.
- Identify opportunities to leverage memberships, subscriptions, and/or reengagement campaigns to increase customers' purchase frequency.
- Improve customer onboarding and identify ways to improve customer experience perception.
- Review your organization's approach to churn and communications with accounts that may be in danger of attrition.
- Determine the right approach to managing referrals and empowering your customers to spread the word.

20

Assembling Your Deep Customer Profile

Over the last few parts of this book, we've explored the ways in which brands can and should build their understanding of their customers. By collecting the data that helps profile, analyze, and customize their messaging and content to their customers, brands can gain a competitive edge over competitors who know less about their customers and therefore don't offer as personalized or relevant content and messaging. But it's not as simple as collecting individual attributes about a customer. To be truly effective, we need to make sure that we're collecting data about the customer that speaks to their emotional states (as we saw in Part Three), taps into the communities that influence them (Part Four), and helps us to build a deeper relationship with them than the competition does (Part Five). Furthermore, we need to map this information against the customer journey and in conjunction with the potential customer lifetime value of the customers.

Reflecting on the Key Components of Your Customer Profile

As we've seen throughout the book, there are many different ways to collect data. Understanding when and how to use first-party (brand-owned), second-party (trusted partner), and third-party (external source) data to ameliorate your customer profiles is essential to building robust customer profiles. At the same time, it also allows you to make sure you're building rich data about your customers without overstepping your bounds.

Demographic Data

While most demographic information about your customers will be first-party data that they provide when they engage with you, as we've seen with second-party platforms like Netline (Chapters 16 and 19), which allow you to tap into existing profile data, trusted partners can be powerful resources for shortening the process of collecting this data, and they can also help you ensure higher-quality (cleaner) data as the information has been confirmed through third-party data hygiene and match-back tools. In fact, that's the key to successfully leveraging these data fields: Good hygiene, consistency of data entry, and regular maintenance. Making sure that your organization checks in with customers consistently about changes in demographic data and leverages tools to streamline and safeguard against errors (such as mistyped email addresses or phone numbers) ensures that your records remain valuable.

Geographic Data

Geographic data can give us input on language, cultural considerations, specific legal and regulatory needs (for B2B businesses), and more. As brands increasingly leverage IP detection to capture this first-party data, it's also useful to implement ways for your audience to confirm their locations and language preferences. This can be as simple as presenting options during their online experiences or account setups, or giving options to confirm preferences during their onboarding processes.

Behavioral Data

In research I conducted with Convince & Convert and ICUC, we found than less than half (44 percent) of marketers collect behavioral data (2023), even though current behavior is one of the strongest predictors of future behavior. Behavioral data isn't just about purchase history or purchase behaviors, but also about the consumption of content and engagement with marketing campaigns before, during, and after purchase. Making sure that your organization is tracking your customers' behavior, not only on your site but also elsewhere (as we saw in Chapter 19), can help you to anticipate their needs, and even understand when there's a risk of customer churn. Running marketing campaigns—including those with trusted partners—to engage your customers before, during, and after purchase to help them get more out of your products, your brand communities, and your learning resources helps to increase customer lifetime value and also reduce churn. Furthermore, using advertising platforms that tag behavioral attributes allows you to test and continue to append your behavioral data. Here are just a few of the many examples of attributes you may find within digital advertising platforms including social media, search engines, and display advertising platforms:

- purchase behaviors
- travel behaviors
- affinities
- sports engagement behaviors
- device usage
- gaming behaviors

Since behaviors are observed patterns, rather than individual characteristics, this kind of information is better identified and tagged by your team as attributes, rather than existing as individual data fields.

Psychographic Data

In our research, we also found that fewer than one in three marketers are currently collecting psychographic data about customers (Convince & Convert/ICUC, 2023). It can seem like a difficult thing to capture and analyze, due to the perceived complexity of psychographic or attitudinal considerations, but there are three ways we can do so. First, as with behavioral data, marketers can observe and identify patterns of behaviors that fit with specific psychographic profiles and supplement customer profiles with this segmentation. Second, as we saw in Part One of this book, there are also opportunities to build psychographic segments based on attitudinal surveys. With that in mind, allowing customers to self-identify based on their priorities gives brands the ability to confirm with customers their psychographic archetypes. Building deliberate checkpoints to allow customers to choose the archetype that best describes them is a valuable tool that lets companies get more specific and personal with customers. That may include presenting options when they visit your website to select what's most important to them, when they create a profile to make their purchase, or during the onboarding process as a series of email automations. Finally, we continue to see more third-party tools that allow companies to leverage their existing databases on customers' profiles to serve up messaging based on their psychographics (such as with Persado's Motivation AI product). This means that even if you don't have your own psychographic data available, you can take advantage of this kind of information to shape and inform your personalization.

Customer Relationship Data

Brand-owned data on customer inquiries, interactions, service requests, and feedback (including customer satisfaction, loyalty and referral, and sentiment) is one of the most powerful elements of data that companies can leverage to drive more contextual and personal marketing interactions. Yet, we found that while the majority of marketers (67 percent) indicated that they collected customer relationship data, that still means that one-third of marketers don't (Convince & Convert/ICUC, 2023). How can we improve this situation? Making sure that this first-party data is shared across your organization—from your customer experience, customer service, sales, and/or account management teams to marketing and vice versa—is critical for being able to offer more data-driven personalization. The issue that most organizations face is that they currently don't make this data available in a structured and usable manner for the purposes of marketing.

Channel Preference Data

Whether you're using first-party profile, behavioral, and survey data, or using third-party data via advertising partners, channel preference data can help you to serve more meaningful messages based on the context of where and how your customers engage. Allow your customers to set their preferences within their profiles, append their records based on the channels in which they engage the most (e.g., email, SMS, phone, chat), and integrate findings from surveys and other platforms into their records. As with demographic data, making sure that you proactively update customers' channel preferences on a regular basis (e.g., every year or two years) will ensure that you are continuing to engage with them in the most appropriate channels.

Technographic Data

For brands in B2B spaces, as well as industries like gaming and software, or brands that offer apps, making sure that technographic data is captured accurately and updated on a regular basis allows for accurate targeting and messaging. Self-reported (first-party) data will be most useful and can come from customer onboarding, customer preferences, and/or progressive profiling through email automations. But it can and should also be captured at other touchpoints, such as customer service. Advertising campaigns that take advantage of this kind of data on third-party platforms can also be used to append customer profiles—just make sure that you're tracking click-throughs from advertising targeted at each type of technology (e.g., operating systems).

Social Media Data

Depending on your industry and needs, how much social media data you need to collect about your customers will vary. But using a combination of collection within customer profiles, running campaigns with trusted partners, and leveraging third-party platforms can allow you to build a robust picture of the places where your customers engage with your brand and others on social media. While capturing information about individual social media accounts is particularly valuable for brands that intend on building referral programs, affiliate networks, or customer communities, for most brands, social media usage can be treated similarly to behavioral data: Observed patterns that are tagged as attributes, rather than as individual data fields.

Consent and Communications Preference Data

Of course, none of this matters if we don't have accurate and well-maintained consent data. In today's age, privacy policies and terms of service are often opaque or buried, but that doesn't bode well for trust or for customer experience. As we've seen with examples such as Lemonade Insurance, our case study in Chapter 10, making transparency in consent part of a brand's approach can pay dividends in terms of customer satisfaction and trust. Companies like Meta (owner of Facebook, Instagram, and WhatsApp) and Google have gone as far as making it easy for customers to update the attributes that are used to target them for advertising, so they can opt out of advertising that they don't want to see—such as in the Mother's Day examples we also discussed in Chapter 10. Making sure that consent is clearly and voluntarily given is crucial, as is making it easy for customers to update their preferences at their convenience.

EXERCISE
Determine Your Data Gaps

Review the data fields in your customer profiles: What data is rarely used? What data is missing that can and should inform your marketing approach? Based on the methods we've discussed here, identify what are your best opportunities for capturing that data using first-party, second-party, and third-party sources.

What are the barriers that you currently face collecting that data? What's the most important data to capture based on your gaps? In considering the responses to these two questions, create a priorities list of the data that you should capture along with what it will take for your team to implement these recommendations. Now you have a framework that you can use for planning and resourcing.

Putting It All Together

If you're wondering whether you absolutely need to have all of these elements within your customer profile, the answer is no. Certainly not at the start, and perhaps not ever. The data in your customer profiles should be as specific to your company as your products or services. But making sure that your database is structured to be able to capture the right data and that it is designed to ensure good data hygiene is the recipe for success. The more usable the data is, the more your team can append the customer profiles with additional attributes, and the more your team can query your database to learn about your audience, the better.

Collecting Data Throughout the Customer Journey

In addition to thinking about what data to collect, we also need to think about when we look to acquire it. In Chapter 7, as we discussed capturing data within the customer journey framework, I asked you to consider: What should you learn about customers at each stage that will help you to deliver on the company opportunity? Thinking about how we should consider customer data vis-à-vis time is important because customers aren't static and what they need or value will change throughout their lifecycles. Let's look at how brands can and should engage with customers to collect data at different customer journey stages.

Beginning of the Journey: Awareness and Problem Identification

Early in the customer journey, customers will be more reticent to share their data—collecting observational data, such as behavioral, geographic, and technographic (based on targeting through third-party tools) will be much simpler than asking for their information. Allowing them to demonstrate their needs via their selection of content or resources on your brand's website or through a second or third party will be most likely. In other words, pairing your data collection with a content marketing approach that delivers value to customers as they build awareness for brand category will be most successful. What kind of content marketing will serve them best at this stage? One focused on education, on norms (within their industry or interest area), and on the problems they may face.

Middle of the Journey: Consideration and Comparison

As customers become more interested in the brand category, they'll be increasingly willing to share more personal information that helps them to get the information that's tailored to them. Offering quizzes and other self-evaluation tools can be a powerful way for your company to build your customer profile data. Collecting data on referral sources (such as different search queries, paid campaigns, affiliates, etc.) also provides a great deal of information about how and why customers have engaged with your brand. By connecting the dots for customers—through nurture sequences via email, messenger, SMS, or even chatbot—gives them more information that's personalized to their needs, while also allowing your brand to better understand them.

Purchase and Onboarding

It can seem like purchase and onboarding are the perfect opportunities to round out your customer profiles, but beware of asking too much of customers during this critical period. Instead, mete out your asks for information over time. For instance, brands may offer a single question each time customers log in, which allows them to collect additional information about customers without overwhelming the customers with too many inquiries at once. In other words, during onboarding, make sure that critical information about the customer (contact information, consent and communications preferences, as well as other data pertinent to their product/service experience) are addressed. The goal is to identify the information that will be most useful to delivering them a high-quality purchase or onboarding experience.

Post-Purchase: Loyalty and Referral

During the post-purchase period, continuing to build your knowledge of your customers is vital to increasing lifetime value, as we discussed in the prior chapter. Making sure to not only collect behavioral data, but also continue to engage with your customers through content marketing (focused on helping them get the most out of their experience with the brand), allows you to continue to identify the traits that you can leverage to improve your marketing. Furthermore, at this post-purchase stage, collecting survey, customer satisfaction, and customer relationship data comes into play in augmenting your customer profiles.

Anticipating Change: Taking a Balanced Approach

Here's the thing: Building this deep knowledge of your customer to offer better personalization than the competition isn't a short-term approach. It's a long-term investment and a strategic approach to marketing that pays dividends through higher relevance, increased conversion, and improved customer lifetime value. It will take a methodical, organized, and concerted approach to collect data, use it to personalize and test marketing messages, and improve results.

When will you have built the ideal database? The truth is that this is a job that will never be finished. Like any good relationship, the one between your brand and your customers will require you to continue to learn from each other. You may find that your customers continue to surprise you as they evolve along with the world around them. And that's why refreshing the data is so important. We should not assume that our customers will stay the same; in fact, we should anticipate that their needs will change, their priorities will change, and their preferences will change. That's why we must build in checkpoints into our marketing approach that allow them to continue to review and modify the data we have within their profiles. With this understanding of how we build deep—and dynamic—customer profiles, we can move into the final part of this book, in which we'll talk about how we can build teams that are empowered to leverage this data to power your personalization efforts and drive business results.

RESOURCES RELATED TO THIS CHAPTER

Transforming Customer Data into Insights by George Mount, Lynne Capozzi, and Karen Wood—While I don't go into depth about customer data platforms (CDPs) in this book, they're an extremely useful tool for managing the kind of profiles we discuss. For a primer on this technology and how it can be deployed within your organization, check out this short book by George Mount and colleagues, available from O'Reilly.

CHAPTER 20 SUMMARY

Summarizing the frameworks in Parts One through Five, we reviewed the key types of data that we should be capturing in our customer profiles and how they could be captured via first-, second-, and third-party sources. We also examined how time (in the form of the customer journey) should be factored into our decision-making when prioritizing what data to capture when.

Actions

- Inspect current customer profile data fields to identify gaps.
- Prioritize key types of data to collect, based on impact and resource constraints.
- Review how data can and should be captured throughout the customer journey.
- Consider how your organization can implement mechanisms for updating customer profile data on a regular basis through customer login questions, surveys, email automations, etc.

PART SIX

Empowering Your Data-Driven Personalization Team

21

Fostering a Culture of Curiosity

Too often, when we talk about data-driven marketing and personalization, we focus on the technical aspects: The tools, the technology, the processes. But building a data-driven marketing practice that offers highly personalized messages to your customers isn't just about the data infrastructure that you set up. It's also about how you cultivate a team that can make the most of that data and turn it into actionable insights.

Ultimately, data alone doesn't drive business results. It's the analysis, the insights, and the strategy that come from the data that will give your organization a competitive advantage. In Part Six of this book we focus on how business and marketing leaders can build teams that can make the most of data. After all, as technologies to collect the data and even interpret the data are improved through AI and machine learning, the work of measuring *should* get easier, more accessible, and less expensive. But the work of being curious, asking perceptive questions, and developing shrewd experiments requires an astute understanding of the customers and a strategic approach to marketing. In other words, the technology will continue to evolve, but the strategic work remains. So, how should you arm your team with the skills they need?

In my work consulting with major brands in industries from travel and hospitality to tech to finance, I've worked with many marketing teams that are well resourced. Many have access to a wide variety of enterprise software, data warehouses in place, and even have analytics teams. And yet, so often, when I ask even basic questions about their target audiences and best customers, I get the response, "That's a good question. We've never looked into it." The team just weren't motivated to think deeply about their customers, and therefore they didn't ask questions that would help them get more strategic.

To get the most out of your data, you must strive to foster a culture of curiosity. No matter the industry, every marketing manager and business leader can and should create the kind of learning environment where everyone is empowered to act as an analyst and everyone is incentivized to ask good questions. All too often, what happens is that marketers and other business leaders are solely focused on the metrics to which they're held accountable. But, as we've seen throughout this book, insights about our customers often come from places that aren't necessarily producing direct marketing or sales results—instead, they come from places that impact customer experience and the customer journey. How do you get beyond this issue? How do you incentivize your team to strive for curiosity, not just to achieve specific metrics? Let's take a look at three key components.

Creating a Learning Environment

First, it's important to build a team that's empowered to learn. Rather than focusing solely on what your team members bring to the table in terms of skills and experience, put emphasis on the entire team, building new skills on an ongoing basis. Not only does this empower people to master new skills (since, as we've seen in earlier chapters, "mastery" is a key motivator), but it also creates a norm in which everyone is striving to learn at all times. After all, data isn't about just recording and measuring what's been achieved, it's about identifying new things to learn and understand.

Creating a learning environment is also about putting emphasis on the customer and their lives. To center the work on your customer, you must make sure that your team not only has access to deep customer research that we talked about in Part One of this book, but is also steeped in that knowledge. This may look like a "customer bootcamp" or training for new hires. Or it may take the form of a "customer room" with physical or interactive representations of your customer journey maps, as we discussed in Chapter 7. It may also look like a program to consistently refresh your customer archetypes with annual or biannual surveys, focus groups, anthropological studies, etc., with corresponding trainings or presentations across your organization.

Developing an environment focused on learning also requires managers to hire for a curious mindset. Managers must seek to hire people whose track record demonstrates that they're not only going after the tasks that they're assigned, but that they're also identifying key questions or problems to solve and then proactively and independently finding ways to get the information needed to address them. How can you identify people with the potential to think strategically about your customers? Let's take a look.

HIRING FOR CURIOSITY: INTERVIEW QUESTIONS

When it comes to hiring for a strategic mindset, looking for people who are interested in finding the insights within the data—who are curious about the deep questions—is vital to building a team that has the skills to succeed long-term. After all, machine learning is making it easier to parse the data and connect the dots. But understanding what questions to ask, what experiments to run, and which dots are worth exploring further—those exercises identify the insights that will provide your brand with a competitive advantage. Here are a few questions you can ask in interviews to better understand your candidates' potential for strategic, curious thinking:

- Tell me about a time you've challenged the status quo in your work. How did you go about understanding the situation and making the case?

- What's an example of a time you've had to go above and beyond to gather insights or additional information to solve a business problem or achieve a business result?

- Tell me about an experiment you designed and ran. What were the actionable insights you learned from this experiment?

- What was an issue or challenge that your customers were facing, and how did you use data to solve or address the issue?

- Tell me about a time that you used data in an unexpected way.

- If you had access to all of our customer data, what are the three things you'd want to look at to improve what we're doing now?

- What's a question that you think we're probably not yet asking about our customers but should be?

Cultivating Questions, Not Just Answers

Second, to encourage curiosity, understand that it's important to cultivate thoughtful questions, not specifically the search for answers. In other words, often times, the act of asking questions and seeking to answer those questions can give you a great deal of insights, even if the answers are not straightforward or don't exist. For instance, I was recently working with one of my engineering firm clients and someone on their team asked about demographics and psychographics of a specific customer segment within one particular region. In looking at the available data, we found that we couldn't answer the question directly with what existed. However, the conversation around who these customers were, what content they consumed, and information they needed allowed us to find a different path forward. We were able to use social listening data based on the social media following of a region-specific publication that was highly relevant to this customer segment to approximate their psychographics and then compare the demographics to a third-party source to confirm the overall profile. The questions led to more questions, but that ultimately allowed us to get to the answers.

So how can you cultivate more questions? Here are a few methods:

- *Start by leading by example.* Marketing leaders should not only ask questions, but also encourage people to ask questions in planning meetings, discussions, and as part of regular exercises.

- *Use data to kick off your marketing meetings.* When my team at Convince & Convert works with clients on their processes for content planning, we often recommend that the insights about the previous campaigns or last planning period are reported out first. This sets the tone for the meeting and gives the team perspective as new content is planned.

- *Encourage questions, proposing hypotheses and defining experiments as part of the planning process.* Set the expectations that curiosity is part of the plan.

- *Promote knowledge-sharing.* Fostering an environment in which team members share both questions and answers with each other breeds a more transparent, creative, and insightful team.

- *Embrace failure.* Not every experiment will lead to gains, but even failed experiments provide information and learnings. Be sure to make failure a normal part of the experimentation process, so that your team is willing to take risks, rather than to simply play it safe.

When the Walls Are Up

What happens when teams are afraid of failure, and therefore afraid of questions? When I spoke to co-founder and Chief Data Scientist of Trust

Insights, Christopher Penn (whom we heard from in Chapter 7), he shared with me a story about one of his clients. With an extremely siloed organization, he said, "Marketing were not allowed to see any sales data whatsoever." This made it very difficult for them to calibrate their marketing campaigns, and his consultancy was brought in to help solve some of the issues. When he dug into the issues at hand, he found out that the sales team didn't want to share any of their data because they were very ineffective with a poor close rate. But this lack of transparency also hindered the organization's ability to improve its marketing efficacy. Penn shared this takeaway, "So it's people and it's processes. In a lot of cases, yeah, there are technological issues, but they are rarely the root cause of the problem" (2023).

Ultimately, it's better for an organization to incentivize its teams to share data and insights, even when they show failure, because at least the organization can then learn and improve. When these failures stay hidden, no one can improve and nothing ever changes.

Rewarding Curiosity

What else should leaders do to build a culture where everyone feels empowered to ask perceptive questions? Here are two opportunities: (a) acknowledge when good insights are gained through these questions; and (b) reward your team for the learnings. To do the first, be sure to give credit where credit is due and highlight success stories and learnings that were gained through the efforts of your individual team members. Reporting out key insights within your planning meetings? Identify the people whose questions or research drive the identification of those key insights.

To do the second, think about how you can create concrete rewards for their work; this isn't simply about providing a "carrot" (versus a "stick"; see Chapter 11), but rather about incentivizing through purpose and mastery. Much like tech companies offer "bug bounties" to incentivize white-hat hackers (ethical security hackers) to identify issues with their programs and report them for the purposes of shoring them up or fixing them, leaders within organizations can set challenges with rewards to encourage team members to identify questions, challenges, and opportunities that can be solved through the analysis of data. Encouraging this kind of stress-testing of your current efforts inspires your team to consistently look for ways to iterate, improve, and experiment.

Build Mechanisms for Curiosity

Third, a culture of curiosity isn't just about encouraging questions and a desire to know more. It must also be supported through processes and mechanisms that make it possible to find answers, do research, and take action. For instance, make transparency a key tenet of your metrics and analytics. Give access to shared dashboards, so that team members can easily understand what's being measured and how performance is changing over time. Create shared "question boards" (a shared physical or virtual board with key questions listed) to ground your team's planning cycle on a few key questions that the whole team is keeping in mind as it identifies learning opportunities, designs experiments, and looks for insights.

Provide the tools to ask good questions and get answers: Whether this is direct access to your data mart or creating a simple ticketing system for individuals to make requests of your data analysts, the right approach will depend on the size of your organization, your bandwidth, and your governance practices. But with the right training and culture, I believe that making it simple for your teams to ask questions and get answers will allow you to foster that curious spirit and more quickly improve your marketing practices. Moreover, as AI makes natural language queries against databases simpler and more affordable, more teams will be able to empower non-analysts to look at the available data and sift for opportunities. Again, I think of the example of Target and its pregnant customers that we discussed back in Chapter 6. AI tools make it simple for a team to do something like this: Identifying a segment of customers based on a specific characteristic and then using cluster analysis to understand what makes them alike and what shared traits or behaviors they have.

Finally, consistently use exercises focused on training your team's curiosity "muscles" in your quarterly planning sessions. Making this practice part of your regular thought processes will set expectations for your team and encourage everyone to open up to new insights and possibilities. Let's take a look at a few exercises that you can incorporate into your processes.

EXERCISE
Curiosity Thought-Starters

Each of these exercises is a simple way to get your team to dig a little deeper, open up to new possibilities, and explore questions with curiosity. With each exercise, be sure to set ground rules. Encourage all voices to participate. Don't let any one voice dominate, and—at least in the first round—have any leaders/ managers in the group speak last to give the opportunity to other team members to voice their opinions without groupthink.

In the first rounds, these exercises should come in with a focus on generating ideas, not necessarily winnowing those ideas down. Winnowing down ideas can be the focus of the final rounds of these exercises, but keep in mind that you may not necessarily come away from these exercises with immediate actions, so much as new questions to explore.

- *Curiosity mapping:* This is an exercise that helps to reinforce the culture of curiosity by highlighting what the entire team is curious about and identifies ways for your organization to support team members in their learning and discovery process. Start with the questions, "What are you curious about currently? What do you want to learn more about?" This could be around open questions about your customer, about your brand/products/services, or even about life in general. Have your team brainstorm responses on a whiteboard (virtual or physical). Then organize the responses into groups by categories and, together, brainstorm and identify resources to help them learn more. The resources they need may go beyond the data your team has available; it may be books, courses, training, and/or other resources.

- *The five whys:* This tactical exercise has your team to come to the table with a problem statement and asks "Why did this [problem] happen?" The team will brainstorm answers to this question for five minutes, then discuss the possible answers. The team will come to a consensus around the most likely reason and then ask the question "why" or "what caused this issue" about that statement. Repeat this process three more time (a total of five rounds) to get deeper into the issue and identify the areas that your team needs to go research further, build experiments around, or address.

- *"What if" scenarios:* Ready to stretch your team's creativity and get outside the box? Take a page from author, cartoonist, and engineer Randall Munroe, who wrote a popular blog and two books around "what if" questions. His book *What If? Serious scientific answers to absurd hypothetical questions* takes a deep, science-based approach to exploring the answers to wild hypothetical questions, like what would happen if everyone on Earth pointed a laser at the moon (2014). The idea here isn't necessarily to ask whacky questions, but to encourage your team to think about blue sky questions without limits and with serious discussion: What if we had an unlimited budget for advertising? What if our main competitor suddenly shut down? What if we suddenly had 100 percent name recognition among our key customers? Identify a "what if" scenario and work through the hypothetical next steps. Doing so can identify questions and opportunities that your team don't think about day-to-day because of the limitations that are placed upon them or restrictions that they face.

Throughout this book, we've talked about the ways that behavioral psychology and behavioral economics can be leveraged to drive actions and change minds. Even within our own teams, these principles hold true. By cultivating a team that is motivated to make the most of data and to serve the audience through personalization, we can future-proof our marketing practices. By focusing on questions, we can stay strategic and gain ground against our competitors. In the next chapter, we'll continue our exploration of how we can build teams that successfully leverage data and effectively reach your key customers. We'll also explore how you can find the rightsized approach for your budget and your industry.

RESOURCES RELATED TO THIS CHAPTER

The Workplace Curiosity Manifesto: How curiosity helps individuals and workspaces thrive in transformational times by Stefaan van Hooydonk—With a combination of real-world examples and case studies, van Hooydonk (founder of the Global Curiosity Institute) goes deep into how to not only build a workplace that encourages curiosity, but also why companies need to embrace curiosity and a startup mindset to survive and thrive in today's quickly changing world.

CHAPTER 21 SUMMARY

To build a data-driven marketing practice, you don't just need tools and processes; you need people who ask the kind of insightful questions that will drive effective marketing strategy. In this chapter, we explored how marketing managers and business leaders can foster a culture that leads to these purposeful questions and strategic thinking, including hiring practices, exercises, and planning mechanisms.

Actions

- Reflect on your current culture: Do you encourage curiosity in the way that your teams plan, analyze, and engage?
- Identify places where you can improve your planning process to include more question generation.
- Review the resources needed to help your team learn more, including shared analytics dashboards, question boards, planning sessions, and budget for education.
- Consistently incorporate exercises that help spark your team to think outside the box and integrate curious thinking into your regular planning processes.

22

Equipping Your Data-Driven Personalization Team for Success

Throughout this book, we've taken a look at how organizations, big and small, can benefit from learning about their customers through the capture and collection of data *and* from using that information to increase the relevance of their offerings, messages, and experience for their customers. But achieving a strategic approach to data-driven personalization is as much about your team as about your data infrastructure, governance, and marketing strategy. In the previous chapter we talked about the importance of fostering a culture where everyone is invested in leveraging your data to gain insights and learn more about your customers and opportunities. In this chapter we'll explore what it takes to embed data-driven personalization into your marketing strategy.

Build Consensus and Support

First things first. To build a data-driven personalization practice as part of a customer-centric marketing strategy and customer experience, you can't go at it alone. Because marketing teams almost never own all of the operational components of data infrastructure and governance or technology implementation, you absolutely need to get executive buy-in to bring these initiatives to life. Demonstrating to your leadership team how you will build competitive advantage through personalization is key. You can use the frameworks in Chapter 19 to help you make a concrete business case for implementing personalization as a centerpiece of your marketing strategy. But beyond getting the necessary support for the initiatives, understand that it's vital to establish a cross-disciplinary team to make these initiatives a success. Data-driven personalization touches much more than marketing; it impacts sales, customer retention, customer service, operations, and technology.

Furthermore, throughout the book, we've explored the ways in which personalization is really just one facet of a customer-centric approach to business. If your organization is not already taking an active look at its customer experience, use your personalization initiatives as a springboard. Customer experience brings the same players together as the above but broadens the scope and remit of those teams to truly thinking about what is delivered to customers, not just what messages are presented to customers.

Ground Your Work in the Strategy

This may seem obvious, but making sure that your marketing strategy—and how data and personalization fit into it—are clearly documented for both your team and your broader organization is vital. It allows you to ensure that this work is consistent, omnichannel, and well-integrated into the customer experience. It may seem obvious, but many marketers don't have documented marketing strategies. For instance, year after year, my friends at the Content Marketing Institute and MarketingProfs (both organizations I've done work with) ask B2B and B2C marketers about their content marketing strategies in particular. In their 13th annual survey, only 40 percent of B2B marketers and 37 percent of B2C marketers said that their content marketing strategies were documented (Content Marketing Institute/MarketingProfs, 2022). This lack of specificity and clarity can lead to teams being disorganized or making assumptions about the purpose, approach, and measurement of the marketing strategy.

To avoid this kind of confusion and make sure that institutional knowledge is captured and shareable as the makeup of your team changes, be sure to document the frameworks and processes that your organization has put in place. Particularly, document clear objectives around both the collection and usage of data, as well as the practice of personalization. This will help you to set parameters or guardrails that make sure that your tactics are purposeful and measurable. Furthermore, document how your organization will measure, test, and learn from these operational practices. Finally, make sure that systems for feedback and learning—not only in testing, but also in the training and support of your team—are part of your written strategy and planning. In other words, to successfully implement data-driven personalization as a core tenet of your marketing strategy, create a playbook that makes it easy for anyone (or at least clear to anyone) in your organization how it fits into the practice of that marketing strategy in serving your business goals, your customer needs, and your market positioning.

Assembling Your Team

Because every marketing team can and should have data and personalization integrated into its practices, how that team should be staffed shouldn't be a surprise. If you have an unlimited budget, the ideal marketing team would include:

- *strategists* to align your tactics to your business objectives and customer needs
- *content creators* like writers and editors, video and multimedia producers, and graphic designers
- *data scientists and analysts* to make sense of both the data collected and the performance of your marketing efforts
- *cultural anthropologists* to gain deep insights into your audiences
- *channel specialists* to optimize and run specific channels, as well as key areas such as paid advertising or even SEO/website content

But, as we discussed in the previous chapter, the goal should be to make sure that everyone within your marketing team is steeped in a culture that encourages all members of the team to be curious, to ask questions, and to encourage each other to dig for the insights that will improve the performance of the team and the organization as a whole.

Furthermore, I recognize that most organizations—even most of the major multinationals that I've worked with over the years—have constraints when it comes to hiring. If you cannot hire strategists, data scientists and analysts, and cultural anthropologists on your team, make sure that you are hiring for people who think strategically, who are curious and willing to dig into the data, and who understand the importance of pursuing a deep understanding of your customers. In today's world, hiring people who are well-versed in the usage of AI and machine learning—who are comfortable developing precise prompts, leveraging tools, and learning new technologies—is particularly valuable, as more of the sifting through the data can be done by machines. The value won't be in building the queries, but in asking the right questions that get at the insights.

Finally, keep in mind that the ideal marketing team isn't always built; it may be trained over time. Ask yourself: How can you deliberately hire people who have the potential to learn the skills to think strategically about your data-driven marketing practice? Ask your organization: How can we put our money where our mouths are and support our team through the resources for continuing education and training?

Developing an Ethical Practice of Data

As data storage and processing continues to get less expensive for organizations, the drive to collect more and more data continues. But, as we discussed in Chapter 10, it's no surprise that the public and governments continue to grow more wary of the overreach of organizations in collecting data. More restrictions on how organizations collect and store data is likely to come as we continue to navigate the ambivalence between a desire for convenience and a desire for privacy. While I encourage you throughout this book to make the most of your data, this doesn't mean that you should collect data indiscriminately and without thought towards what's needed, what's useful, and what could potentially be harmful to your customers.

Brands must take a responsible approach to data, one that includes having clear governance around the collection, access, usage, and storage of data. Furthermore, brands must foster a culture of ethical usage of data through training and guidelines. Data privacy and data ethics go well beyond the marketing team within an organization. Your organization must consider data privacy compliance and regulations, data retention, data transparency, and data security.

But as your marketers exercise their curiosity and think through how they can take an impactful approach to personalization that helps your brand stand apart from the competition, it's important to make sure that your marketing team has guidelines and guardrails in place to keep your marketing approach valuable and beneficial. Your marketers should seek out information that helps our customers to get more out of their relationship with our brands *without* revealing sensitive information to others or causing harm. In my conversation with Robbie Fitzwater (2023), the founder of digital marketing agency MKTG Rhythm, whom we heard from in Chapter 8, he shared a simple framework for how he thinks about the most important data to collect for the purposes of personalization and learning, "We don't want to just collect data for the sake of collecting data. I always think about: What's a primary segmentation variable we can focus on? What is going to be the biggest 'unlock' for us that is going to help us define who our customers are and how we serve them uniquely and differently?" To Fitzwater's last point, I would add "how we serve them ethically" to the considerations.

What If You Don't Have All the Resources?

I hope, by this point in the book, you've seen that my approach is all about balancing technology and a strategic understanding of customers. For those with small teams—or even who are teams of one—there is still so much you can do to take a data-driven approach to personalization and marketing. It's all about finding a balance between investing in developing a marketing strategy that puts the most resonant messages in front of the right customers and the technologies that can help you execute on that strategy *and* learn from the results. We live in an age where even Mailchimp, an email service provider aimed at small businesses, allows you to suggest products to individual customers based on their past shopping behaviors. But chasing after individualized messaging isn't effective if you cannot extract the learnings to help make better strategic decisions in the future.

I spoke to Shafqat Islam, Chief Marketing Officer of Optimizely, a software-as-a-service platform that allows companies to conduct A/B testing and multivariate testing on their web content. As a leader in testing and experimentation, Optimizely offers machine-learning-driven recommendations that are specific to the individual customer. And yet, Islam told me, "It's a very easy trap to try and personalize too much, down to smaller and smaller cohorts, at which point you're running so many personalization experiments you kind of lose track—you can't see the forest for the trees—of what's working and what's not." Ultimately, he said that the key is to find the "Goldilocks zone" where the experiments are giving you insights that are actionable because they're scalable (2023). In other words, don't run all the experiments and don't try to personalize every message everywhere. Instead, focus on the persuasive messages that matter the most.

Way back in Chapter 5, we explored the reasons why personalization is so powerful: All customers use mental shortcuts to make decisions—and making your messages align with their needs makes it more likely that they'll say yes. Identifying what are the key places to intervene in their customer journeys (Chapter 7) with which forms of persuasion is the best way to focus your time and resources. Again, you don't need every aspect of your customers' experiences to be specific to them. After all, many of your customers will share experiences. And, as we've seen in Chapter 13, social proof is influential because there is power in the experiences of others. Instead, focus your resources on the places to step in where a tailored message will have an outsized effect on making them pay attention, feel understood, or buy in.

Start and End With People

Ultimately, this book is about people: Your customers, your organization, and your team. To equip your team for success, you need to make sure that your marketing strategy starts and ends with people. Data and personalization are mechanisms to understand your customers better and to provide them more value. Your team must put them at the heart of your strategic approach, your measurement and experiments, and, ultimately, the way you turn your learnings into insights to improve their experiences.

RESOURCES RELATED TO THIS CHAPTER

Marketing Strategy: Overcome common pitfalls and create effective marketing by Jenna Tiffany—This hands-on book not only presents frameworks to develop your marketing strategy, but also includes practical exercises to help you document your marketing strategy effectively.

Marketing with Strategic Empathy: Inspiring strategy with deeper consumer insight by Claire Brooks—Need another resource to help you ground your strategy in the people it serves? This thoughtful book is a practical resource that brings these principles to life.

Agile Marketing: Unlock adaptive and data-driven marketing for long-term success by Neil Perkin—Perkin brings the principles of Agile from technology into the world of marketing, with practical examples from well-known organizations.

CHAPTER 22 SUMMARY

Integrating a data-driven approach to personalization into your marketing practice isn't just about the technology, it's also about building consensus, documenting and socializing your strategy, assembling your team, and cultivating an ethical approach to data. In this chapter, we looked at the ways you can set your team up for success by establishing a strong scaffolding that goes well beyond marketing alone.

Actions

- Review how you can gain buy-in from your leadership team for the practice of data-driven personalization through a compelling business case.

- Evaluate your current marketing strategy and document or update it to reflect how data-driven personalization integrates into the approach—if you can't do it all, prioritize based on the needs of your audience and the impact for your business.

- Consider the makeup of your current marketing team and identify gaps and opportunities for future hires and/or training.

- Examine your current guidelines and governance around data—what can be improved to make sure that your organization stays ahead of the curve, when it comes to data compliance, privacy, and ethics?

23

Assembling Your Tech Stack

While much of this book is about the strategic frameworks and executional considerations of data-driven personalization, we've seen throughout that technology and the toolstack play significant roles in making this approach successful. That's because to collect the right data and organize it in a usable, accessible, and transparent fashion, you need the right tools for your organization. Not every organization has the same needs or the same budget, so the point of this chapter isn't to prescribe tools to you and your team. Rather, the goal is to make sure that you have a firm understanding of which types of tools are needed to achieve a highly personalized approach to digital marketing and how you evaluate the tools effectively.

What Technologies Do You Need?

While every organization will be different and every industry will have unique considerations, there are a few broad categories that your organization will need technologies to address. For small/medium companies, you may want to select technologies or platforms that can play multiple roles. For larger organizations, you may find that you have custom-built technologies already in place that serve some of these roles. Again, understand that these are broad guidelines—how you put them into practice will depend on your organization's parameters, as well as the evaluation process we just went through:

- *Infrastructure:* At the end of the day, if you're going to have usable data, you need somewhere to put it. Larger organizations will want to implement data warehouses or data lakes, in conjunction with data marts (see Chapter 6 for a primer on these terms) so that they can see data across teams in a unified place. But just about every organization should have same kind of customer data platform (CDP) that collects and unifies the organization's first-party customer data with the other data collected. A CDP should be the repository of all of the different types of data we talk about throughout Parts One and Two of this book.

- **Delivery:** Once you have the data, you need to be able to use it to deliver marketing messages and content to the customers in meaningful ways. The tools that help you deliver marketing messages include your website platform and personalization software, email service providers (ESPs), text/SMS tools, customer-facing apps, and even your POS systems. As you're evaluating your delivery tools, you must make sure that they integrate as tightly to your CDP as possible, so that you're capturing your marketing data within your customer profiles. At the very minimum, every organization needs an ESP that has strong integration with your CDP and your website, so that you can use transactional and content consumption data (parts of your behavioral data set) to personalize your emails.

- **Testing/experimentation:** As we've seen throughout the book, testing and experimentation is a cornerstone of a data-driven approach. We need to learn through doing. And to facilitate this approach, we need to have tools and technology that allow us to conduct useful experiments. Experimentation tools should allow your organization to conduct A/B testing (testing two versions of an experience with one single variable) as well as multivariate testing (testing multiple variables at the same time) in your most important mediums.

- **Insights/business intelligence:** While many of the tools above will give you analytics, it takes an insights or business intelligence tool to bring these analytics into one cohesive view and make them usable for your team to learn. Too often, teams rely on a variety of different platforms and report out metrics *without* gleaning the insights. Throughout this book we've talked about the ways in which you must connect the dots if you are to gain a competitive advantage through data. To empower your team to take this approach, an insights platform is key—preferably one that leverages AI to make it more accessible for your team to query the data to find the valuable insights.

CASE STUDY
How Optimizely Simplifies the Integration Process

When it comes to your toolstack, more isn't always more. In fact, more tools usually come with more complexity. And when it comes to structuring a successful tech stack, you need to make sure that all the tools "talk" to each other, share data well, and empower your team and organization to have visibility into the results of the experiments they facilitate. I talked to Shafqat Islam, the Chief Marketing Officer of Optimizely (whom we heard from in the previous chapter), about some of the common challenges that he's seen organizations face, what he calls "too many systems," and how Optimizely—as an experimentation platform—has addressed these issues.

Islam, who was CEO and co-founder of Welcome/Newscred prior to its acquisition by Optimizely, shared an experience of his own, "I was trying to figure out, 'How do I do something as basic as show customers something and show prospects something else?' And it was pretty difficult to even do that level of personalization because the only way we know if someone is a prospect or not is from our Salesforce database. So, all of a sudden, you've now added at least one tool—Salesforce—[plus] potentially a personalization tool, potentially a CDP. Then you have your website. And now you're wrestling with five or six different tools to personalize. And, again, it makes it very difficult to figure out what isn't working and makes it difficult to iterate."

To address these challenges, the Optimizely team were able to leverage their own suite of fully integrated tools for the CDP, personalization on the website, as well as experimentation. Islam told me, "So now I have Salesforce data going into our own CDP—we have what we call ODP: Optimizely Data Platform—to create those segments. And then I have a very simple personalization technique on my website where I can personalize based on any ODP segment. So now, all of a sudden, I've shrunk down this problem to just: Is Salesforce connected to Optimizely products? If so, the rest takes care of itself" (2023).

Technology companies like Optimizely are continuing to vertically integrate these capabilities into their own services, making it easier for brands and marketers to implement tools to address their various technology needs more simply. As you consider building your tech stack, look for platforms that serve multiple roles or are already tightly integrated into the existing tools your organization leverages.

How Should You Evaluate Prospective Technology?

In Chapters 6 and 7 we explored how resilient data systems and thoughtful customer journey mapping require the participation and cohesion of teams throughout the organization. Because technology must facilitate the tracking of the information collected and the delivery of experiences based on that information, it too requires marketers to cooperate and work alongside of other teams including IT, sales, customer experience, customer service, and operations. As a marketer, you may or may not be leading the discussion about *technology* evaluation. But being informed and knowledgeable about the requirements-gathering process will allow you to effectively participate in and shape the discussions.

To make this process simple, I've broken it down into three key categories: Fit, cost, and people.

Fit

The first set of considerations is around fit—does this particular software or technology fit your organization's needs, budget, capabilities, and resource constraints? It's not only about what it can do, but also about rightsizing the fit. Think about purchasing a home: Sure, two people could live in a 6,000 square foot house with five bedrooms in the middle of the woods, but would that be the best use of their money? Perhaps they would rather purchase a smaller home in a metropolitan area that gives them better access to arts and entertainment. I've seen many organizations purchase or subscribe to technology platforms that are either too powerful and seriously underutilized because of their complexity or too limited and that stymie experimentation and learning. Finding the right fit takes careful review by all parties that will use the technology actively day-to-day. Here are the areas your cross-functional team must discuss:

- *Business needs assessment:* What are the main challenges that the organization needs to solve for? What business case(s) will be addressed in the process of implementing this technology? What are the requirements of the main users?

- *Functionality and features:* What are the essential and high-priority features that the main users need access to? What are challenges the users want to address but may not know the right features to address? Keep those in mind as well.

- *Compatibility, integration, and customization:* Does the technology easily integrate into the existing toolstack and/or other technologies that are being considered? How easy is it to integrate? Can the necessary customizations be done, if applicable, and at what cost? Consider whether there are open APIs for developers, whether there is an existing community of third-party developers who are familiar enough with the tool to build the connections needed. Take into consideration not only the cost of integrations and customization, but also the time that it will take.

KNOW WHAT IT TAKES TO CUSTOMIZE UP FRONT

In one of my first professional roles, I worked at a company that had a very popular website that served both as a brand destination and an ecommerce store. The original website had been custom-built over a decade, bit by bit, but the company wanted to move to an existing ecommerce platform to take advantage of best-in-class existing technologies and have access to more existing integrations. So, the leadership brought in a consultant to help with the needs assessment and documentation, brought in designers to create wireframes, and then started to look into how to replicate the existing functionality and customizations of the website.

However, the original website was custom-built and dreamed up by a single developer, and it had some very unique but very useful features that were beloved by customers. And the new ecommerce platform was selected without a deep dive into the cost and complexities of customization. So, as the team got into the process of how to migrate the data, build the site, and keep these features, it soon became apparent that this new website/ecommerce platform wasn't going to be a good fit. It also meant that more than nine months of work and at least six figures were wasted preparing for a website platform that wasn't right for this organization. Plus, this revelation scuttled the organization's efforts and it would take more than another *two years* before the team was able to finally get a new site built and launched. All of this time, money, and effort could have been saved if the organization had considered the customization piece early in the evaluation process. Don't make those mistakes—consider that integration and customization should be part of the discussion early in the process, not at the end.

- *Scalability and flexibility:* Will this technology easily grow with your organization? What are the cost implications of that growth? How easily can this technology adapt to changing business needs?

- *Security and compliance:* Does this technology meet best-in-class security standards like encryption, redundancy, access controls, audit logs, etc.? Does it comply with industry-specific regulations and data-protection laws in all markets that your organization operates in?

- *AI and machine-learning:* Does this technology currently integrate AI or machine-learning where appropriate or applicable? Does the organization have a roadmap for how they will use AI and machine-learning to improve the technology in the future?

MAKE AI PART OF YOUR CONSIDERATION SET

Over the last few years, the conversations around AI have increasingly captured the public imagination, but AI has been integrated into a wide variety of marketing tools even before ChatGPT became mainstream. While not every technology requires AI or machine-learning, the truth is that these disciplines will continue to be integrated into just about every technology you touch. Therefore, it's important for you to understand how it impacts new technologies you're considering subscribing to or purchasing.

I spoke to Chris Lu, co-founder of Copy.ai, an AI platform that helps businesses of all sizes scale their work and bring their ideas to life, about what he sees as the opportunities around personalization and AI. Lu told me, "Historically the main reason personalization has been hard is due to effort and time. With AI, this ability to personalize should become much easier. This will allow smaller companies with smaller budgets to still be able to personalize in a very powerful way." Lu is right—while teams that have the resources for analysts or content teams may be less concerned about access to technologies with AI, smaller companies and teams will benefit from selecting tools that have AI built in, because they make it easier and more accessible to access data, create workflows, and/or personalize messages.

I also asked Lu for his advice to companies who want to future-proof their marketing efforts. He focused on AI fluency, saying, "Invest time and money into learning about AI. AI will help develop repeatable systems that allow scaling very rapidly at a fraction of the cost" (2023).

Cost

Cost isn't just about monetary considerations. It's also about opportunity cost, time investment, risk assessment, and also switching costs. That isn't just the cost of switching *to* the technology, but also the cost if—for some reason—you need to switch away from that technology in the future. With all of that in mind, there are many dimensions of cost that need to be considered up front. While many organizations are eager to invest in new technologies and only consider the upsides, I think it's incumbent on us to have a clear picture of what the costs will be. The more detailed an assessment we do up front, the better our organization can plan and the less likely the organization will be to go over budget.

- *Cost considerations:* As we've seen, cost goes beyond just the cost of the technology itself; it includes the cost of implementing/migrating (see below), integrating, and customizing, as well as the cost of training and/or additional headcount to make use of the technology. Therefore, be sure to take into consideration the true costs of your technology.

BE SURE TO CONSIDER END-TO-END COSTS

In implementing a new technology, it's easy to focus on the main costs of the technology—the big-ticket item; the single biggest investment. But in doing so, your organization may miss the true costs around consulting services and training, customizations, integrations, etc. Let me give you an analogy: When my husband and I were renovating our apartment in New York City, we got several bids from contractors on the work and materials. This was the big-ticket item. But we also kept in mind the cost of the architect, the engineer, and other ancillary services (the human pieces), as well as the light fixtures, appliances, and the cost of furniture (the customizations and extras). Because our overall budget considered all of the costs associated, when we ran into some surprise construction issues (which, if you've ever done any construction or renovation work, you know is bound to happen), we were able to adjust other areas of our spending (tightening our lighting and furniture budgets) to make up the difference. This meant that our entire project came in within budget, which—I've been told—is a rare feat.

- *Implementation and transition:* In addition to the monetary costs of implementation and/or migration to a new technology (i.e., you may need a consultant or specialist to help port of data or set up your data structure, for instance; you may pay up-front fees to the company to help you get up and running on their platform), consider the time investment from your team to make this project happen. What are the opportunity costs? In other words, what will your team need to give up or *not* work on in order to work on this project? Are there other initiatives that will need to fall by the wayside?

- *Risk and exit strategy:* What are the risks of moving to this new technology? Are there situations where you may need to roll back to your old technology? What if you decide to switch off of this technology in the future? Consider the switching costs, especially if this particular technology is highly integrated into your other systems. How difficult will it be to exit if you need to?

People

The final category of considerations when it comes to technology evaluation is the people piece. How will your people interface with this new technology? How simple will it be for them, and what are the things that the technology company has implemented to make this process smooth for them? Consider these three areas:

- *User experience and learning curve:* What is the ease of use of this new technology? Is it well-designed and intuitive? How steep is the learning curve? How does the technology company support onboarding within your organization? Do they provide ongoing training or resources as you hire/experience turnover?

- *User feedback and reviews:* What do current users say about their usage experience? Go beyond team leaders to understand the reviews of the everyday users. If there is a big disconnect between the value of the technology and the pain it causes its current users, that's something that you should flag and review. A great experience for your team's users will ensure that you get the most out of the technology, because you'll have a higher rate of adoption and usage.

- *Support, documentation, and maintenance:* What is the support and documentation like for the technology in question? Is it fast and easy to get the support your team needs when something goes wrong? How strong is the available documentation? Is there a support community? Also consider the maintenance requirements: How often does this technology need to be upgraded or maintained? How smooth or disruptive is that process? We've all had the experience of team members delaying the upgrades of software on their devices, and we've all seen the news reports of organizations hacked due to the lack of follow-through on these basic software hygiene practices. Make sure you know up front what the maintenance process will look like.

Just as technology in and of itself will not enable your organization to strategically leverage data and personalization, even a good strategy for data-driven marketing will be thwarted by a lack of technology infrastructure. To set your team up for success, engineering a strong tech stack that addresses the key needs and unique use cases of your organization is essential.

RESOURCES RELATED TO THIS CHAPTER

The Martech Handbook: Build a technology stack to attract and retain customers by Darrell Alfonso—To delve more deeply into the work of assembling a technology stack, be sure to check out this book, which is a robust resource for understanding and evaluating the tools you need to bring your marketing strategy to life.

CHAPTER 23 SUMMARY

What are the tools you need to have in place to effectively support your data-driven marketing approach? Broadly speaking, the categories are: Infrastructure, delivery, experimentation, and insights. But more than just knowing what tools are needed, you need to have a strong understanding of how to conduct an effective evaluation of the tools in question. To do so, you must consider criteria in three categories: Fit, cost, and people.

Actions

- Evaluate your current toolstack and identify the gaps or shortfalls.
- Identify the key opportunities to implement new technologies or upgrade existing technologies.
- Assemble a team to build out your evaluation criteria.
- Use the framework in the chapter to create a robust evaluation set, prior to choosing and evaluating technologies.

24

Putting It All Together

Creating Your Action Plan

You've made it—the final chapter. Are you feeling inspired to develop or overhaul your approach to collecting, analyzing, and leveraging data to personalize and improve your customers' experience with your brand? Over the last 23 chapters we've explored how to better understand your customers and build nuance based on their decision-making processes, their emotions, and what influences them. We've also explored how your organization can collect a wide variety of different data to understand your customers' behaviors and motivations. In this final chapter we'll review the key takeaways from each part of the book, we'll work through an exercise to help you build your action plan, and I'll answer some of the questions that I've received from real-world marketers as I've been presenting the research and frameworks from the book at conferences and workshops.

Building the Case For Having a Seat at the Table When Making Data Decisions

Here's what you need to get across when you're trying to get buy-in within your organization: Over the last two decades, we've seen our customers become digital-first. And with that, their expectations of both customer experience and how brands communicate with them has shifted to match. My research shows that 88 percent of US adults believe it's important for brands to remember past interactions and engage with them based on that shared history, and 85 percent believe that it's important for brands to share personalized recommendations with them (Researchscape, 2023). That's the reality that marcomm professionals now operate in.

Collecting the Right Data

Yet, in many organizations, marcomm professionals aren't involved in the strategic decision-making of how data is collected, what data is collected, and why that data is being collected. And when they are involved in how data is collected—usually in the form of lead forms, advertising campaigns, surveys, and/or pixels—often there isn't a clear strategic imperative in place to shape how this data comes together, how it's organized, or how it's tagged for analysis. As David Fortino, Chief Strategy Officer of Netline (whom we heard from in Chapter 16), told me, "Unstructured data is worthless data [...] If you're building a database full of disparate values, none of which have the same naming conventions, and so on, you'll never get to being good at personalization or contextualization, because all of it is random" (2023).

Fortino is absolutely correct. Without a deliberate framework and plan for collecting data and organizing or structuring that data, the data is unusable. As we saw in Chapter 1, more than four in ten marketers say that data quality and accuracy issues is one of the challenges they face when using data for personalization (Convince & Convert/ICUC, 2023). To address this, marketers must make a case for laying out the framework for collecting data so that it's purpose-built for marketing use cases.

Getting More Out of the Data

But for marketers, having a seat at the table isn't just about delivering on the expectations of the customers; it's also about making marketing and communications measurable and insightful. In the same research, we saw that only about one-third of marketers somewhat agree that their company is able to use VOC data to strategically inform marketing messages, content, and/or segmentation and only one-fifth strongly agreed with this statement (Convince & Convert/ICUC, 2023). That means that, on the whole, marketers aren't getting nearly as much valuable, strategic information out of their current data resources as they should. And it also means that a lot of organizations are flying relatively blindly when it comes to what truly resonates with their audiences. When marketers are part of the research process, the organization is able to build a true feedback mechanism between the communication with customers and the perception of customers about the communications.

Developing a Competitive Advantage

To gain a competitive advantage in the marketplace, you need to know more about your customers than your competitors, and you need to deliver a more relevant, valuable, and personalized message to those customers in the places and spaces where they are primed to receive those messages. Data-driven personalization is about integrating a customer-first approach to marketing and customer experience that leverages data on an ongoing and proactive basis. You cannot treat customer research as static and still maintain a competitive advantage. The lessons of this book must be implemented consistently as a part of the normal operations of your marketing communications organization.

Refresher: Reviewing Chapter Takeaways

As you've read the book, you've probably encountered frameworks that you're familiar with and others you haven't encountered or haven't thought about in a long time. Hopefully, with the help of the case studies and business examples, you've also seen how brands, both large and small, have put these frameworks and methodologies into practice. Recognizing that you may have read the book over time—or even jumped around it as you've read—here are the key takeaways from each part of the book. And remember: Every chapter has a summary and action items at the end, so you can go back and reference each chapter as needed.

Part One: Understanding Your Audiences

Every organization needs to understand its audiences, but in this foundational section, we discuss how many organizations either have insufficient research or treat their research as an exercise done in the past—perhaps gathering dust in a proverbial drawer somewhere, rarely referenced, and usually not refreshed in ways that are useful to the marketing, sales, and executive teams (Chapter 1). In Part One, we discuss why every organization needs to be more deliberate in both choosing key audiences strategically and collecting data that helps to segment and identify these audiences. We also discuss the importance of bringing together our data ecosystem across first-, second-, and third-party data sources to research and profile our customers (Chapter 2), as well as how we can use technology such as AI to help make our audience segmentations and personas more useful as tools to power our marketing efforts (Chapter 4). We outline the basic categories of data that organizations must collect (Chapter 3), and we discuss how organizations can be strategic in using existing data to segment and prioritize our audiences, as well as how we can engage them in the feedback/data collection process (Chapter 4).

Part Two: Building the Toolkit for Personalization

Part Two contains some of the key frameworks of the book. We discuss why and how you must build a strategy for data-driven personalization and how to leverage behavioral economics and behavioral psychology to make your brand the default choice for your customers (Chapter 5). We talk about how your organization can set up resilient, strategic systems for data (Chapter 6). We also explore how to layer data collection and customer research onto your customer journey maps (Chapter 7) to deliver more relevant content (Chapter 8) and build seamless omnichannel experiences (Chapter 9) that meet customer expectations. Finally, we explore the key considerations that every organization must have when it comes to privacy, ethics, and personalization (Chapter 10). This is a useful section to review as you're building your action plan.

Part Three: Fostering Emotional Resonance

The customer and what matters to them is at the heart of why personalization is so important to customer experience and marketing communications. In Part Three, we explore the motivations that impact customer decision-making and how we can capture that through structured data (Chapter 11), how data can be used as a persuasive tool in messaging (Chapter 12), and how data in the form of captured reviews and social proof can be leveraged to persuade your audiences (Chapter 13). We also explore the ways in which we should develop and test our messaging to make sure that we use a measurable approach to improving our marketing communications over time (Chapter 14). In Part Three of the book, we connect the dots between emotions, measurement, and strategic improvement to build our competitive advantage.

Part Four: Tapping into Community

Whereas Part Three focuses on the internal motivations of our customers, Part Four discusses the ways in which external influences in the form of perceived community motivate our customers. Not only do we explore how data can inform how we identify communities to engage with, but we also discuss the benefits of building a community to both gather more data and also deepen your brand's relationship with customers (Chapter 15). We then discuss how to improve community engagement and get the most value from a strategic point of view out of these rich entities (Chapter 16), and we explore how community-builders (power networkers, advocates, and ambassadors) can be empowered to spread the word (Chapter 17). Part Four demonstrates how data can be collected from sources outside of typical customer relationship data and/or content consumption, as well as how you can get the most out of your data to identify people whose voices influence others.

Part Five: Deepening Customer Profiles

Collecting valuable data about your customers is more than simply passively identifying what data to collect. It's also about creating mechanisms that incentivize your customers to share their data. In addition to leveraging communities, as we explore in Part Four, in Part Five we discuss additional methods and tools to help deepen your customer profiles. We explore how to leverage the behavioral psychology of status to improve customer relationships and reward your best customers (Chapter 18). We consider how to improve customer lifetime value and examine how you can make the business case for how data-driven personalization and improved customer experience can increase CLV (Chapter 19). We also re-examine the different types of data that were introduced in Chapter 3 to consider what's valuable for your organization to track, understand, and leverage in personalization.

Part Six: Empowering Your Data-Driven Personalization Team

Finally, in Part Six, we consider the infrastructure needed to succeed with a data-driven marketing strategy that is powered by personalization. In this section, we first reflect upon how your organization must cultivate a culture of curiosity to truly enable your marcomm team to get the most out of data, automation, and personalization (Chapter 21). Second, we examine the ways in which your team must rally around a strategic approach to data-driven personalization (Chapter 22). Third, we look at the technologies needed to succeed in this data-driven approach (Chapter 23). In other words: To set your organization up for success you need the right people, you need alignment around a strategy, and you need the right tools to empower the work.

BUILDING AND ORGANIZING YOUR ACTION CHECKLIST

Before we jump into the exercise, I encourage you to go back through and collate the action items from the end of each chapter that you have identified as gaps in your current practices. Pull them together and organize them by topic areas. As you've seen, because the chapters are purposefully intertwined, there may be checklist items from different chapters that relate to each other. Go back through and sort your action checklist so that you have categories that make sense for your organization and team. This will also set you up for success in the upcoming exercise.

FIGURE 24.1 A SWOT analysis is a useful tool for auditing your current state and identifying the areas that your team may need to address or want to leverage

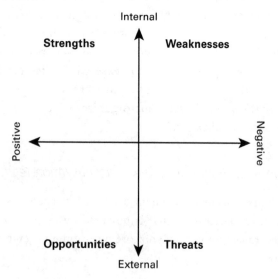

Assembling Your Action Plan

With that review of the book under your belt, it's now time to put together a plan to implement the recommendations in the book.

SWOT Analysis

If you're not sure where to start, I encourage you to start with a SWOT analysis—a framework for understanding your strengths, weaknesses, opportunities, and threats (Figure 24.1). Using the book's summary (above) and your action checklist as references, identify your brand's strengths, weaknesses, opportunities, and threats, when it comes to implementing data-driven personalization.

ACKNOWLEDGING INTERNAL AND EXTERNAL FACTORS

While many organizations use SWOT analyses for a market analysis and auditing their current work, many don't correctly apply the categories based on the axes of the matrix. SWOT matrices consider positive and negative areas of both internal and external origins. This is particularly important to keep in mind as "opportunities" and "threats" should address considerations identified based on external forces or circumstances. By considering the internal capabilities, as well as the external considerations, you can identify the areas that you have more or less control over, as well as the areas that may shift based on landscape conditions. This differentiation will help you in the next exercise—prioritizing initiatives to move forward based on your limited resources—since external factors may impact your decision-making process on what's possible, what's strategic, and what's doable.

Prioritize the Initiatives That Have the Most Potential

Once you have created your SWOT analysis, you will have a clear matrix of the areas that you can capitalize on, the weaknesses your organization must address, the opportunities you should take advantage of, and the threats you must fortify yourself against.

Identify a few key points from each quadrant of your SWOT analysis and find the related action checklist item from your end-of-chapter list. Alternately, rewrite the SWOT item to describe the activities you and the brand should take on. For instance, if you've listed "Depth of existing customer data" as a strength, you might rewrite that as "Build a plan for analyzing existing customer data to refresh customer profiles." Or perhaps you jotted down a threat like "New entrants in the marketplace have more industry-specific content than we do"; you might rewrite that as "Gather industry-specific knowledge to create thought leadership content specific to our key target audiences."

Once you've identified and rewritten the actions, map them against how quickly they can be implemented in your organization:

- *Immediate initiatives:* Actions you can do in the next 90 days or so.
- *Mid-term initiatives:* Something that will take some organizational buy-in and may require additional steps to implement; achievable within the next year or so.
- *Long-term initiatives:* Projects that will take significant organizational buy-in and resources; achievable within the next two to three years.

I recommend that you try to plot all of your key initiatives within this time-frame, since behavioral psychology tells us that people are bad at planning for the future. If we make the time horizon too far out, it's more likely that you will find your initiatives abandoned or that inertia causes your team not to act. Instead of planning further out, focus on breaking bigger projects into smaller tasks, so that you can get buy-in and start moving within the three-year time period.

Identify the Buy-In You Will Need to Implement Your Initiatives

As we've seen throughout this book, marcomm is hardly the only team that is involved with the capture, use, analysis, or support of good data. One way to mobilize your organization is to bring teams together with a task force to move your data-driven personalization efforts forward. In doing so, it's also vital to gain executive support. Identify the person or people within your organization who would be a valuable executive champion. What are the key metrics and considerations that they would want to see to help push these projects forward? Keep that in mind as we build the business case (coming up shortly).

Determine the Resources Needed

In the last few chapters, we looked at the ways your organization should build the people, the teams, and the tech stack that empowers a marketing strategy grounded in data-driven personalization. Identifying what gaps exist in terms of resources and how to address those gaps is vital. Again, the frameworks and concepts in this book can be executable at every budget. You can be a small business and collect the data you need to personalize, and you can be an enterprise organization. What you must determine is what are the tools and who are the right team members to help you bring your goals to life.

Outline the Measurable Goals/Return on Investment

With your action items and initiatives in hand, you must then map them to business goals and marcomm objectives. What are the key metrics that you will measure to determine success? How will you tie them to business performance? What tracking will you need to have in place to capture results? This is a great place to go back to Chapter 19 to look at CLV and how personalization initiatives can produce results for your organization.

Make the Case to the Right People

With these steps done, it's time to make the pitch to the stakeholders and the executive sponsor. Present your action plan, your prioritization, the measurable goals and return on investment, as well as the resources you will need to bring the plan to life. If your stakeholders aren't yet ready to greenlight the full scope of projects, specify which parts of your proposal could be initiated as a pilot program or limited test. In doing so, you should also clearly define what the metrics of success will look like and what the next steps will be if/when success is achieved.

Launch, Measure, and Report Out

As you roll out your first few initiatives or your pilot program, you'll uncover areas of opportunity, as well as areas of friction. Be sure to treat the initiatives list you've created based on this chapter as a living document; update it as things shift and priorities change. In this initial phase, it's important to not only identify wins, but to build momentum for your future projects. Create a framework for consistent storytelling about the data you collect and the impacts of personalization: What are you learning along the way? What kinds of improvement are you seeing to CLV? As we've seen throughout this book, outputs are only as good as your inputs. Be sure that you have the right tracking mechanisms in place to weave a compelling narrative based on your progress. Internal data storytelling is critical to building consensus around the value of your initiatives.

Roll Out Phase Two and Repeat

As you rally support for your initiatives, you will be able to continue to improve the mechanisms within your organization (see Part Six) to support your data-driven personalization strategy. Think of this work as climbing a proverbial stepladder. At each rung, you'll need to adjust your weight distribution, check your balance, and make sure that you clearly see how to navigate to the next rung. With your plan in hand, you'll no doubt be able to make the climb with confidence.

Questions From Marketers Like You

As I've been writing this book, I've had the privilege of giving both in-person and virtual talks that feature some of the frameworks, case studies, and examples that appear in its pages. Whenever I speak at these events, one of my favorite parts is getting questions from the audience. Whether I'm speaking to small business owners, enterprise marketers, or folks that are somewhere in between, I find that I both learn a lot from their questions and am challenged to think on my feet. Maybe it's my days as a faculty lecturer at Columbia University and the City College of New York that make me fond of being put in the hot seat and taking questions on the fly. Here are just a few of the questions that I've gotten that might come up in your conversations with your own team:

My organization has been collecting a variety of data, but it's not the right data for being able to better personalize our marketing. What now? It can be frustrating to realize that the data that you have is not very useful, but think of it as an opportunity. Knowing what doesn't work makes it easier for you to identify what *will* work. First audit your data for hygiene: Is the quality of the data poor or is it just not the right information to offer the kind of personalization you think would benefit your audiences? If the quality of the data is poor, it's time to clean the database and identify ways you can encourage or even incentivize existing customers to update their information.

If you don't have the right information to develop personalization campaigns, such as interests or pertinent information, build a plan of action to create points of engagement for your audiences to provide that information. Whether you decide on surveys, pop-up questionnaires on your website, or choose-your-own-adventure content in email automations, there are many different ways to develop content that allows you to collect more data about your customers. Be sure to review Chapter 8 for more on this topic.

What if my organization has purchased lists from data brokers and they aren't the best quality? How do we engage those contacts and improve the data about those prospects?   For businesses in many industries, list brokers can seem like a useful tool. After all, they supply the contact information of people who meet your demographic and geographic criteria. But, as you've probably seen, there's no guarantee that these customers meet the right psychographic criteria or are at the right part of their customer journeys for your outreach to be relevant to them.

If you have purchased lists, being deliberate in developing content marketing campaigns (again, see Chapter 8) that help to address their unique needs—and allow them to identify their use cases or challenges—is a good way to engage them meaningfully while collecting more data about them. For instance, you might create an email automation whose first message asks what's their biggest pain point and features three buttons, one for each of the three options. Each button clicks through to a resource that helps to address that problem, but it also gives your company more data for the second round of automation to be more personalized to their needs. Using gated content (see the case study in Chapter 16) or events (see the case study in Chapter 4) can also be valuable methods to engage prospects further through resources, while also capturing more information about them and their needs.

My team and I only own one part of the data process—we're focused on analysis and tactics, not strategy. How do we convince our organization to involve us in the strategic planning, since we're the ones who see how the data gets used?   It's not uncommon for practitioners to recognize the need for stronger strategy in their practices. Start by making the case: Identify the areas where your current data demonstrates that there is room for improvement. Propose to the owner of those areas to conduct a team review to help educate them and the broader team about what you're seeing. Plan this session as not only a read-out, but also a brainstorming session or workshop. Together, identify ways that the organization could make improvements and/or run tests to learn more. Make sure that you and your team, as the data owners, provide direction and expertise on how you would design these experiments and/or tag the data to produce valuable outputs and insights. By providing both the analysis to set up the session and guidance on the measurement that frames the output of the session, you'll be seen as a strategic partner. For more on building a culture that takes a strategic approach to data and personalization, be sure to go back to Chapter 21.

We have limited resources; how do we convince our leadership team that we need to make investments in a marketing strategy that focuses on data and personalization?   Ultimately, customers' expectations are shifting, and the vast majority of customers want more relevant recommendations from brands. Your customers are getting bombarded by messages every day, and they make snap judgments about what to pay attention to and what to ignore. They ignore the messages that don't serve them, and they may give a few seconds to the messages that feel somewhat relevant to them. You need to not only be in the second camp, but you need to go further than your competition. When you have limited resources, it is even more important to have a marketing strategy that leverages knowledge and delivers insights— you only have so much bandwidth. Wouldn't you rather spend it on the initiatives that truly speak to the audiences that convert? To bring your leadership team on board, focus on the chapters of this book that speak to strategy and results (Chapters 1, 2, 6, 19), and make sure to work through the exercises in this chapter to make your case compelling. Selling to your internal audiences is as important as selling to external audiences.

What can I use as a starting point for my team to rally them around the concepts in this book?   In presenting the ideas from this book, I have found that it's important to focus on the areas that need to be addressed by your specific team. Identify what are the biggest pain points and start from there. Particularly, Chapter 6 lays out several key frameworks and opportunities that translate well to a workshop or presentation format. You'll also find more resources, including the research shared throughout the book from our team at Convince & Convert, as well as my friends at Researchscape, along with videos and a webinar version of Chapter 6 at datadrivenpersonalization.com. I hope to see you there.

Turning Ideas Into Action

I believe in you. I believe that you've read this book because you understand that marketers need to make dramatic improvements into the way they measure, the way they test, and the way they personalize in order to gain a competitive advantage and set the marketing strategy of the future.

My final advice for you is simply: Take action step-by-step. There are so many businesspeople whose plans go awry because of inertia, other more pressing business needs, or limited resources. But everything can be done if you break it down into doable steps. And remember: You don't have to go it alone. I have included a wide variety of resources, as well as case studies from experts and brands that I respect, throughout the book, to help you find your way. This road has been traveled by others, so you can be assured that you can do it too. And guess what? I'm also just a message away. Find me on social media or through my websites (zonteehou.com and datadrivenpersonalization.com). I'm in your corner.

ACKNOWLEDGMENTS

Throughout my career I've been lucky to work with business leaders who have nurtured my skills and cultivated my interests. I'd particularly like to thank Ilana Rabinowitz, Kelly Santina, Jay Baer, Ann Handley, Pam Didner, Mark Schaefer, Jason Keath, Nicole Dalonzo, and Andy Crestodina for their support, mentorship, and camaraderie over the years. I'd also like to thank my incredible Convince & Convert crew and alumni—Amanda Stevenson, Anna Hrach, Anthony Helmstetter, Chris Sietsema, Daniel Lemin, Gini Roberts, Jennifer Harmon, Jenny Magic, Jess Tyson, Kim Corak, Lauren Teague, Lisa Loeffler, Mary Nice, Megan Gilbert, Sunny Hunt—you all make me better at my work every day, and I'm grateful you have my back. I must also thank the fantastic team and alumni of Media Volery—particularly, Brandyce Pechillo, Nai Chen Liu, and Maddie Jager. As a marketer, it is so important to have a community with whom you can bounce ideas— thank you to those folks who have helped me think through this book at various stages: Chris Johnson, Nancy Harhut, Robert Rose, Robbie Fitzwater, David Fortino, and Christopher Penn. And, of course, there would be no book without the likes of Bronwyn Geyer, Jeylan Ramis, and Donna Goddard—many thanks to the whole team at Kogan Page.

I wrote this book during the first year of my daughter's life and, as you can imagine, it has impacted not only the examples that I've included in this book and my mindset as a consumer, but also when/where/how I've written the book. So I absolutely have to thank my supportive husband, Hadrien, and my wonderful daughter for their support and understanding during this doubly busy time in my life. My long-time friends—Lauren, Alex, Liz, Michelle, and Patty—you're always inspiring me and heartening me. Thank you for listening to me—and letting me share your stories and anecdotes too. My parents, Gloria and Joe, my brother Timothy, as well as my parents-in-law, Monique and Roland, have been a constant source of strength in my life. They are my biggest cheerleaders. Although I'm saddened that Monique isn't here to see this book completed, I'm grateful that she was with us when I set off on this journey—and I draw inspiration from her as a storyteller and writer, every day.

Finally, I want to thank my many students and clients over the years. Your questions, your feedback, and your thinking have challenged me, made me laugh, made me think, and made me a better marketer. I hope you see in this book many of the frameworks, ideas, and questions we've explored together over the years.

REFERENCES

Chapter 1

Barron, T (2023) Interview by Zontee Hou, October 17

Content Marketing Institute/MarketingProfs (2021) B2C content marketing benchmarks, budgets, and trends: Insights for 2022, Content Marketing Institute. contentmarketinginstitute.com/wp-content/uploads/2021/10/B2B_2022_Research.pdf (archived at https://perma.cc/9ZTN-XMRA)

Convince & Convert/ICUC (2023) The state of data-driven personalization in marketing: Opportunities and challenges in AI, social media and more, ICUC. lp.icuc.social/ebook-2024state-of-data-driven-personalization-in-marketing (archived at https://perma.cc/VW4E-5WWU)

Fitzwater, R (2023) Interview by Zontee Hou, May 11

Heitman, S (2022) What happens in an internet minute in 2023: 90 fascinating online stats, LocalIQ, May 5. localiq.com/blog/what-happens-in-an-internet-minute (archived at https://perma.cc/9AR7-AWQ2)

Lu, C (2023) Interview by Zontee Hou, May 14

Researchscape (2023) Media Volery omnibus 230818 weighted report, Researchscape, August 21

Chapter 2

AdAge (2023) Across the pet-verse: Building essential brands with data-driven personalization, AdAge. adage.com/article/digital-experiences/across-pet-verse-building-essential-brands-data-driven-personalization/2501076 (archived at https://perma.cc/3UP2-X6DS)

Researchscape (2023) Media Volery omnibus 230818 weighted report, Researchscape, August 21

Chapter 3

Baer, J and Brown, A (2023) How Sam's Club creates community with social media, Convince & Convert, April. www.convinceandconvert.com/podcasts/episodes/how-sams-club-creates-community-with-social-media (archived at https://perma.cc/794Z-NF7K)

Convince & Convert/ICUC (2023) The state of data-driven personalization in marketing: Opportunities and challenges in AI, social media and more, ICUC. lp.icuc.social/ebook-2024state-of-data-driven-personalization-in-marketing (archived at https://perma.cc/GNQ2-QVLS)

Walmart (2023) Real-time intelligent retargeting launches on Sam's Club member access platform (MAP), Walmart, February 28. corporate.walmart.com/about/samsclub/news/2023/02/28/real-time-intelligent-retargeting-launches-on-sams-club-member-access-platform-map (archived at https://perma.cc/5CHL-A547)

Chapter 4

Barron, T (2023) Interview by Zontee Hou, October 17

Crestodina, A (2023) How to create AI marketing personas with 8 powerful prompts, Orbit Media. orbitmedia.com/blog/ai-marketing-personas (archived at https://perma.cc/93WT-R7W9)

Chapter 5

Aristotle (2007) *On Rhetoric*, translated by G A Kennedy, Oxford University Press, New York

Damasio, A (1994) *Descartes' Error: Emotion, reason, and the human brain*, Penguin Books, New York

Kahneman, D (2011) *Thinking, Fast and Slow*, Farrar, Straus and Giroux, New York

Patagonia (2023) www.patagonia.com/home (archived at https://perma.cc/T2GS-KGTM)

Chapter 6

Adams, L, Burkholder, E, and Hamilton, K (2015) Your guide to winning the shift to mobile, Think With Google. thinkwithgoogle.com/marketing-strategies/app-and-mobile/micromoments-guide-pdf-download (archived at https://perma.cc/LA43-U4EQ)

Clapp, R (2021) Covid-19 causes digital consumption to rise by over 30%, forming new and lasting consumer habits, WARC, April 30. www.warc.com/newsandopinion/opinion/covid-19-causes-digital-consumption-to-rise-by-over-30-forming-new-and-lasting-consumer-habits/en-gb/4209 (archived at https://perma.cc/FA3M-49ST)

Duhigg, C (2012) How companies learn your secrets, *The New York Times Magazine*, February 16. www.nytimes.com/2012/02/19/magazine/shopping-habits.html (archived at https://perma.cc/NZ5C-SKVA)

Gerards, F F, Goodin, C, Logan, B, and Schmidt, J (2018) Powerful pricing: The next frontier in apparel and fashion advanced analytics, McKinsey & Company, December 13. www.mckinsey.com/industries/retail/our-insights/powerful-pricing-the-next-frontier-in-apparel-and-fashion-advanced-analytics (archived at https://perma.cc/E5PA-9XC3)

Gordon, R (2022) Seeing into the future: Personalized cancer screening with artificial intelligence, MIT News, January 21. news.mit.edu/2022/seeing-future-personalized-cancer-screening-artificial-intelligence-0121 (archived at https://perma.cc/3ARA-THGG)

IBM Cloud Stories (2015) FreshDirect slices and dices more sharply than ever—how about them apples? Medium, December 7. medium.com/@ibmcloud/fresh-direct-delivers-personalized-food-to-your-door-thanks-to-ibm-cloud-experience-one-9f6399afa8bf (archived at https://perma.cc/VCD9-FDM3)

Selligent Marketing Cloud (2020) Leading online grocer FreshDirect selects Selligent Marketing Cloud to drive personalized service and engagement, GlobeNewswire, February 25. www.globenewswire.com/en/news-release/2020/02/25/1990261/0/en/Leading-Online-Grocer-FreshDirect-Selects-Selligent-Marketing-Cloud-to-Drive-Personalized-Service-and-Engagement.html (archived at https://perma.cc/BXA9-T768)

Shaw, N, Eschenbrenner, B, and Baier, D (2022) Online shopping continuance after Covid-19: A comparison of Canada, Germany and the United States, *Journal of Retailing and Consumer Services*. www.sciencedirect.com/science/article/abs/pii/S096969892200193X (archived at https://perma.cc/PJ5P-M7EL)

Singer, N (2014) Intel's sharp-eyed social scientist, The New York Times, February 15. www.nytimes.com/2014/02/16/technology/intels-sharp-eyed-social-scientist.html (archived at https://perma.cc/XU3N-9C9D)

van Assche, K, Beunen, R, Duineveld, M, and Gruezmacher, M (2021) Adaptive methodology: Topic, theory, method and data in ongoing conversation, *International Journal of Social Research Methodology*. www.tandfonline.com/doi/full/10.1080/13645579.2021.1964858 (archived at https://perma.cc/N6SW-N4WR)

Chapter 7

Bliss, J (2015) *Chief Customer Officer 2.0*, Jossey-Bass, San Francisco

Penn, C S (2023) Interview by Zontee Hou, May 8, 2023

Chapter 8

Carr, D (2013) Giving viewers what they want, *The New York Times*, February 24. www.nytimes.com/2013/02/25/business/media/for-house-of-cards-using-big-data-to-guarantee-its-popularity.html (archived at https://perma.cc/55BL-KPNE)

Content Marketing Institute/MarketingProfs (2022) B2B content marketing benchmarks, budgets, and trends: Insights for 2023, Content Marketing Institute. contentmarketinginstitute.com/wp-content/uploads/2022/10/b2b-2023-research-final.pdf (archived at https://perma.cc/U44D-W9MC)

Dixon, S (2023) Media usage in an internet minute as of April 2022, Statista, February 14. www.statista.com/statistics/195140/new-user-generated-content-uploaded-by-users-per-minute (archived at https://perma.cc/Y5BB-HFQ5)

Fitzwater, R (2023) Interview by Zontee Hou, May 11

Mutiny (2023) Carta increased seed stage signups by 80% with targeted messaging, Mutiny. www.mutinyhq.com/customers/carta (archived at https://perma.cc/9JBX-2N5A)

Chapter 9

Chartier, D (2010) Nike releases new Nike+ GPS app for runners, Macworld, September 7. www.macworld.com/article/207560/nike_gps_iphone_running.html (archived at https://perma.cc/H7GV-SBAB)

Fernandez, C (2020) Inside Nike's radical direct-to-consumer strategy, Business of Fashion, December 7. www.businessoffashion.com/case-studies/retail/inside-nikes-radical-direct-to-consumer-strategy-download-the-case-study (archived at https://perma.cc/ZK4C-Z75Z)

Monllos, K (2019) Why insurance startup Lemonade built an in-house creative agency, Digiday, August 22. digiday.com/marketing/insurance-start-lemonade-built-house-creative-agency (archived at https://perma.cc/5R4J-9WGU)

Penn, C S (2023) Interview by Zontee Hou, May 8

Salesforce (2022) State of the connected customer, 5th edition, Salesforce. www.salesforce.com/eu/resources/research-reports/state-of-the-connected-customer (archived at https://perma.cc/R5GX-S5CS)

Zoghby, J, Tieman, S, Perez Moino, J, and Falconer, E (2018) Personalization pulse check, Accenture Interactive

Chapter 10

Auxier, B, Rainie, L, Anderson, M, Perrin, A, Kumar M, and Turner, E (2019) Americans and privacy: Concerned, confused and feeling lack of control over their personal information, Pew Research Center, November 15. www.pewresearch.org/internet/2019/11/15/americans-and-privacy-concerned-confused-and-feeling-lack-of-control-over-their-personal-information (archived at https://perma.cc/GK5P-XN6M)

Crawford, K (2014) The anxiety of big data, The New Inquiry, May 30. thenewinquiry.com/the-anxieties-of-big-data (archived at https://perma.cc/C5N7-R5GE)

Duhigg, C (2012) How companies learn your secrets, *The New York Times Magazine*, February 16. www.nytimes.com/2012/02/19/magazine/shopping-habits.html (archived at https://perma.cc/NZ5C-SKVA)

Hawkins, E, and Tyko, K (2023) Brands allow customers to opt out of Mother's Day marketing, Axios, April 30. www.axios.com/2023/04/30/mothers-day-2023-marketing-holiday-email-opt-out (archived at https://perma.cc/9G79-2RNB)

J D Power (2022) Bundle fumble? Rising auto insurance premiums are killing home bundles, J D Power finds, J D Power, September 20. www.jdpower.com/business/press-releases/2022-us-home-insurance-study (archived at https://perma.cc/LSY8-96HK)

Lemonade (2023) Lemonade's data privacy pledge, Lemonade. www.lemonade.com/privacy-policy (archived at https://perma.cc/SPM7-5P6Q)

Prasad, A (2020) Unintended consequences of GDPR: A two-year lookback, Regulatory Studies Center, George Washington University, September 3. regulatorystudies.columbian.gwu.edu/unintended-consequences-gdpr (archived at https://perma.cc/7R6D-4HRF)

Salesforce (2022) State of the connected customer, 5th edition, Salesforce. www.salesforce.com/eu/resources/research-reports/state-of-the-connected-customer (archived at https://perma.cc/N7Q6-BZCZ)

Schwartz, K (2023) Developing proactive security measures: Lessons from Lemonade, *ITPro Today*, April 24. www.itprotoday.com/compliance-and-risk-management/developing-proactive-security-measures-lessons-lemonade (archived at https://perma.cc/D8BJ-UYDY)

Watson, S (2014) Data doppelgängers and the uncanny valley of personalization, The Atlantic, June 16. www.theatlantic.com/technology/archive/2014/06/data-doppelgangers-and-the-uncanny-valley-of-personalization/372780 (archived at https://perma.cc/9WF7-A27X)

Zoghby, J, Tieman, S, Perez Moino, J, and Falconer, E (2018) Personalization pulse check, Accenture Interactive

Chapter 11

Faverio, M and Anderson, M (2022) For shopping, phones are common and influencers have become a factor – especially for young adults, Pew Research Center, November 21. www.pewresearch.org/short-reads/2022/11/21/ for-shopping-phones-are-common-and-influencers-have-become-a-factor-especially-for-young-adults (archived at https://perma.cc/7HNK-M5PS)

Maheshwawri, S (2023) For Gen Z, playing an influencer on TikTok comes naturally, *The New York Times*, May 17. www.nytimes.com/2023/05/17/ business/tiktok-influencers-gen-z.html (archived at https://perma.cc/9FCA-7C7G)

Maslow, A H (1943) A theory of human motivation, *Psychological Review*, 50 (4), 370–96

Pink, D H (2011) *Drive: The surprising truth about what motivates us*, Riverhead Books, New York

Suarez, M (2023) Interview by Zontee Hou, June 7

Willige, A (2021) People prefer brands with aligned corporate purpose and values, World Economic Forum, December 17. www.weforum.org/agenda/2021/12/ people-prefer-brands-with-aligned-corporate-purpose-and-values (archived at https://perma.cc/9FCA-zzzz)

Chapter 12

Apple (2023) Close your rings, Apple. www.apple.com/watch/close-your-rings (archived at https://perma.cc/VK8Y-8G2F)

ClearVoice (2019) What's your biggest challenge with content: 2019 marketing survey, ClearVoice. www.clearvoice.com/resources/biggest-content-challenges-survey-results (archived at https://perma.cc/SB8D-7E7M)

Crestodina, A, and Hou, Z (2022) Find – and publish – your missing stat, Convince & Convert, June 8. web.convinceandconvert.com/find-your-missing-stat-on-demand (archived at https://perma.cc/M86P-5PDX)

Curology (2023) curology.com (archived at https://perma.cc/8L2S-RU5P)

Feehan, B (2023) 2023 social media industry benchmark report, RivalIQ, February 21. www.rivaliq.com/blog/social-media-industry-benchmark-report (archived at https://perma.cc/2RMP-WCJJ)

Frane, A (2016) Things you didn't know about Chivas Regal, Thrillist, April 27. www.thrillist.com/drink/nation/facts-about-chivas-regal-scotch-whisky (archived at https://perma.cc/YWZ5-37CU)

Glater, J D and Finder, A (2006) In tuition game, popularity rises with price, *The New York Times*, December 12. www.nytimes.com/2006/12/12/ education/12tuition.html (archived at https://perma.cc/CQQ2-T37N)

Tal, A and Wansink, B (2016) Blinded with science: Trivial graphs and formulas increase ad persuasiveness and belief in product efficacy, *Public Understanding of Science*, 25 (1), 117–25

Thaler, R T and Sunstein C R (2009) *Nudge: Improving decisions about health, wealth, and happiness*, Penguin Books, New York

Chapter 13

Baer, J (2016) *Hug Your Haters: How to embrace complaints and keep your customers*, Portfolio, New York

Baer, J and Lemin, D (2018a) Chatter Matters: The 2018 word of mouth report, Talk Triggers. www.talktriggers.com/cm (archived at https://perma.cc/59UV-FSYZ)

Baer, J and Lemin, D (2018b) *Talk Triggers: The complete guide to creating customers with word of mouth*, Penguin Publishing Group, New York

Cialdini, R B (2006) *Influence: The psychology of persuasion*, revised edition, Harper Business, New York

Convince & Convert (2020) SharpSpring, Convince & Convert. www.convinceandconvert.com/clients/sharpspring (archived at https://perma.cc/48JU-Z2LQ)

Hanlon, P (2012) If Sir Dyson doesn't believe in brands, why has he spent millions building one? Forbes, 6 May. www.forbes.com/sites/patrickhanlon/2012/05/06/if-sir-dyson-doesnt-believe-in-brands-why-has-he-spent-millions-building-one (archived at https://perma.cc/2RK5-ZNRT)

Indiegogo (2021) Lomi: Turn waste to compost with a single button, Indiegogo. www.indiegogo.com/projects/lomi-turn-waste-to-compost-with-a-single-button (archived at https://perma.cc/U2S8-XQ49)

Kharraz, O (2013) The importance of patient reviews (and why doctors should leverage them), Zocdoc, March 12. www.zocdoc.com/resources/doctors-should-leverage-online-patient-reviews (archived at https://perma.cc/25HS-54ET)

Ries, T (2023) 2023 Edelman Trust barometer: Global report, Edelman. www.edelman.com/trust/2023/trust-barometer (archived at https://perma.cc/W6VJ-LD4B)

Woods, K (2022) Spotify Wrapped: What marketers can learn from the viral campaign, Sprout Social, December 7. sproutsocial.com/insights/spotify-wrapped (archived at https://perma.cc/CE5M-H6K6)

Chapter 14

Content Marketing Institute/MarketingProfs (2023) B2C content marketing benchmarks, budgets, and trends: Insights for 2023, Content Marketing Institute. contentmarketinginstitute.com/wp-content/uploads/2023/01/B2C_2023_Research_Final.pdf (archived at https://perma.cc/5LM4-6H98)

Garcia-Navarro, L (2020) How the University of Arizona is handling Covid-19 on campus, NPR, September 6. www.npr.org/2020/09/06/910194892/how-the-university-of-arizona-is-handling-covid-19-on-campus (archived at https://perma.cc/M9MH-LQDK)

Persado (2023) www.persado.com (archived at https://perma.cc/TH37-CDP7)

Chapter 15

Bark Box (2023) www.barkbox.com (archived at https://perma.cc/RZ7H-8PDX)

Drum, M (2023) Interview with Zontee Hou, June 29

Farm House Tack (2023) www.farmhousetack.com (archived at https://perma.cc/GB6J-967E)

Lego (2023) What is LEGO Ideas about? LEGO. ideas.lego.com/howitworks (archived at https://perma.cc/S4GJ-NJNM)

Maslow, A H (1943) A theory of human motivation, *Psychological Review*, 50 (4), 370–96

Chapter 16

Convince & Convert (2022) Texas Exes: Alumni association for the University of Texas, Convince & Convert. www.convinceandconvert.com/clients/texas-exes-alumni-association-case-study (archived at https://perma.cc/YFS2-GSYP)

Creative Cloud (2023) Learn Photoshop, Creative Cloud. creativecloud.adobe.com/learn (archived at https://perma.cc/7FRF-3XZD)

Dachner, A M and Makarius, E E (2021) Turn departing employees into loyal alumni, *Harvard Business Review*, March–April. hbr.org/2021/03/turn-departing-employees-into-loyal-alumni (archived at https://perma.cc/66QY-KRDM)

Fortino, D (2023) Interview by Zontee Hou, July 18.

Microsoft (2023) Welcome to the Microsoft support community, Microsoft. answers.microsoft.com/en-us (archived at https://perma.cc/8DKM-952F)

What to Expect (2023) What to expect: Community groups, What to Expect. community.whattoexpect.com/forums (archived at https://perma.cc/T5UN-U237)

Chapter 17

ActiveCampaign (2023) Affiliate, ActiveCampaign. www.activecampaign.com/partner/affiliate (archived at https://perma.cc/4H37-X4A3)

Baer, J and Lemin, D (2018) Chatter Matters: The 2018 word of mouth report, Talk Triggers. www.talktriggers.com/cm (archived at https://perma.cc/YJ44-ZNWU)

Fiverr Forum (2023) A home for meaningful connections, peer support, and professional growth, Fiverr Forum. community.fiverr.com (archived at https://perma.cc/J3SH-GNRP)

Habitat for Humanity (2023) Volunteer, Habitat for Humanity. www.habitat.org/volunteer (archived at https://perma.cc/436B-QK3T)

HubSpot (2023) HubSpot User Groups, HubSpot. www.hubspot.com/hubspot-user-groups (archived at https://perma.cc/CE4Y-HE82)

Chapter 18

Anderson, C, Hildreth J A D, and Howland, L (2015) Is the desire for status a fundamental human motive? A review of the empirical literature, *Psychological Bulletin*, 141 (3), 574–601

Baer, J and Brown, A (2021) Social pros: How Sam's Club quadrupled down on social care, April. www.convinceandconvert.com/podcasts/episodes/how-sams-club-quadrupled-down-on-social-care (archived at https://perma.cc/ZDW4-8VAD)

Gingiss, D (2023) This is a simple and inexpensive way to celebrate an anniversary with a customer…, LinkedIn, July. www.linkedin.com/posts/dangingiss_customerexperience-activity-7085629104623886336-CQha (archived at https://perma.cc/T2GN-BNG8)

Griff, Z (2023) Wow: Inside Amex's glistening new Centurion club in midtown Manhattan, The Points Guy, March 4. thepointsguy.com/reviews/american-express-centurion-club-new-york-tour (archived at https://perma.cc/VZH5-Z5U4)

Livescault, J (2022) My Starbucks Idea: An open innovation case-study, Braineet, May 22. www.braineet.com/blog/my-starbucks-idea-case-study (archived at https://perma.cc/6PHY-F75J)

Pincombe, M (2021) Chewy sends loyal customers custom pet portraits in appreciation, Daily Paws, January 6. www.dailypaws.com/pet-news-entertainment/pet-news/chewy-sends-customers-custom-pet-portraits (archived at https://perma.cc/AV2B-Q3ZT)

Russell, A (2023) Forks, *The Bear*, S2, E7, dir. Christopher Storer, Hulu, June 22

Sam's Club (2021) Meet Nathan, our Sam's Club cookie taster…, Instagram, January 26. www.instagram.com/p/CKhVhojjNBb (archived at https://perma.cc/D2RR-7FZN)

Settembre, J (2023) Your waiter is creeping on your Instagram: Top restaurants trawl social media to please guests, *New York Post*, June 28. nypost.com/2023/06/28/your-waiter-is-creeping-on-your-instagram-top-restaurants-trawl-social-media-to-please-guests (archived at https://perma.cc/BDZ2-FJQG)

Chapter 19

Fortino, D (2023) Interview by Zontee Hou, July 18

Tardi, C (2023) The 80–20 rule (aka Pareto Principle): What it is, how it works, Investopedia, March 7. www.investopedia.com/terms/1/80-20-rule.asp (archived at https://perma.cc/Y7J4-WT94)

Chapter 20

Convince & Convert/ICUC (2023) The state of data-driven personalization in marketing: Opportunities and challenges in AI, social media and more, ICUC. lp.icuc.social/ebook-2024state-of-data-driven-personalization-in-marketing (archived at https://perma.cc/7SKW-54CM)

Chapter 21

Munroe, R (2014). *What If? Serious scientific answers to absurd hypothetical questions*, Houghton Mifflin Harcourt, New York

Penn, C S (2023) Interview by Zontee Hou, May 8

Chapter 22

Content Marketing Institute/MarketingProfs (2022) B2B content marketing benchmarks, budgets, and trends: Insights for 2023, Content Marketing Institute. contentmarketinginstitute.com/wp-content/uploads/2022/10/b2b-2023-research-final.pdf (archived at https://perma.cc/K5GN-KCYP)

Content Marketing Institute/MarketingProfs (2023) B2C content marketing benchmarks, budgets, and trends: Insights for 2023, Content Marketing Institute. contentmarketinginstitute.com/wp-content/uploads/2023/01/B2C_2023_Research_Final.pdf (archived at https://perma.cc/6MJ9-KGFS)

Fitzwater, R (2023) Interview by Zontee Hou, May 11

Islam, S (2023) Interview by Zontee Hou, July 24

Chapter 23

Islam, S (2023) Interview by Zontee Hou, July 24

Lu, C (2023) Interview by Zontee Hou, May 14

Chapter 24

Convince & Convert/ICUC (2023) The state of data-driven personalization in marketing: Opportunities and challenges in AI, social media and more, ICUC. lp.icuc.social/ebook-2024state-of-data-driven-personalization-in-marketing (archived at https://perma.cc/FAA5-XK8Z)

Fortino, D (2023) Interview by Zontee Hou, July 18.

Researchscape (2023) Media Volery omnibus 230818 weighted report, Researchscape, August 21

Salesforce (2022) State of the connected customer, 5th edition, Salesforce. www.salesforce.com/eu/resources/research-reports/state-of-the-connected-customer (archived at https://perma.cc/HJY7-S9JE)

INDEX

Page numbers in *italic* indicate figures or tables

Looking for another book?

Explore our award-winning
books from global business
experts in Marketing and Sales

Scan the code to browse

www.koganpage.com/marketing

Also from Kogan Page

ISBN: 9781398606487

ISBN: 9781398607644

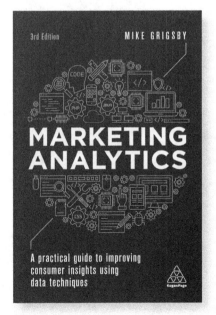

ISBN: 9781398608191

ISBN: 9781398612631

www.koganpage.com

Printed in the USA
CPSIA information can be obtained
at www.ICGtesting.com
JSHW010732270424
61990JS00004B/18